Amidst times of social upheaval, racial tension, and changing values, how to prepare young people and their teachers for social living is a topic of increasingly urgent debate. An experimental project, under the sponsorship of The Ford Foundation, was mounted recently in the Boston area. Over a four-year period it studied school programs in social education that dealt with drug abuse, sex, and racial prejudice. The project got under way at a time when black children were being bussed to white suburban schools, when growing drug abuse and the controversy around it was at its height, and when the impact of "the pill" and the resulting changing sexual mores were becoming apparent.

From their initial pilot project the authors came to the conclusion that efforts to teach social subjects by providing factual information or "enlightened attitudes" were at best inadequate and at worst myth-perpetuating. They therefore decided that a group approach which emphasized the *process* by which people attempted to learn and express their attitudes was more functional than one which focused on the *goal* of acquiring more knowledge. They avoided prescriptions for "good" behavior and instead encouraged participants to study *themselves.*

Over a three-year period this approach was tested in a course called "Social Education" that was offered to seventh-to-eleventh-grade pupils in a heavily populated suburban area. Similar group seminars were given to teachers from inner city schools whose students were being bussed to suburban school systems, and to teachers from the schools receiving them. By using relatively untrained people as group leaders, the authors hoped to make their approach useful on a wide scale.

Boris is a consultant in psychological methods at Boston's Beth Israel Hospital, where she is adapting some of the basic approaches discussed in this book to the care and treatment of the medical patient.

TEACHING SOCIAL CHANGE

A Group Approach

Norman E. Zinberg, Harold N. Boris,
and Marylynn Boris

Manufactured in the United States of America

The Johns Hopkins University Press, Baltimore, Maryland 21218
The Johns Hopkins University Press Ltd., London

Library of Congress Catalog Card Number 75-26746
ISBN 0-8018-1771-4

Library of Congress Cataloging in Publication data
will be found on the last printed page of this book.

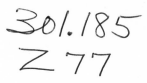

CONTENTS

Part III

ACKNOWLEDGMENTS

To say simply that this project was made possible by the financial support of The Ford Foundation is insufficient. Such a statement would not convey the generosity of time, energy, and sustaining spirit which Stanley Brezenoff, Howard Dressner, Hilary Feldstein, and Mitchell Sviridoff offered us at all times. And "at all times" includes those times, of which you will read, when the project clearly was not functioning in the way they hoped it would. In addition to expressing our appreciation for these multiple supports, we also want to express our gratitude for the existence of The Ford Foundation and other organizations like it which continue to favor ideas out of the mainstream. Whatever the reader may think of this particular work, our culture would be far poorer if researchers could not turn to a variety of sources for help.

Two people who merit our most intense gratitude and without whom this project could not have taken place are Dr. Bert A. Roens, then superintendent of the Arlington (Massachusetts) Public Schools, and Ruth M. Batson, then executive director of the Metropolitan Council for Educational Opportunity (METCO). They were the bulwarks, and they helped convince superintendents of sixteen other school systems to allow our project to take place. We thank them all.

Next to thank are the 209 teachers from all these school systems and the 207 junior high school and senior high school students who were in our groups. They somehow put up with our research and went on with their own work despite us. These groups were led bravely and faithfully by Suzanne Albert, Jane Amsler, Alan Fisch, Philip Helfaer, Inge Hoffmann, Florence Shelton Ladd, Mayfield Peterson, Roy Thompson, and Margaret Wood on the METCO side, and by Anthony Bale, Anthony J. Balski, Mary C. Barry, Winifred Behlan, Robert F. Berman, James S. Brown, Bradford Clough, Barbara Elwood, Donald J. Fortunato, Susan N. Hafner, Thomas Latshaw, Mary M. Leary, David E. Moore, Lois Pharris, Donald Richardson, Jeanne Talbot, and Patricia Trainor on the

Arlington side. During the life of the project, Lucille Kurian, Marcia Millman, Nicki J. Nichols, Jerrold M. Starr, and Dora Zelnicker Ullian ably assisted us with the research.

It is impossible to list the various principals, supervisors, teachers, METCO coordinators, representatives from the Council for Public Schools, and students who at one time or another gave us a hand above and beyond the call of duty, but we wish them to know of our gratitude.

Our editor, Catherine D. Martin, worked unceasingly and valiantly with us on the preparation of the manuscript, and at the end we also received assistance from Philip M. Rich. And last but not least, Miriam Winkeller not only typed our material and administered the project with effectiveness during its life and in its final preparation but also provided a sincerity and dedication without which the job would not have been completed.

INTRODUCTION

From 1968 through 1971, under the sponsorship of The Ford Foundation, the authors of this book ran an experimental project studying groups. The groups, composed of teachers and students, dealt with emotion-laden topics like bigotry, drugs, and sex. They met at a time when racial tension and anxiety about drugs and sexual behavior were causing much public unrest (as, in fact, they still are). We undertook the project in one frame of mind, with many of the conventional aims of research before us. We finished it, having discarded much of our "research" apparatus, in quite another.

In a sense, then, this book reports the beginning, middle, and end of a research project. It did not succeed entirely, but success in research is not the same thing as *doing* something, or drawing clear conclusions about what was done, or having a conviction that others might find what happened and what we have pulled together from these events interesting. Often, in research, there are no "hard" data, no quantifications, no figures, no tables, not even a series of 1, 2, 3, 4 conclusions. A project like ours, concerned with matters like sex, drugs, and prejudice, cannot be a "pure" study of isolated phenomena; it must also be a study of social history. These matters have so aroused our citizens that our mores, our approach to education, our philosophy, ideology, and even politics have been influenced. Hence, we offer this book as a case study in a problem of research that partakes of social change, with all the accompanying tribulations, and a study of how the participants in this project experienced it.

In Part I we discuss the evolution of our project. We began with the idea that it is hard, if not impossible, to "teach" grownups or kids about prejudice, drugs, sex, family life, growing up, and the like. We guessed that in the effort to teach people about these highly charged, emotional subjects, ideas would solidify about what was right and better, and so about what one should or ought to do. This, we thought, would in turn make people feel that as human beings they were insufficient or bad and that they had to strive to change themselves and be better. We thought, further, that efforts to teach these subjects are inconsistent with another alternative, and in fact neutralize it. That alternative is to help people to see what keeps them from knowing about prejudice, etc.—from learning, that is, from experience, both their own and that of others. Right from the beginning, we thought that efforts to "teach" these things minimized the human condition, and that our task was to see what stopped people from accepting themselves more readily as they are (not, however, like Henry VIII, who prayed to God every morning that everything he did that day would be God's will so that he could do exactly as he pleased).

In Part II we present a subjective report on the groups' experience. It aims for disciplined subjectivity, coherence of argument, and sharing of experience. We do not claim a new, definitive, psychoanalytic theory of groups, nor do we insist that our approach can be widely used as a new form of social education. Knowledge of these and many other areas that this project has touched on is badly needed. The need in the real world for direct help to teachers and students is great, but providing it was beyond the powers of the authors and this project. In Part II, for instance, it is not possible, at any point, to be unaware of the real struggles of the real participants in the real group. Yet, in order for us to understand certain aspects of that struggle, we chose to pay little attention to tangible anxieties within the external group. This emphasis on abstraction does not deny the external world. It is simply what we chose to look at.

Chapter 20 presents a piece of group theory which, in the light of the complexity of the groups as we found them, is only a small part of the puzzle. For the authors, however, it represents a bit of light. We also include an excursion into larger "natural" groups to see whether our project experience and our theories help explain some curious behavior.

We have the notion that our study of how individuals experience a group—how, in fact, a group is processed within individuals—has larger implications for social change projects of all kinds. We also feel we have some valuable observations about our difficulty with the research and evaluation of the project. The authors, as well as the project sponsor and evaluator, had hoped that the program would afford a chance both to evaluate groups dispassionately—a kind of "pure" research—and to effect pragmatic social change. The authors found conflict between pure and pragmatic research. This conflict is a useful subject for discussion in a day when social research and evaluation are words "writ large." We do not mean to add our book to the public flood of research findings in the area of social change. We do hope our work may help others gain a little perspective on research itself.

Throughout this book—and particularly in Part II—we ask the reader to avoid preconceptions and, above all, not to look for systematic proofs of one thing or another. We will tell him what we derived from our experiences with the teachers, children, and other professionals and non-professionals who served as group leaders, and try to tell him how we got there. But that requires the reader's willingness to put aside what he thought before, at least until afterward, and join us as we try to make sense of some very complex phenomena.

One of our findings (which is not new—it has been of great importance in the thinking of Bion [1961, 1962, 1963, 1965, 1970], Klein [1932, 1948, 1952, 1957, 1961, 1963], Klein, Heimann, and Money-Kyrle [1955], Laing [1967, 1969a, 1969b], Meade [1934], and others [Foulkes and Anthony 1957; Segal 1964; Whitaker and Lieberman 1964]—and proved to be much more important in our groups than we had expected) was that each group member had in his head his own group. This internalized group of previously significant and modified "others"[1] played a vital part, in our opinion an enormously influential part, in each member's functioning in his (or her) social education and external groups. The reader will see how intricate each moment in the group interaction can be for anyone who is trying to make sense of it. For one thing, it is hard to keep the *dramatis personae* straight. At different times we may be looking at (or for) an individual, or the members of each individual's inner group, or his interactions with the external group, or the external group as a whole, or the group leaders, or the authors, who were the project directors, or all of these at once.

As the very idea of an internal group is an abstraction, a hypothesis, it requires a willing suspension of disbelief. In the beginning of the project we wanted to follow conventional research methodology, but, as we shall demonstrate, being rigorous simply didn't explain much of what we thought we saw in the groups. Since we are asking the reader to let us lead him through this project and its groups as we experienced them, we felt free to select from the group sessions what we regarded as the essence, that which helped us to understand what we felt was occurring. Appendix I contains two recorded group sessions for anyone who wishes to check our bowdlerizing; but, in our opinion, sessions which are recorded word for word, whether by machine or human being, flat tape or video, are no closer to the experiential real thing than are our abridgements.

Is this introduction defensive, a word much used today at cocktail parties as well as in professional journals? Are we projecting onto others our own concerns about failing in research by preparing readers

---

[1]Although originally the internal group consists of parents, other figures and subsequent psychological development add to the internal group and revise the positions of the original figures.

too carefully for the limitations of the report which is to come? The authors' rationale for this beginning comes directly from our group experience in the project. Most of our participants went into the groups with enormously high hopes for real answers, for formulas that would allow social change that would transform individuals, that would alter their attitudes and even their behavior. They wanted the whole loaf so much that they paid little attention to half-loaves, no matter how succulent, until a lot of work had been done. Sometimes preparation cut down the time it took for them to appreciate what was there instead of bemoaning what was not.

A final word: material in Part II, the documents, is essential to the establishment of our argument but may be of too great length for the lay reader. The latter may direct his attention to the analyses and conclusions by the authors, as they occur in each chapter of Part II. These should provide an easy overview of the progress and evolution of all dynamics of the groups.

Part I

CHAPTER ONE

HISTORY OF THE PROJECT

The history of a complex social experimental project represents the interaction of an individual or group with the social history of the period. Considered this way, it is difficult to say just when our project originated. For a number of years two of us had been interested in dynamic group work and in its applications within social institutional structures. Norman Zinberg (1969) had helped organize for the Massachusetts Association for Mental Health a one-day institute for teachers from all over Massachusetts. The institute, which has been held every year since 1952 (Berman 1956), featured two long group sessions. Participants from these institutes could, and many did, join fifteen-session weekly seminars whose goal was greater understanding of self and of self within the group process (Zinberg and Shapiro 1964). Harold Boris (1966a, 1966b) had studied a rural Vermont community by interesting citizens in attending regular group sessions. Both these efforts began independent of each other and were similar in using a group approach roughly based on the principle that understanding what went on in groups at the latent (i.e., unconscious) level and the manifest (i.e., conscious) level and the interaction between these states of consciousness added to our knowledge about the operating psychology of teachers, parents, schools, and communities. It was also thought that if this understanding were shared with the participants, they might find it interesting and possibly useful in their everyday functioning. Thus a great deal of groundwork had already been done by two investigators.

As a result of his work with teachers and the Massachusetts Association for Mental Health, when the issue of bussing black or white children from one school to another became a matter of public concern in Boston in 1965, Zinberg was asked to organize a one-day institute for teachers (Zinberg 1969). The underlying philosophy of the institute was already established, and in his report on this day, Zinberg (1967) states: "Once an educational process becomes an attempt to shape the opinions and judgments of its students, no matter what the aim, it is potentially an instrument of regimentation and reduces rather than increases the individual's capacity to choose."

In an essay on groups published not long after, H. Boris (1970a) independently points out:

Dynamic consultation, however, like dynamic psychotherapy, is difficult—not methodologically but personally. The neutrality it requires means that its practitioners have to renounce the luxury of getting people to change in ways that make them, the practitioners, feel better. Its objective is not this or that, but the freedom compounded of outer possibility and inner option to elect either. The consultant's client may make a choice other than that which the consultant needs, likes or deems wise, leaving the consultant with what may feel like the poor satisfaction of having helped create an option only to see its potential frittered away. But the alternative may really prove to be worse.

Both men were drawing on their past group experiences to describe an approach which would allow participants to learn about how they *felt* about an issue, whether it was bussing, school salaries, principals, or community activity, without attempting social indoctrination. (In Vermont communities, parents wanted desperately to know how they should behave with their children; in Massachusetts towns, teachers longed to know how to be better teachers.) Boris and Zinberg recognized that all they could offer participants was a colleagual relationship through which people could explore how they felt as parents or teachers and what they did with these feelings. Despite their backgrounds in group work, both were in daily life principally involved in working with individuals. The rationale of the use of groups was not developed easily.

THE PILOT PROJECT

The problem of integrating classrooms by bussing in Massachusetts was at that time becoming an extremely tense social issue. Deep fears and high hopes divided schools and communities (Zinberg and Boris 1968). At the same time, drug use among secondary and younger school children loomed as a source of great anxiety among teachers, parents, and the public at large (Abrams 1973; California Teachers Association 1968; Ohio Department of Education 1968; School Health Education Study 1967). These concerns led, too, to considerable discussion in these communities about that area of education where the cognitive knowledge about subjects such as prejudice, sex, drugs, and family living is minimal, while feelings about the subjects are intense and full of highly personal details garnered by innumerable responses to inner and outer stimuli since birth.

As a result of these discussions, formal courses began to be introduced in sex education and drug education for students (Assimakos 1965; Bennett, Taylor, and Ford 1969; Reiss 1968; *Students Speak on Drugs* 1974). At the same time, courses in black history and the black experience were being developed for teachers, school administrators, and other community members (Beisser and Harris 1966; Pinderhughes 1969).

All of Zinberg's growing experience in this area of education led him to believe that it was how people dealt with their feelings about these matters that determined their response, not how much factual information was available to them. This attitude, in 1967, went much against the conventional wisdom (Child Study Association of America 1954). People were becoming increasingly committed to the possibilities of using drug education courses in the high schools, junior high schools, and even elementary schools to halt the spread of nonmedical drug use (*Report to the Massachusetts State Legislature* 1967).

At that time drug education courses were just beginning to increase in number, and they were modeled on the already considerable efforts at sex education (Reiss 1968; Fayette County Public Schools 1968; Maryland State Department of Education 1968; National Association of Independent Schools 1967; North Carolina Department of Public Instruction 1968; School District of Kansas City 1968). The programs Zinberg studied were clearly designed to frighten people away from drug use (Abrams 1973). The best of them told the "facts" about drugs (the facts are virtually nonexistent and could be covered easily in one session) and went on to dwell on the dangers. A good instructor left plenty of time for discussion. He tried to answer the complex moral and philosophical questions that arose about excessive penalties, the right to stop people from doing something that hurts no one else, the effect of the drug experience on the development of spiritual and religious values, and so on. Some courses emphasized the idea that drugs are strong and people weak, some spoke of the anxieties and pressures of modern society, some stressed the evil of harming the body and clouding the mind. No matter what the emphasis, the final message was inescapably NO. The teacher wanted *for* his students a clear mind in a strong body and *from* his students abstinence from nonmedical drug use (Lewis 1970).

Zinberg was puzzled by this use of the public classroom for a clear, righteous, moral imperative and by this use of education for social indoctrination. He turned to sex education, thinking that because the subject had been taught longer, a more neutral presentation might have been worked out. Alas, no. Most of the sex education courses he studied had the same effect of arousing fear (Reiss 1968). One important difference was that instructors could be positive on this topic, as they never could be on the subject of drugs, although they modified their approval with phrases like "when you're ready," "at the right time," "with the person (always singular) you love" (Lerrigo 1962).

These courses made much of conveying information and offered considerable factual knowledge about human anatomy and physiology. Yet some instructors showed no awareness of the contradiction in first insisting that nothing in the human body should be considered shameful or undesirable and then a few sessions later delicately indicating that having sexual relations with several people before marriage was the result of "emotional problems." One could not fail to get the message that there were better or "right" ways about sex which were only slightly more elastic than the conventional moral stereotype. The teacher wanted *for* the student a healthy, fertile, frequently orgasmic, heterosexual marriage, and *from* him (or her) the rejection of "excessive," perverse, or illicit relationships.

A few of these courses took an altogether different tack. They seemed afraid of fear and set out to demonstrate that there should not be *anything* anxiety-provoking about sexual activity. One course, for example, intended for thirteen- to fifteen-year-olds, provided a huge chart which listed the varieties of sexual contacts. It began with holding hands and kissing, and gradually moved through the various possiblities of intercourse, ending up with fellatio-cunnilinguism and anal intercourse. A serious and competent teacher who believed in this approach and in the course material was asked to account for the embarrassment and giggles of some children and the number of other youngsters who fell asleep during this provocative presentation. He quickly blamed it on excessive punitivism in their families and defended his course as a needed antidote. Zinberg thought the course material was anxiety-provoking and excessive. In attempting to force sophistication and acceptance of every sexual practice on the students, it demanded as much of them as did the frightening courses, and it paid equally little attention to what *they* felt about these matters and how *they* viewed their choices and alternatives.

Zinberg also interviewed intensively a number of students who had participated in drug education and sex education courses. The interviews made it plain that none of the courses was constructed to pay attention to how the information presented was used or not used. One male eighteen-year-old veteran of a drug education course turned out to be shooting heroin four to six times a day. When detoxification was mentioned in the course of the discussion, he announced that "cold turkey" would kill him. He heard this myth when he first began using drugs, and although nothing in his extensive street experience confirmed this false belief, he clung to it. He also denied, inaccurately, that the subject was ever discussed in his course. But presenting the "truth" to him and telling him he was mistaken did nothing to shake his misconception.

Another of the interviewees was sixteen and pregnant. She had been given an "A" in what was generally regarded as the best "family life" course offered locally. It did not seem unreasonable to ask her why she hadn't made use of the wealth of contraceptive information presented in her course. She answered plaintively, "My sister [eighteen] told me you couldn't get pregnant if you did it standing up." These examples are exceptional, but myths just as tenacious if not as striking are common among young people.

Myth and misconception, Zinberg concluded, could only be dispelled by the kind of discussion period in which the basis for these misunderstandings might emerge. Even the best courses did not seem to recognize the real power of myth and of inhibitions against knowledge—how facts can be selectively overlooked and how even the reports of one's senses ignored.

All of this preliminary study and survey of what was going on in the socially controversial areas of education coincided in time with, and gradually came to be seen as more and more congruent with, the emotional issues raised by the busing of black children to the white suburbs (Coles 1972; Jerome 1970; Herndon 1970). Issues of sex and drug education and issues of prejudice in the school system were the subject of grave public concern. Both were not going to go away. Both involved every aspect of the social system of schools and school personnel, parents and children, and both were in the process of change and available for the study of that process. Above all, both had more to do with how people *felt* about things than with any specific area of cognitive knowledge.

In 1965, Zinberg led a one-day institute on integration in Arlington, Massachusetts, because Dr. Bert A. Roens, who was then school superintendent there, shared with Zinberg and the Massachusetts Association for Mental Health an interest in how teachers were dealing with their jobs as the responsibility for implementing social change fell more and more squarely on their shoulders. Mrs. Ruth Batson, then associate director, later director, of the Metropolitan Council for Educational Opportunity (METCO), the organization which was bussing children from the ghetto to suburban school systems, helped recruit the teachers for the institute. All three felt that, although one day was too short a time to indicate anything, the content of the group discussions and the impact on the participants was enough to warrant further pursuit of the idea. Black and white teachers talking these issues over in groups might learn more about what feelings led to trouble for them and for their students. Also, just as the teachers might understand better how they responded to newly integrated classrooms in a highly charged atmosphere, so too might youngsters in high school understand more fully how they were responding to drug use in an equally emotional climate of opinion.

Once Zinberg became aware of these responses in both teachers and children, he decided to go ahead with an action-oriented research project consisting of two parts, one to do with youngsters and one with teachers (Zinberg and Boris 1968). In the spring of 1968 Mrs. Batson arranged a small grant, through METCO, to pay for the services of two group leaders and an observer-assistant for fifteen sessions and helped recruit thirty-five black and white teachers from urban and suburban schools. The two people selected as leaders had professional training and some experience with therapy groups and open seminar situations, which are not quite the same as self-study or dynamic groups. One leader was black and one white; the groups were made up of approximately half urban and half suburban teachers, half of whom were black and half white (Carkoff and Pierce 1967). To continue the symmetry (which in retrospect seems ridiculous, but which didn't to us at the time and which to many people still seems important), one-half of the sessions were to be conducted in an urban school, characteristically run down; the other half were to meet in the far more attractive building of a suburban school. The two leaders met weekly with a supervisor (Zinberg) and an assistant who observed both groups.

For the adult teacher part of the program, there was no question about working with Mrs. Batson and METCO. For one thing, METCO was the only such program. More than that, it was the organization most concerned with the emotional response of teachers and as such seemed the natural partner in this project. Despite the early cooperation of Superintendent Roens, there were many questions about where to do the "social education" part with youngsters, and Zinberg tested several systems and grade levels. In some schools a preoccupation with race and poverty overshadowed all else; in others, self-consciousness and guilt about affluence would have skewed the sample; in yet others, the systems' authoritarian rigidity made working conditions difficult. The interesting sociological mix of the Arlington school system, plus the knowledge that there would be dependable administrative cooperation, finally dictated the choice of that suburb. Its school system was good but not extraordinary. It had no ghettoes, but no strong opposition to integration, little poverty, few areas of high income, and an educational policy that was flexible but traditional, since the system was not wealthy enough for expensive, innovative schools or programs.

For the youngsters' side of the program, we had a different—but equally effective—arrangement. Dr. Roens arranged for Zinberg to give a series of six discussions with any interested teachers at the Arlington high school on the general topic of the influence of the classroom on these fears of affectful education. The series was well attended and the discussions lively; eighty-five teachers, about 70 percent of the faculty, attended, and

three-quarters of those present volunteered to teach/lead a social education class/group. After considerable discussion about how to inform
students about the fourteen weekly social education classes—a printed
notice would be too formal, announcement by administrators would be
too frightening, announcement by Zinberg would be too psychiatric—the
English department agreed to announce the class and provide brief
explanations of its purpose. The course could be taken in place of a
regular hour in study hall. There were many volunteers, and the selection
of participants and teachers was made by computer. The sole criterion
was availability: fifteen to twenty students with the same study hour were
matched with a volunteer teacher who was free at the same time. Roens
and Zinberg felt that if this sort of class/group could only be run by
specially selected teachers with a gift for or experience with this sort of
work, it would have little widespread applicability. These leaders, too,
met weekly with Zinberg.

Obviously there were great differences between a project with teachers
from urban and suburban schools who were adult professionals and the
Arlington project which dealt with adolescent kids, but the principle
behind the work was the same. All participants had to make daily,
repeated decisions about how to conduct themselves in areas that were of
deep personal and social concern. Each participant, it was assumed, had
already had the opportunity to learn a great deal about these areas. It was
not that we believed that this rational knowledge would lead to the same
feelings or decisions in different people: some teachers would use their
knowledge to be more authoritative, some less, just as some adolescents
would decide to try a joint or kiss a friend while some wouldn't. But we
surmised that many had not acquired the knowledge available to them
because they perceived selectively or repressed quickly, or that they had
distorted whatever they did know into myths or misconceptions that
better fit some aspect of their emotional reactions to these issues. If
people, adults and youngsters alike, had the chance to explore not so
much what they knew as how it was that they did not know more or that
they used what they knew in such a distorted form, they would have a
fresh chance to grapple personally with these complex issues. Teachers
would have a chance to know more about how they developed their
attitudes toward black children in the classroom, rather than learning
about black children; and adolescents could recognize how they came to
believe that, e.g., the Army puts saltpeter in the food to reduce soldiers'
sexual interest, rather than discussing the physiological gymnastics of
semen and gonads.

One serious problem, which was recognized during the pilot project,
arose from METCO's sponsorship. The invitation to participate in "A
Group Consultation Program for Teachers" noted carefully that the

groups were about the participating teachers and their feelings and
reactions as teachers and people, and *not* about black children, race, or
integrating classrooms. This point was made again by the group leaders at
the start of the groups. Yet the fact that the groups were sponsored by
METCO made it very difficult to keep the emphasis on self-study and
away from race, prejudice, bigotry, and so on.

Much of the work was hard sledding, indeed, and the one thing that
saved all those associated with the project from despair and a sense of
worthlessness was an awareness from the beginning that we were not
setting out to be saviors. Indeed, we felt the teacher was the odd man out
in the school racial crisis, as children, parents, superintendents, legisla-
tors, jurists, and the rest decided how their classrooms must be run. In the
same way Zinberg felt that courses dominated by traditional teaching
methods and conventional values did not adequately respond to the
extent of contemporary change in mores and values relating to sex and
drugs. We wished to find out whether these hypotheses were correct; it
was not our aim to find the definitive way to solve either problem.

The leaders' approach to their groups was roughly similar in both
projects; only the wording was changed. They all said that the group was
not like an ordinary class or seminar, as the teacher would not in any way
offer direct material or guidance but would only comment on the
proceedings if it seemed appropriate. The leader explained that no one
was under any coercion to say anything that he didn't feel reasonably
comfortable saying. But, as everyone had joined this group/class in order
to understand better how he responded to a variety of issues that were of
great importance to his professional/everyday life, it would be hard to
understand where and what his conflicts were if he did not speak more
freely than in an ordinary bull session. Then the leader suggested that, to
start getting to know each other, each person might say who he was and,
if he chose, what prompted him to join this group/class. The leader
usually began by giving his name and stating that he had long been
interested in groups/classes that allowed one to understand oneself and
others. Then he nodded to the next person, but remained silent from then
on. The supervisor had prepared the leaders for silences, questions, and
other technical problems and had asked them to keep their own opinions
to themselves and comment only on what was happening in the group.
The two pilot projects got under way more or less smoothly. In the
crowded high school there was no room for social education to meet, and
the group ended up in a closet or the serving room; many teachers did not
want to change from the comfortable suburban school to the uncomfortable urban one; but leaders and participants seemed interested in the
proceedings. Batson, Roens, and Zinberg decided to try to study the
group process with more care and in greater depth than they could on the

funds available. The Ford Foundation, already backing a project on affect in education (Weinstein and Fantini 1970) and interested in the process of school integration, seemed the natural place to turn, and negotiations were set up.

THE FORD FOUNDATION PROPOSAL

Ford sent a program officer to Boston to interview all three researchers and to sit in on the supervisory sessions with both teams of group leaders. That she was, at that point, very positively impressed there can be no doubt, for the grant was made. In retrospect, it is equally clear that the seeds of later problems were already being sown. The program officer particularly liked the use of nonselected teachers in the Arlington project. These three women and one man were clearly representative of the broadest spectrum of teachers. The man was a young, married science teacher, serious, somewhat authoritarian, not unsympathetic to the young but without a wish to be "with it"; one woman was a young, unmarried history teacher who had lived her entire life in the community, had gone to that very high school, had great empathy with her pupils, and was much involved in extracurricular activities such as taking students to plays and exhibitions which were not always those most approved by the school committee. Another woman was middle-aged, married, with three children; she taught English but had always wanted to teach sex education or family living. She was new to the community and was much at odds with the head of her department. The last was an older, single woman who had taught social science or its earlier equivalent at that school for decades. Well liked by the students because of her pleasant disposition, she had been much protected by them before these groups began to meet and spent each supervisory session admitting how hard it was for her not to display the shock she felt about the content of the discussions. All of these teachers were managing to function as leaders and expressed their feeling that their group experience was aiding them as classroom teachers by making them more aware of group mechanisms and by offering the students a chance to interact with their peers and a grownup in a way they ordinarily could not.

The program officer visited just after Martin Luther King's assassination, and the teachers' groups, particularly the one with a black leader, were profoundly moved and moving. Any technique that could channel that level of emotion was worth finding out about, she reasoned (Feldstein 1969), and she recommended the project to the Ford vice president in charge of national affairs pending the submission of a research proposal.

At this point Harold Boris joined the team, and the proposal that was submitted listed him as codirector. Boris and Zinberg (Zinberg and Boris 1968) wanted to find out what teachers' attitudes were toward integrating classrooms and what happened to these attitudes during the course of the group, just as they wanted to know what the youngsters knew about sex and other "sensitive" subjects and how they used and expanded their knowledge during the groups. The groups were to be observed, pre- and post-group interviews were to be conducted, control groups were to be interviewed, and so on. In other words, there was much that could be considered a formal research approach.

From the start The Ford Foundation was concerned about the research evaluation component. Mitchell Sviridoff, the vice president in charge of national affairs, arranged for a research consultant to meet with Zinberg. The consultant advocated interview protocols, questionnaires to participants, and the like. As it turned out, this consultant, who was most interested in quantification, could not continue. Boris, who ran the project singlehanded in 1968–69 while Zinberg was in England, never met her (Boris and Zinberg 1970b). So it all led to nothing except a vague awareness that the program officer and project director had not reached an understanding about the project goals.

This might have been made explicit had the project people seen then the excellent memorandum Sviridoff wrote recommending the project, but it was an internal communication. The "Social Education" project was funded as part of a package concerned with youth—with the "strength, militancy and agony of middle-class youth" and the search of all youth for answers to such questions as "who am I inside?" and "what am I capable of?" and, for black children, the burning question of whether they could make it in desegregated educational settings. The Ford Foundation never seemed to wonder about the influence of impersonalization and bureaucratization, affluence for some and the parading of that affluence in front of the have-nots on television, and the continuing problem of middle-class white attitudes toward race and poverty.

Both the METCO (adult professional teachers with experienced leaders) and the Social Education (young adolescents with teacher group leaders) pilot projects were part of an effort to test "the effect of a group approach in the development of attitude and attitude change." The ultimate concern of Sviridoff's memo, however, was whether the proposed programs would have an impact on the students. The Arlington project was seen as "intending to assist adolescents to explore the issues of concern to (them) with maximum freedom, to identify misconceptions and to come to terms with themselves as individuals and to experience a considerable amount of personal growth." The teachers' project was seen as aiming "to assist teachers in understanding their reactions when operating in a classroom during this period of intense social pressure . . . and when working with newly integrated groups of lower-class black children and, therefore, to improve the educational experience for the children." The memo goes on to say:

The most important element of this project is evaluation. It is also the most difficult as the goals of teacher behavior and student maturity are subjective and dependent on a number of variables.

The most difficult objective is to identify the impact, if any, on the children of the participating teachers. This section is the weakest part of the evaluation. We expect as the project continues to identify additional ways to measure the impact on the children without prejudicing the unstructured nature of the group sessions.

Obviously, during his discussion with Zinberg, Sviridoff had captured the spirit of the project sensitively and accurately and had gone further and recognized the inherent weakness of the project as research. He knew as well as Zinberg and Boris that the teachers were a crucial and a weak link in the integrating classroom, just as he knew that most of the efforts at sex and drug education were a disaster. But he backed their efforts not just to study *how* the process occurred but *what* happened and what could be done to facilitate the change resulting from such a project.

THE PROJECT BEGINS

The proposal included both METCO and Arlington. For METCO it promised to "help teachers identify and work through the interpersonal factors affecting their ability to teach and cope with their classes, both generally and in the face of the presence of black urban children, as the service aspect of the project, and to continue to identify those factors, especially in their social function, as the research aspect" (Zinberg and Boris 1968). For Arlington, the plan was to use "the group discussion method to teach young people that they can communicate with each other about topics and feelings usually kept to oneself regardless of personal differences," with the ultimate aim of making "members sufficiently aware of their own unconscious motivations and sensitive to the feelings of others to permit more rational reality testing" (Zinberg and Boris 1968). The proposal was approved, and in September 1968 the project was in business. There were eight teachers' groups meeting, and nine social education groups—five in the senior high school and four in the junior high school, with two each in the seventh and eighth grades. (For a diagrammatic representation of the entire project, see the figure at the end of this chapter.)

The decision to move into the junior high schools came after much thought. At this stage the project was still concerned with attitude formation, and we had found that the attitudes of the senior high school students in the pilot project were already well developed. They possessed considerable knowledge about all the key areas, albeit with many misconceptions, and thought they knew how they felt about them. Hence, the project team hoped that by working with thirteen- and fourteen-year-olds they might see firm attitudes develop from more inchoate beginnings. As one project member had worked with a variety of age groups preliminary to the pilot project, this move was taken with full awareness that these early adolescents would form quite different groups from the middle adolescents. Even the difference between seventh- and eighth-grade groups was considerable, for the younger people had one foot in childhood, and, when words failed, as they often did, giggling, touching, punching, crying, sleeping, moving about, and general physical and emotional chaos were readily available (Boris and Zinberg 1970c).

In the Arlington school three of the four pilot project people continued, and the new person was added from the old list. A notice was posted in the junior high school, and many teachers volunteered. The existence of the project was now well known throughout the Arlington school system and had aroused much interest. The Ford grant made it possible to pay five hundred dollars to all participating teachers to compensate them for after-school meetings with their supervisors and for preparing brief, written reports on each meeting. None of the volunteers knew of the stipend in advance; it simply came as a pleasant surprise, and was not a motivating force for joining the project.

The group leaders for the teachers' groups were recruited from local graduate schools and social agencies. Neither of the METCO pilot project leaders could return. There was a concerted effort to get two black leaders, but not much emphasis was placed on specific training. The principle mentioned earlier still held: part of the research aim was to find out how well people without special training could do in these groups. To what extent does the group carry the leader or does the leader propel the group?

Supervision of all the leaders in the pilot project followed the same pattern. Leaders and the observer in the teachers' groups described what had happened, and everyone went on to discuss what they thought was going on in the group, what reasoning had led the leader to intervene or not, and how the leader might proceed from there. There was little or no emphasis on what was going on within the leaders themselves. When the first year of the formal project got under way, Boris, who was supervising, began in the same way. Very quickly he began to feel that the teacher/leaders were too inexperienced to carry a full-year group of thirty to thirty-five sessions by direct supervision. He decided to carry on the supervision group as a dynamic group, and rather than advise them about what was going on in the group or what techniques they might use, he would help them to see how people operated in a group by acting as a group leader. Then they might be able to translate their experience with him into their own group leadership. With some misgivings the teachers accepted this, and that year's supervision with them became one more group. However, supervision with the leaders of the teachers' groups proceeded as before.

Each half of the project had a research assistant who observed two of the groups and took comprehensive notes. The group participants were told that the observers were part of a research team who were interested in groups, not individuals, and that anything specific said in the group would be kept completely confidential, although general observations about the group as an entity would be made. Once in a while people would comment on the observers, but on the surface their presence was accepted uneventfully.

The first year had no more than the expected share of trials and tribulations—there was trouble finding rooms, there were mixups of meeting places, one leader of the teachers' group seemed unsatisfactory and was replaced in the second term, and so on. Observer and leader reports were gathered; some pre- and post-interviewing of participants was done. Regular meetings were held with Mrs. Batson and her associates and with Superintendent Roens to take up reactions to the groups. The METCO people reported some teacher satisfaction and some dissatisfaction; METCO wanted the groups to be run in school systems where there was trouble, and they were a bit unhappy but understood when it was pointed out again that the groups themselves were not direct mechanisms for social change. In Arlington, when the word got around to parents that there was a class in school where the kids were permitted to use foul language and talk about sexual activity and drug use without their teachers condemning such acts, there was a mild flurry of protest. Roens refused to back down; he told parents that he did not know what was said in these classes and that it was none of their business either. And, indeed, one interesting finding was how little the group participants talked to their parents about the groups, although there was obviously considerable peer discussion.

One matter caused considerable concern throughout the teachers' groups. Participants were recruited through notices posted in each school by that school's METCO representative. The notice stated:

Groups for teachers, sponsored by METCO and supported by The Ford Foundation, are being offered to all classroom teachers who wish to undertake, together with others, an examination of the effects of today's social issues on themselves and their classrooms. The work of the groups will center on exploring the relationship between self, professional role and teaching function, and the inevitable demands placed on teachers as mediators of social issues.

Each of the groups will meet for 15 weekly sessions . . . [here followed the practical details] (Boris and Zinberg 1970b).

Despite this explanation of the work of the groups, when the participants arrived, many of them expected to be told about black children, how they grow and how they were to be cared for and taught. It seemed that each of the groups met for a fair number of sessions before this misconception could be faced, and some of the disappointment and anger remained unresolved and appeared almost reasonable to the participants. We had thought that word-of-mouth explanations of the group work, from teacher to teacher within the school systems, might help to modify these kinds of expectations. But in the fall of 1970, despite what other teachers might have conveyed of the content of the previous year's meetings and despite what we thought was the careful wording of the notice above, these misconceptions reappeared vigorously. Hence, in January 1970, in preparation for the next series of meetings, Boris and Zinberg sent out the following letter to individual teachers and to each school system:

Dear _____ :

This time the regular group consultation program (supported by The Ford Foundation) will be preceded by a general meeting for you and other concerned teachers.

The purpose of this preregistration meeting, at which Norman E. Zinberg, M.D., Project Director, and Harold N. Boris, Program Director, will preside, is to present the program's purposes and procedures so that you can decide the program's suitability for you—in advance. (The group program itself will begin the week of March 9.)

Two such meetings will be held in order that their size may be small enough to permit discussion. One will be on February 25 from 4–5:30 P.M. at Newton South High School; the other on February 26, also from 4–5:30, at the Lecture Hall in Lexington High School.

COFFEE AND DOUGHNUTS WILL NOT BE SERVED. BUT
    if you, as a teacher, are feeling the turmoil of today's social transitions,
    if teaching seems more difficult than it has a right to be, and
    if coming to know and learning to manage some of what, if anything, in you
    adds to the difficulty, would seem to you to be of use,
by all means do come to one of the meetings (M. Boris 1971).

Each of the two preregistration meetings took place in a school situated in the middle of a region, so that teachers from several systems could attend easily. The project format was explained with particular emphasis on the opportunity for each teacher to explore his own personal response to his job in the midst of so much social and emotional pressure. Questions were answered carefully, and from the nature of the response, Boris and Zinberg believed that the people who were *not* interested in this sort of experience would not volunteer—that they would not be misled by a misconception that they were joining a seminar on the black experience. As we shall see in Part II, this careful preparation helped very little. People continued to expect that the groups would be whatever they hoped they would be and found it very hard to accept them for what they were.

QUESTIONS ABOUT RESEARCH

As the project proceeded into the second year, Boris and Zinberg began to have doubts about their original research aims. At about the same time The Ford Foundation was worrying about the same thing. In keeping with the interest in high-quality work that they maintained throughout the project experience, in January 1970 Ford hired Dr. James Laue, an astute investigator with considerable research experience, to analyze the current research status of the project. Laue was particularly interested in how the research could be quantified and the methodology evaluated (see Chapter 5 for the effect of his report on the project and the eventual thinking of the authors). By this time Boris and Zinberg had revised their thinking on research, as they wrote in a report (May 1970) to Ford, entitled "Are Piano Lessons Different from the Appreciation of Music?" (Boris and Zinberg 1970a):

In setting our inquiry in this direction—the question of what enables group members to be freer in proceeding toward their *own* initial or stated objectives— we clearly had to set aside the question of what they *do* with their enhanced freedom. Rather, the questions posed for us were such as these: What are the manifest or behavioral indices of a freer style, a more volitional ego, an activated disposition? Are these made evident in the fact that group members are better able to reach their own objectives? Will they become more or less prejudiced to blacks—or drugs—or drug takers? To do justice to our undertaking, its participants, its sponsors, and its hosts (not to speak of ourselves), changes in the direction of freedom have not only to be done, but to be seen to have been done.

And yet the behavioral equivalents of inner change in the direction of freedom to make choices proved equivocal. For instance, Mr. A enters a group spouting prejudicial attitudes and is surprised that others in the group do not share these attitudes, because the reference group to which he has been accustomed has shared those attitudes. Fifteen weeks later he leaves the group spouting liberal principles. Is this an index of change, or an example of "plus ça change . . ."?

To this question our own answers have changed. Our own experiences as subjects of consultation (psychoanalysis) was that with the modifications of our own ego autonomy in the direction of awareness, activity, and volition, we became more tolerant, less prejudiced, more "liberal." It seemed reasonable to imagine, then, that so would others. Thus, while we would never take Mr. A's conversion to be an unequivocal manifestation of a deeper change, we did tend to focus on attitude change in general. We puzzled for a fair while on how to dispel the equivocal elements.

Though a futile exercise in terms of reducing the uncertainty of our research measures and conclusions, this process of puzzling proved immensely useful in another respect. Through it, we moved further and further away from our preoccupation with attitude change and the behavioral counterparts of changes in attitude. Put in other terms, we moved away from considerations of *what* to considerations of *how*. We are now quite squarely focused on how people process experience and no longer on what they do as a result.

Without question, Boris and Zinberg had developed grave doubts about the ability of formal research to turn up much that meant anything. A compromise with the Ford investigator was decided upon. Boris and Zinberg could continue to focus on how a member in the group was processing the experience. What from within him goes into the choice of speaking or not speaking, to whom, after whom, to what effect? When does he "tune out"? And do these change? This model of research was roughly an ethological one. Members of the group were to be studied in their (natural) habitat, the group. At the same time Boris and Zinberg hired a research director who would administer pre- and post-questionnaires designed to test bias in perception, "closed"- and "open"-mindedness, how participants felt about the group, the effect of the total experience on them, and other presumably quantifiable indices.

Except for the addition of the research measures in the spring of 1970, the second year was much like the first. Two leaders of teachers' groups were replaced, and one new senior high school and two new junior high school leaders were found without much trouble. Both research assistants left the area, and new ones were hired. This time the teachers' group leader supervisory sessions as well as the social education sessions were run in a group fashion. The two full years of the projects supplied far more data than can be used.

During the second year of the project another area of consultation was undertaken—consultation to superintendents of many of the school systems whose teachers were invited to join the teachers' groups and to Arlington, which had both teachers and students in groups (M. Boris 1971). Our notion was that to engage a superintendent in a consideration of his own aims and goals in his work and of how and to what extent they were being met might provide him with a real sense of what teachers in our groups were doing. It would be both a parallel experience and a means for deciding himself whether that experience was one he would like to see offered to more of his teachers over several years. For this to happen he would have to choose to find the means to support the project after the second year, when the Foundation support would end.

Since we wanted to meet a number of times with each superintendent, we determined to work with no more than six. Out of ten superintendents initially visited, six were interested in exploring the possibility of developing their own community-sponsored dynamic group program for their teachers. Of these six, one, after three consultations, decided that what could be presently provided within the school system for teachers was adequate to their needs. Another superintendent had us work for some months with one of his staff who was developing a proposal for "Teacher Orientation—Race, Culture and Human Relations." We shared our notions of what might work drawn from our thinking and our experience. He had his own differing notions, such as wishing to include a course in "Black Heritage" for all teachers and making the group work subtly mandatory (through administration expectation) for all teachers. His proposal did not receive foundation funding.

The remaining four superintendents we worked with for almost two years. After five initial consultations to determine whether they wished to choose to work to implement community-sponsored groups, all four opted to do so. A major task ahead was to try to find funding. We followed as many avenues as were open to us, working particularly on federal funding through the state Department of Education. Proposals were submitted, discussed, revised, and resubmitted. What became clear in late 1969 and early 1970 was that there were fewer funds available for projects in education than there had been earlier. Superintendents were also feeling tremendous pressure from their communities to cut costs. When, therefore, three of the superintendents tried every means of allocating funds from within their school systems for a small version of the group programs, it was not surprising that only one did finally find some funds. This was Arlington, which ran a half-size program in social education for one more year.

We were interested in what happens when consultation is offered to superintendents. Our objective was to explore thoroughly with them their initial interest in group work for teachers and students, necessarily exploring at the same time their other aims and objectives as superintendents so that they could ultimately choose to do what they deemed useful concerning such a program. As with the teachers and students in our groups, we wished to offer superintendents, on an individual basis, the opportunity to choose. We went, so to speak, door to door to offer this opportunity. Among all the superintendents we visited, both those with whom we consulted a few times and those with whom we worked at length, we noticed a lingering hope for clear and dramatic solutions to

problems they saw in contemporary education, problems such as drug abuse, student unrest, conflict in race relations. The active solution had a strong pull of appeal: an education collaborative, for instance, offered a course designed "to train teachers to deal honestly and openly with the racial problem as it affects the lives of students." Beneath such an offering lies the assumption that such a hope—that people, teachers, can be trained to be honest and open—can be fulfilled in some concrete, quantifiable way (Boy and Pine 1971; Bruner 1960; Caswell 1964; Clark and Erway 1971; Holt 1972; Postman and Weingartner 1969). It is to a study of this hope itself that we have devoted much of our work.

CHAPTER TWO

WHY GROUPS?

It could be successfully argued that, when this project began, a dividing line was only sketchily drawn between a pure research project on the one hand, intended to investigate how people develop the attitudes they do toward emotion-laden subjects, and a social change project on the other, designed to change people's attitudes in these areas, so that they had more freedom of choice by virtue of knowing and accepting themselves better (Zinberg and Boris 1968). Undoubtedly, it can now be seen that, as we were considering how to carry out the project, we attempted initially to deal with both, according to the goals set out for us by Sviridoff of The Ford Foundation. This focus shifted. Pure research grew to be our main interest as we began to doubt the very idea of teaching, in whatever form, social change. How we diverged from Ford goals will be discussed in Chapter 5. In retrospect, it can be seen that at this stage we principally concerned ourselves with the aspect of the project concerned with social change/greater freedom of choice by self-knowledge. There was a sort of unspoken assumption that, once we could think through our method of approach, ways to test and measure could then be ingeniously devised. Hence, when considering how to go about the project, we concentrated on what goes into our ordinary methods of doing therapy —teaching, sensitizing, "changing," training—when dealing with feelings and not facts.

Both Boris and Zinberg were basically trained in one-to-one therapy. Both had had considerable experience with a wide variety of groups. Another factor emerged which was of critical importance: much of their experience was with middle-class patients, students, clients. This fact figured prominently both in the choice of a group technique and in the choice of Arlington as the site for the social education groups.

Some of the material in this chapter appeared in different form in N. E. Zinberg, "The technique of confrontation and social class," a chapter in *Confrontation in psychotherapy*, ed. G. Adler and P. G. Myerson (New York: Science House, 1973).

Among the principal concerns of the project were prejudice and integration of black and white kids in different school systems. Why not do some of the work in ghetto neighborhoods? And, in fact, when we were planning for the social education groups, some preparatory discussions were held in ghetto schools. These early discussions confirmed what we had already suspected: most thinking about therapy, or group work, had been done by middle-class professionals working with middle-class people. This created no problem with the teacher groups because even those teachers who originally came from low-skilled, working-class backgrounds had become socially mobile, acquired an education, and aspired to and acquired middle-class values, customs, and ways of thought (Jersild 1952). But the children in low-skilled, working-class neighborhoods had not made this shift (Conger and Miller 1966; Hollingshead and Redlich 1958). We began to look at the structural factors that go into the various approaches—one-to-one and groups—and to take class differences into account. We recognized that, given the undefined nature of social education, to achieve reasonable communication across a gap of class, values, and age would be a separate project of its own. Hence, a middle-class school, although one with as broad a range of students as possible, seemed necessary. Let us turn to the possible approaches and our reasoning.

MEANS AND ENDS

Today a wide range of models of intervention are grouped together as psychotherapeutic techniques—one-to-one therapy, group therapy, dynamic groups, family therapy, "confrontation" groups (Chance 1971). Patients and members of such groups come from a variety of social backgrounds as well: since the Community Mental Health Act of 1964, psychotherapy is no longer only for the middle class (G. A. P. Report 1968; Jackson 1963). Community psychiatry, drug addiction, and political radicalism have all contributed to a desire by psychiatrists to work with low-skilled, working-class patients (Bernard 1965; Zinberg 1973). Yet many professionals, whether they describe themselves as concerned with "emotional problems of living," "acquisition of mental health," "social and psychological deviancy," or even old-fashioned "emotional problems" and "mental illness," have not taken social class into account when thinking about their field. These "mental health workers" (for lack of a better term) have tended to rely on what we feel we know about working with people without noticing that all too much of this knowledge is based on middle-class therapists working with middle-class patients (Zinberg 1972). A look at the various techniques—group or individual —which define the relationship between therapist and patient, leader and member, may enable us to see how these techniques are means and to what ends. Means and ends tend to get confused when middle-class-dominated professionals try to work with low-skilled, working-class clients.

As Harold Boris said (1971):

It is not seen that this group (the working class) has other ways of doing things, another culture and social organization, another form of personality patterning; rather it is seen that this group, lacking our own folk-ways and mores, is considered deprived or, more sociocentrically still, disadvantaged, and so we want things for them. Sometimes it is clear—almost—that we want things from them: to get off the streets and stop making trouble or off the relief rolls and stop costing us our hard-earned money or to stop their profligate impulse-serving behavior so that we can stop contending with our unconscious envy.

It is a general principle that, in any therapeutic interaction, if it is to be effective, a differential equality must be maintained between the participants; that is, each person has his own area of special contribution that is different but not inherently unequal. In one-to-one psychotherapy, for instance, the doctor is a specialist in the general principles of how people work, and the patient is a specialist in himself. Differential equality requires a degree of social and/or psychological distance between leader and members, or doctor and patient. We argue that this distance cannot be zero, but it also cannot be too great, or there is no communication.

When we speak of treatment techniques, what are we talking about? How are the tasks of therapist/leader and patient/member differentiated?

INDIVIDUAL THERAPY

One-to-one psychotherapy is the usual therapeutic model. Doctor and patient roles are clearly defined. The patient seeks out the doctor, makes an appointment, and explicitly agrees that he has an emotional conflict to discuss. Generally this procedure requires some similarity of life experience between the patient and the therapist which permits them to work out a shared level of ego perceptions and verbal representations. Thus, the therapist's expectations—that is, what he wants for the patient and from the patient—can be made fairly explicit.

With the recent growth of community psychiatry and case-finding, the therapist may venture into the community as part of a community health or case-finding team. Usually he goes into working-class neighborhoods, where the populace is less likely to seek counseling; but case-finding is appropriate among some middle-class groups as well. He goes to seek out troubles, and he maintains a clear view of his position as doctor. Who is to be considered "patient" may be less clear, and this must be defined before a therapeutic situation can be officially established. When the therapist takes the initiative for the therapeutic encounter, there may be confusion about what he wants from the patient or for him.

The position of the therapist in most individual situations has remained essentially as it was defined by Freud (1913a). The therapist, in effect, leases time to the patient: Freud made an analogy with a music teacher who brought his skills to the time during which he was hired. This view of the therapeutic situation stresses the total voluntariness of treatment and the resulting equality between teacher and pupil. The patient-pupil decides whether he wants therapy lessons; he can stop at any time, but he is responsible for the time that has been contracted. Thomas Szasz (1968), particularly, has stressed equality through contract. Two equal individuals with similar rights and privileges, although not identical tasks or responsibilities, work together on a common problem. It is in this sense that they may be called colleagues. The therapist will do this work for an agreed fee during agreed-upon hours, and he will not save hours that are not paid for but neither will he lease the contracted hours to anyone else.

This clarity about arrangements ensures the equality of the participants. If the therapist were to set aside time and not charge for that time when a patient is called away or suffers a long illness, out of his humanistic, subjective concern for the patient, he would be behaving as though he were a philanthropist—a benevolent spirit who graciously provides for the needy patient. Freud believed that such a therapist, who was convinced that what he had to offer was so "good" for the patient that he could not in all conscience withhold it, raised questions about what he wanted from the patient in return. While the payment of a fee does not per se guarantee that some therapists will not want and indeed feel entitled to returns of gratitude, the patient's moral betterment, or simply "improvement," it at least sets the stage for an objective, colleagual relationship.

This objective relationship calls for the therapist's presentation of himself as relatively invulnerable. No matter how personal or how intense the statements and the feelings of the patient, whether affectionate or angry, the therapist treats them as manifestations of transference. This posture establishes a psychological distance between him and the patient. His benevolent acceptance of the patient's expressions and his attempts to make sense of them are part of the skill for which he is paid. The therapeutic contract protects the therapist's objectivity and offers the patient the freedom to express his emotions without fear. Many people find it harder than one would imagine to differentiate between act and thought, endowing the latter with magical properties. If a patient misses hours because of emotional turmoil or a vacation and desires to continue the therapy, he must pay for those hours. Should he remain silent out of a wish to punish the therapist, he soon realizes that it is his therapy that suffers. The situation is designed to make clear that it is the pupil's desire to learn music that provides the impetus for the lessons, not the teacher's wish that he do so.

While this invulnerability supports the crucial therapeutic neutrality, it also becomes one of the most delicate therapeutic problems. Anyone who can accept without flinching feelings as powerful as the patient regards his own deeper responses to be must be either callous and uncaring or enormously powerful, with the capacity to succor, to retaliate, or to judge. The therapeutic neutrality can be experienced by the patient as degrading or dehumanizing: "You are too weak and unimportant to have an effect on me," the therapist seems to say. The therapist, of course, knows all too well that he is not so totally strong, objective, or invulnerable; he knows that these properties derive from the situation and his skill at his job. But his ability to show the patient that reactions to the therapist's objectivity are part of the work—perhaps the most difficult, though potentially the most fruitful, part—depends upon the invulnerable position of the therapist.

In the one-to-one situation, then, the therapist is objective, committed to the study of the individual case, and invulnerable. He values the shared work of the situation and, without disregarding the importance of nonverbal messages, relies heavily on verbal communication and, eventually, rationality. His generally neat appearance and carefully selected surroundings announce at least some interest in material comfort and the avoidance of any deviant or disruptive social atmosphere. As the overwhelming majority of his patients share the values implicit in these nonverbal announcements, they contain no mysteries or hidden potential. The patient's questioning of the therapist's neutrality occurs over issues on which the patient anticipates conflict or disagreement. This anticipation arises when the patient experiences as coming from the therapist some less conscious aspect of his own conflict. Moreover, such projection is usually sanctioned by old parental attitudes, ideological or religious convictions, or official cultural positions. They range from "stand up straight" and "thou shalt not even wish to kill" to embarrassed confessions of cheating at cards or an illicit sexual act, accompanied by the conviction of the therapist's moral outrage.

Of course, therapists are attacked by their patients for their speech, appearance, and surroundings, but they are usually attacked, not questioned, because in almost every case their patients are people who have shared similar life styles and are expressing their own demonstrable personal conflicts. The therapist's own analysis prepares him with an awareness in depth of his own position on such issues. The nearness of the patient's value system and life style to the therapist's own life, i.e., the lack of social distance, does not interfere with the therapeutic position of functional psychological distance. Thus, by restricting his offering to a discussion of the patient's conflict rather than the manifest reason for the attack, the therapist does not strive for agreement, closeness, or the avoidance of criticism. By not taking the patient's criticism personally, the therapist makes it clear that he does not want anything beyond the contract for or from the patient. This sharp break with the niceties of conventional social interaction is meaningful because both parties acknowledge it as a break. Thus, the working model of two relative equals, one of whom supplies the subjectivity, the other the objectivity, operates smoothly because both know and accept the same social values.

SMALL THERAPY GROUPS

Small therapy groups follow the individual psychotherapy model. The groups are artificial, arising from the shared, stated desires of each member to study himself. While the members test reality against each other as part of an aggregate, the purpose for which the group was created—work with the individual member—is never entirely lost sight of. Nor is there any doubt as to who is the patient and who the doctor, though the various wishes and expectations involved in these roles become a lively part of the therapeutic process.

The positions of therapist and patient are different in one respect, however. As in the one-to-one relationship, the "patient" supplies the individual cases to be studied. The "patient" group hires a leader of similar social class to bring his objectivity and skills to bear on the problems. They consciously or unconsciously accept the broad outlines of how he might proceed and further accept their interest in his actions as part of the process. All of these factors, including the leader's psychological distance and relative invulnerability, follow the original working model of equality and difference. But in the one-to-one relationship, if either party is physically absent no actual therapeutic session can occur. The patient, albeit at a cost, can halt the proceeding, just as the therapist can. In a group, an individual patient loses that equality with the therapist. Group sessions can proceed without any one individual, as long as the leader is there.

As one would expect, such middle-class groups are extremely concerned with the issues of authority and dominance as they relate to the leader and to the issue of closeness among members. When the life of the group depends essentially on the existence in that time-space of that one person, while others are expendable, he automatically becomes endowed with great power. (Leaderless group meetings occur, but unless the group is greatly experienced, such meetings are idiosyncratic and desultory.) So much power, in fact, does the leader have that at some conscious or unconscious level almost any group discussion needs to take him into account. One should never underestimate the force of the transference reaction in the one-to-one relationship, but there are times when the interaction with the therapist is submerged. Individual patients do become involved in their interpersonal conflicts with others outside the therapeutic situation, and they do review everyday decisions they must make with little regard in their associations for the immediate transference implications. Members of a group, on the other hand, find it extremely difficult to minimize in their discussions the constant ongoing emotional relationships to other group members, particularly to the leader, and when they seem to do so, it is usually a transparent defense against a previous or forthcoming group issue.

LARGE PROBLEM-MASTERING GROUPS

Large problem-mastering groups which are therapeutic in intent represent a different model of psychological interaction. Dr. Joseph Pratt of Tufts Medical School first reported formally on this approach in 1902; and he emphasized the search for an active solution to a problem. Today there are many such repressive-inspirational groups organized around a variety of diseases, the best known being Alcoholics Anonymous. The individual is essentially anonymous. Anyone who has found a way to transcend the problem qualifies as a therapist, though he becomes recognizable as a patient again if his mastery over the problem falters. Hence patient-therapist is a variable division, but there is no ambiguity about what would be "better" for the patient—whether it be to stop drinking, adjust to an ileostomy bag, or think cheerful thoughts rather than succumb to the hopelessness of depression. Group members can come from any class background. As the emphasis is more on the "problem" to be overcome than on communication or interactions between leader/member or member/member, class differences seem to matter far less than the willingness to "believe" in the solutions.

DYNAMIC GROUPS

So-called dynamic groups also have a more or less therapeutic purpose, but the aim here is not wholly the study of the individual case. The "patient" is not the individual himself or the symptom but rather a task, for example, knowing more about oneself in order to be more effective as a teacher, psychiatric resident, or group leader. Individuals discuss their conflicts and how they see the world. The focus, explicit or implicit, is not on themselves as patients but on their function in relation to an accepted social institution.

The social distance between leader and member in a dynamic group is clearly less than that between doctor and patients in a therapy group. The group leader is a professional colleague who could easily be socially confused with other members of the group but whose differentiated role within the group creates a distinct psychological distance between him and the other group members. The group goals are considerably less structured than in the large problem-mastering groups like Alcoholics Anonymous, but more so than in individual or group therapy. While it could certainly be argued that it is no easier to say what makes a better teacher than what makes a better person, there are more specific task designations around even jobs as multi-dimensional as group leadership or teaching.

When dynamic groups are assembled by drawing from all over persons who do not know each other, they are artificial, created for the purpose of working with individuals, and are then similar to therapy groups. However, when the group is made up of teachers from the same school or residents from the same hospital, the dynamic group comes closer to a natural group. These people are part of a pre-existing social network and have relationships with each other which are external to the group. In this situation, the stated goal of working toward greater understanding for the individual becomes less sharp. The group behavior of a participant can have direct consequences for him and for his institution outside of the group meeting. Once the need for attention to and preservation of these extra-group networks is recognized by the group, the priority of working toward individual goals receives greater consideration.

This specific inclusion of the social institution in the relationship between group leader and group member thus changes the patient/therapist position as outlined in the discussion of the one-to-one situation. The acceptance in dynamic groups of a social goal other than the study of the individual case suggests the desire of the leader for the members of the group to improve their functioning by greater understanding of their interpersonal relationships. This is a middle-class position echoing middle-class preoccupations. Thus the leader raises questions about his neutrality because he seems to want something personally for and from the group members. By joining them in an effort to be better social workers or to be more learned about groups, he indicates that he knows what a good social worker or group leader is and something about the proper way to become one, and he suggests that to be one is a "good" thing.

The members, for their part, by their very presence in the group, show confidence in their ability to attain a group goal. The leader may have something special to teach them which exalts him, but they can legitimately regard themselves as students with a potential social use for what they learn. The role of student differs sharply from that of patient in our society. "Patient" is a deviant role implying sickness or weakness, while "student" promises achievement and the possibility of surpassing the teacher. In fact, to maintain "student" as a viable social role requires hope and activity, as contrasted to "patient," with its accompanying feelings of passivity and helplessness.

In therapy groups it is a long time before a patient can accept the possibility that what another patient has to say may be almost as meaningful to him as any comment from the leader (Zinberg 1964). He longs for curative interpretation from an omnipotent leader. In dynamic groups, anyone who enters as a neophyte social worker, psychiatrist, or group leader—no matter how ill at ease or uninformed he feels—wants to be seen as a potential contributor. To gain such regard he must give it. Often the regard is given and accepted grudgingly. But no matter how undeserving he may feel, the group member understands that he must solicit the regard of his fellows. Members, by this giving and accepting, confer status on each other and thus restore their position vis-à-vis the leader to one of relative equality, though it is psychologically distinct.

It is difficult enough in a one-to-one therapeutic situation for a therapist of any sort to say undeviatingly to a patient: "Yes, I will help you study yourself, and doing so is often an illuminating procedure which will lead you to a greater awareness of choices and inhibitions. But what choices you make, what being 'better' means to you, is your business and not mine." He carefully keeps in focus the goal of his job as working toward this understanding and does not assume responsibility for the implementation of the understanding. In a dynamic group, once the leader announces (by his presence alone) that he wants the group to achieve a specific state of "betterness," and is willing to work to that end, he will find it much harder to deal with the question: "What should we be doing?" His position as dominant in a magical sense has been eased by the existence of a specific goal and the status that this gives to group members, but the idea that there is a "place" for the group to "get to" makes the leader more of a teacher assigning grades, who wants his group members to implement certain social goals, and less of a neutral therapist.

That the dynamic group leader can legitimately be considered to have ideas about where the group should go does not increase the *social* distance between him and the group members. Rather the opposite: his age, social circumstance, and general demeanor are all similar to theirs, and there is agreement that the group has a purpose or goal more specifically related to a socially accepted goal or value system than to the psychological study of an individual case or the process of therapy. Hence, the *psychological* distance evidenced by the different functioning of the group leader becomes both more necessary (because there is no other distance) and more irksome to the group members: more necessary if the group members are to learn what they want to learn by participating subjectively in the group experience but at times drawing back and observing their difficulties in dealing with each other, particularly with that differentiated other, the leader (of this they are largely unaware throughout much of the life of the group); more irksome because once having agreed upon a goal relating to a third party (pupils, clients), it seems that only the peculiar stubbornness of the group leader prevents them from achieving it. If he would stop his habit of commenting on what is happening in the group—or, worse, remaining silent—and give them straight answers, they might get somewhere. As the group progresses and members become more aware of the hopes implicit in their annoyance with the leader, they tend to shift their attention toward analyzing these hopes and away from the expectation that they be fulfilled. This shift represents an acceptance of the leader's psychological distance. In the dynamic group the leader's position demands this distance not only because of his middle-class social closeness to members but because, by wanting something for them, he trades a degree of objectivity in return for their strengthened identity as goal-oriented professionals.

Thus in a dynamic group much of the group work centers around persuading the group leader to join them, to be more like them in function. It is hard to get group members to recognize that the study of group process and their part in it is an end in itself, which each must apply in his own way to his function as teacher or social worker. The group leader's behavior might be seen as less omnipotent than in a therapy group, but equally incomprehensible. Hence he remains clearly differentiated psychologically.

SYSTEMS THERAPY

The potential importance of the dual concern for individual and system is especially obvious in such therapeutic efforts as couple therapy, family therapy, and milieu therapy. Here the therapist no longer works with the individual, but with the system. A married couple, a family, or the ward of a mental hospital form a natural situation, a small social system, which occupies much of the life space of the individuals involved. In therapy, as in the rest of his current life, the individual appears as part of his usual social setting. The therapeutic endeavor is to preserve the system and to consider the individual's responses only insofar as his communications, positive or negative, reflect on the system which is threatened.

In the actual clinical situation of "marital counseling," for example, the question of what the therapist has been hired to do may not be perfectly clear. Just as a dynamic group of residents from the same hospital learns that their goal of knowing more about their individual responses as beginning psychiatrists may need to be modified to protect the system of a closely integrated residency training program, so a couple who want their marriage treated may find that the study of each of them as individuals intrudes on that goal. Thus, in contrast to individual or group therapy, where the value of studying the individual case is accepted as worthwhile, in systems therapy the study of the individual case may be recognized as destructive of the system and, hence, of the therapy. There is no doubt as to who is the therapist in systems therapy, but conflict sometimes arises from the need to give priority to the system over the individual.

The therapist, by his willingness to work to preserve the system, shows that he accepts the system as valuable. This indeed limits the therapeutic relationship. The more traditional the social structures accepted by the therapist, the smaller the area where he and the patient can meet to consider objectively, without defensiveness, the patient's responses to his social setting.

Thus, even more than dynamic groups, the systems therapies struggle with the value positions implicit in the therapeutic goals. Conducting marital therapy commits the therapist to the value of marriage as an institution, though the therapist may maintain his neutrality about the value of the particular marriage he is treating. Once he is committed to that much of current social convention, is it not fair to wonder what other cultural values and conventional institutions he holds as "good"? If he has clearly defined positions on what these good behavior patterns are, will he not judge deviations?

The situation is clearest in mental-hospital milieu therapy (Zinberg and Glotfeldty 1968). There the therapist is not paid by the patient but by the hospital. The "patient," in effect, is the hospital ward itself, which exists to establish a milieu that is "better" for all. The hospital also operates on the belief that learning is transferable and that a person who achieves improved functioning in a hospital ward should function better in society. The therapist's job has far less to do with individual idiosyncratic responses than with the general demands of establishing a coherent milieu. And that milieu must be coherent within a framework of rules, regulations, mores, values, and principles acceptable to his employer, the hospital. The patient, too, is limited in his expressions because in ward meetings, no matter how free in intent, he does not leave his usual social setting. Despite verbal agreements about objectivity, the participant's responses can have real-life consequences for him. He can please or offend other participants, including the authorities running the meetings, with whom he must contend after the meeting. Hence in the ward group, as in family, couple, or other institutional groups, it is possible to study the workings of a system, how it uses or rejects parts or persons, and the open or closed avenues of communication and the sources of power within it, but at the cost of basic restrictions on the freedom of members to study themselves. There are similar restrictions on the leader's flexibility as he becomes the proponent of "reasonable" behavior. The therapist as an individual dealing with a system is clearly differentiated socially and psychologically from individuals who are members of the system, and no effort is made to close that gap. Doubts as to who the therapist is "for" in systems therapy, and the extent to which he indeed wants, because of the demands of his job, social conformity from the participants, indicate a doctor/patient model quite different from the traditional one-to-one therapy situation with an objective therapist and a defined patient.

ENCOUNTER GROUPS

Encounter or marathon groups, which under the rubric of a therapeutic encounter use confrontation as a technique, place their emphasis on highly charged emotional interactions among participants. Such groups gather together for the purpose of boldly and defiantly telling each other "how it is." They report directly not only on what each participant feels but on their direct emotional responses to what another says or is. Boldness can be humorous, even gentle, and not antagonistic or forceful, but it is direct and related to effect (Myerson 1973). In these groups one member responds to another's statement of feeling by saying, "Make me believe it! You say it but I don't feel it. Make me feel what you feel." These interchanges get tensions out into the open and expressed. The resultant behavioral manifestations of the emotional interchange are accepted and valued (Corwin 1973). Conversely, a reflective study of the individual as a separate entity and of the factors inhibiting his expression of feelings is devalued. In fact, to focus on conflicts within an individual may be conceived of as a derogatory procedure in the encounter situation. All are in the group together and all are there to "give" to others.

In these groups the concept of leader is resisted. Once the person who calls the group together has performed that function, he makes little effort to differentiate himself from other participants. He talks freely about his own feelings and reactions, and bases his relationship with other group members on these highly charged, emotional interactions, just as they do with each other. The impact develops as a result of these direct expressions of feeling.

Once the "leader" participates directly and indicates that he has feelings that can be aroused or hurt, that he will defend or attack just like anyone else, he relinquishes his invulnerability, but this does not prevent group members from being concerned about authority and dominance. Further, if there is a putative "leader," it is he who is the most natural repository for such feelings despite his renunciation of the role. The other group members, paradoxically, find themselves in a position where the free expression that is so valued may have to be curtailed. If a member wishes to please or to attack the putative group leader, he runs the risk of rejection, retaliation, or feeling guilty. He finds this situation very close to an ordinary interactional social situation in spite of the group's emphasis on expression of feeling. For although the decision about what to express may be different in a confrontation situation—hence, loud angry feelings may please rather than offend—the essential focus is on the degree of control or lack of it that one exercises, as opposed to the study of what may now or might originally have inhibited feeling. Little attention is given to understanding past conflicts and inhibitions. Hence, members' reactions to a leader who takes the privileges of a participant, relinquishes control over his own responses, and thus declares his vulnerability are experienced as active, rational, and in the present.

This therapeutic method tries to reduce the psychological distance between leader and participants to zero and frankly wants this for participants. It is considered per se "better" for people to face each other freely and without shame. The groups are supposed to be democratic and to have the idealistic goal of helping group members to cleanse themselves of hidden poisonous feelings so that they can care for and about each other. Here a means/end conflict develops. Is this reduction of psychological distance a means to an end or the end itself? What are the participants in these groups searching for?

Some encounter group participants, particularly those from the middle class, hope that the experience will teach them, force them, to "feel." They express little curiosity as to what may have *stopped* them from feeling, which, after all, is as much a part of the human birthright as breathing. If, in their struggle to experience, this comes up at all, it is given a social rather than a psychological explanation. Confrontation groups assume anthropomorphically that our increasingly mechanized society victimizes individuals by recreating them in its own depersonalized image.

In their case the means, reducing psychological distance, seems to become an end. It is not that participants literally do not feel, but rather that they do not like what they feel any better than they like internal restrictions against some feelings. They want both the process of feeling and the feelings themselves to be "better." They long to be cleansed not only of hate and anxiety but also of greed, lust, cruelty, sorrow, and especially envy, leaving only love and caring for one's fellow man. An ideal human interaction that eliminates dominance or submission requires more than freedom from conflict; there must also be freedom from difference. Differential equality is not enough because where there is difference there can always be jealousy, desire, and disagreement. Should such feelings exist, there is no hope for noetic fulfillment, oceanic gratification, or a mystic oneness with each other.

Certainly dynamic groups of all sorts desire to close the division between group and leader and, by reducing that distance, to achieve a unity that would permit them to relate to an outside, third party (Boris, Zinberg, and Boris 1975). Dynamic group members believe that they cannot be better teachers or group leaders until they can decide together what "better" is. Thus they are intolerant of the leader's insistence that they study their differences and divisions. Unrealistically, the group believes that by confronting each other with their "real" feelings, they can eliminate social and psychological differences. Members hope to eliminate narcissistic barriers (Boris 1973). In answer to the question "Is each man an island?" they want to be able to shout a "no" so resounding that for an instant each could believe that he might truly and totally share another's feelings.

To the extent, then, that confrontation techniques become an ideologically endowed end for those trying to escape internal and external conflicts and inhibitions, the method appears to be a gimmick or a fad. In groups so motivated it is no paradox that the "leader" can become a tape-recorded instruction. What is wanted from the leader is impossible, and hence it matters little what or who he is. Michael Oakeshott (1968) once said: "To try to do something which is inherently impossible is always a corrupting enterprise." If the aim of these confrontation groups is to exalt humanity to a totally loving state, the result is the denial of the dignity of the human struggle. This is *misuse* of the confrontation techniques, and a misunderstanding not only of people but also of the therapeutic process as a process, not an end or an ideology.

It would not be too far-fetched to describe encounter groups as attempts at systems therapy in which the system to be treated is the larger social setting itself. Instead of exploring the inhibitions and fears that might interfere with an individual's ability to adjust in society, these groups assume that unreasonable social conditions have resulted in his present distress. One may well wonder why a middle-class person, who is socially accepted, with verbal and intellectual skills, and with emotional problems of living stemming from a difficulty in using what he has needs to fear such social influences so greatly. This concept makes a good deal more sense when applied to a drug user, labeled deviant by society for his drug use per se, or to an inarticulate, low-skilled, working-class black.

CHOOSING A TECHNIQUE

Choosing the right technique to use with different groups is a complex matter; one cannot always adopt as a rule of thumb the notion that when there is great social distance one should choose a technique that minimizes psychological distance, and vice versa. With groups who have somehow fallen into social crevices, we find some of the same problems as those encountered in systems therapy. Society defines an addict as deviant: not surprisingly, he organizes a relatively coherent identity around what such social institutions as the law, the school, the church, and conventional public opinion think of him. Erik H. Erikson (1959) describes this as a negative identity. The acceptance of himself as an embodiment of bad characteristics protects the addict from internal conflict but as part of the same dynamic process ensures continued conflict with society. He is seen and sees himself as part of a delinquent social subsystem.

When the leader/therapist does something similar and organizes *his* identity around acts which are really only part of a technique, but which he begins to see not as means but ends, then individual interactive elements get lost, and it is system versus system. Traditional therapeutic techniques require the psychiatrist to see his patients as individuals, to listen carefully, and to indicate gently and objectively how he has understood what he has heard. Such techniques are benign and reasonable, hard to fault. However, this behavior leaves the therapist an inviolable, invulnerable, distant thing. Furthermore, at this point in history, these techniques must be viewed not just as the technician intends them to be perceived but as they are perceived by the recipient. For such techniques are now well known and can represent stereotypes as readily as do the acts of the drug addict. The stereotypical view associated this sort of approach with the social desire that the addict get "better." Just as the addict then perceives the leader as only a representative of the reforming social system—the very social system whose repudiation provides him with a raison d'être—so could the youngsters and the teachers in this project view such a leader as hoping to reform them and lead them into "better" ways. This view is a far cry from an objective partnership whose sole hope is some understanding of what goes on in each member and in the groups.

The middle-class therapist/leader has often been called upon to empathize with someone with whom he could not share specific subjective experiences: males with pregnant women, females with men who have premature ejaculations, tall persons with short ones, and so on. Hence his assumption that his invulnerable, relative objectivity permits communication that surpasses difference is rooted in his experience. But what he fails to see is that his experience is usually with people who have sought him out, who see the problem as an intrapsychic one, and who share a large number of perceptions, assumptions, and values, chief among them an acceptance of their relatedness to the social system. Thus the specific subjective experiences that are not shared are surrounded by myriads of shared understandings that slowly overcome mistrust. When a "junkie" or a migrant worker expresses mistrust of people who haven't experienced what he has experienced, it is hard for the middle-class therapist to separate it from similar statements about differences among people when made by members of his own social class. He fails to see that he and the junkie represent two different social subsystems with little shared social experience that might open avenues of communication and begin a working relationship (Zinberg 1975). Too often pupils and teachers also see themselves almost as belonging to different social systems, just as do teachers and principals. In fact, despite the difference in age and status, all of these groups turned out to have views of values, mores, and a basic concept of language use which were more similar than different.

In situations where the social distance is great, the reduction of psychological distance may be necessary. This is true for professionals working with addicts and with troubled, low-skilled, working-class patients; it is also true in our educational projects, where teachers were invited to abandon their traditional roles and act more or less as group leaders with adolescents who wanted to talk about sex, prejudice, and drugs. The social distance between teacher and pupil is so great that if the self-study group leader maintained the usual psychological distance, there could be little communication at all. The leader can readily relax the psychological distance by personal remarks without fear of loss of position, so completely sustaining are the differences in social roles. Surely something of the same sort is involved in child therapy techniques, where therapist and patient play games together.

The confrontation technique allows the therapist/leader to express his personal feelings directly and unequivocally. With addict groups, where so much language is not held in common, feelings serve as a *lingua franca*. The social distance assures separateness and a sense of human individuality between leader/member, communicator/constituent. In their ability to feel similar things and to "make me know it" they establish their common humanity and their potential ability to understand each other.

Here confrontation is a technique—a means, not a gimmick, fad, or end. It is a way of establishing communication. Confrontation techniques become one means for a therapist/leader to indicate that he is not a representative of a system. He confronts his constituent and so becomes a vulnerable practitioner who, despite his social distance, manifestly feels, responds.

Though the therapist may present himself as an individual who feels, this does not negate his awareness that he does not share the powerful impulses which have seemed undeniable to the addict and led him to drugs. The therapist tries to base the working alliance on a mutual recognition of each participant as an individual and not as a member of a system that needs reform by representatives of another system. Once an alliance is established more will be needed, perhaps including the more traditional analysis of why the practitioner's humanity was doubted in the first place. But without an alliance, little or nothing can be done.

A TECHNIQUE FOR THE PROJECT

Use of a technique that might overcome the gaps that would exist if the project moved into low-skilled, working-class schools, and black ones at that, risked creating special difficulties. It is one thing to try out a confrontation technique with addicts; it is quite something else to stir up youngsters in school by trying to reach them directly and emotionally. Once the difficulty of having to use such a technique was faced and a middle-class school decided upon, the choice of technique narrowed quickly. A one-to-one technique was not only too expensive in terms of personnel but was too close to a doctor-patient relationship and outside the usual experience of the participants. Also, the direct transference relationship to parents in a one-to-one situation would probably have to be worked through without the amelioration of a peer group.

When the choice of a dynamic group technique was made, we were aware of the difficulties. The one that preoccupied us most directly was the issue of the leader's not wanting anything from or for the participants (Rosenthal 1955; Sherif 1958). The very act of setting up a group indicated that a teacher, for example, could learn more about how he operated as a teacher, or a student could learn more about how he dealt with information already available. Was the group's leader not implying that a participant with that information would be a "better" teacher or student? Once leader and member agreed that the leader was saying that he knew what might make a participant a "better" anything, was it not "reasonable" for the member to ask the leader how he *should* go about all this? The answer is yes, in part. The second half of this book is in large measure a study of how the group members dealt with their hopes of getting something from the leader.

When we considered dynamic groups, we knew the extent of the emphasis that technique brought to bear on the leader (Stock and Thelen 1958; Whitaker and Lieberman 1964), but it would be fair to say that we still underestimated its extent. We reasoned that preoccupation with the leader, of course, might only represent the way in which the groups were run, or our own unconscious bias, rather than something indigenous in groups like these. We accepted that risk. The role of teacher or student is a normative role, which carries with it a coherent sense of what is fitting within that role, no matter what that person may feel about himself in other ways or at other times. Volunteering for a self-study group meant accepting the principle of self-study. It was an operating hypothesis of the team that the group members' conviction that the leader should tell them how to go about being better would itself turn into something to be studied. We assumed that the members would note the extent of the reality of that conviction. Indeed, the leader had taken the responsibility of calling the group together, but that was all he had done that could be directly construed as saying he knew what "better" was. We also thought that self-investigation might show the extent to which the hope to be better was based on an irrational concern about being defective or bad: a general misconception about, or overestimation, if you will, of what it means to be human.

CHAPTER THREE

THE GROUP CONSULTATION PROGRAM FOR TEACHERS

Part II contains abridged versions of group sessions to illustrate how individuals processed the group experience internally. Because this internal processing came to be the chief focus of the project, we have not written much about the manifest content of the discussions and the participants' more conscious responses. In order to give the reader a general orientation, we have included here and in Chapter 4 general descriptions of the groups, some illustrative anecdotes from the groups and the post-group interviews, and some subjective assessment of what the groups "accomplished."

The teachers' groups follow a fairly general pattern. The participants find it hard to believe that the leader will do what he said he would do, that is, be nondirective. After the beginning, when the members tell who they are, they flounder, first shooting looks at the leaders, then questions. The leaders usually turn aside these questions, implying that the individuals can think about the feelings that go into the asking of the questions (they did *not* respond mechanically, like the stereotype of a group leader: "What do you feel about that?"). This technique is highly frustrating, and particularly so when the questions are of a factual nature about racial issues. If there are black teachers or black leaders in the group, the discussion usually turns to questioning them about how to understand the black pupils now in suburban schools, and often, quite explicitly, how to control them in the classroom.

Cleavages develop in every group, some more distinct than others. There are usually a few white liberals allied with black teachers or operating independently to "answer questions" and challenge what they see as prejudiced attitudes. How these issues do or do not get explored is highly dependent on the group leader. Does he allow, or promote, rancorous conflict? Does he take sides with the liberal wing (no leader in these groups ever came out *for* racial prejudice) and blame someone —other group members, bad principals, citizens, child development methods, society—for the trouble? Or do the group leaders, generally speaking, maintain a relative neutrality and comment on the group splits, the use of projection by individual members, and the like? (See Appendix A to this chapter for an example of such a dialogue.)

Of our eighteen teachers' groups led by ten different leaders—two pilot project groups, four groups each term for two experimental years—we had one group leader who felt it a duty to promote conflict and two who not only took the liberals' side but also felt it necessary to lecture the groups on the evil of racial bias and urged them at all costs first to admit it and then expunge it from their souls and psyches. Interestingly enough, one of these groups was one of the most popular, for reasons that will become clear in Part II. Three other leaders who had one group each could only be described as ineffectual; that is, they did not lecture the group or promote conflict, and they preserved their benign neutrality, but they were not active. They did not point out dilemmas or inhibitions in the group process and their origins and expression in the discussions. At times the groups managed to prompt some member to take over the leader function and to notice general anxieties and resulting inhibitions. But if they could not get this subtle message across to some member or another, these leaders did not help out.

In the other twelve groups the discussions waned and waxed, with fearsome silences. They had specific difficulty deciding what they were there for—goals in these groups are easily and mysteriously mislaid—and how they should go about getting to wherever they wanted to go. More and more of the participants in these groups expressed more and more openly their fears, questions, angers, ambivalences about many things —METCO children most prominently—with a slowly growing ability to achieve greater clarity about their dual feelings, specific concerns, and the roots of their annoyance. Their annoyance, once recognized, spread from bad schools and bad principals to colleagues, to the METCO program, to pupils white and black, to the group leader, and finally to other group members. Most of the groups began to connect some of the intergroup responses with intrapsychic origins.

One way in which the progression showed itself fairly consistently was in the teachers' becoming aware that the students they once had been still influenced the teachers they were now. Their own pupil experience was revived in the group, usually through their relationship to the leader. In one group, for example, a teacher spoke very softly, and when the leader on a couple of occasions asked her to repeat what she said because he could not hear her, she became angry. Other group members noticed her annoyance and asked her about it, with the clear implication that it was unreasonable. She refused to comment then, but the following week she brought up the subject and told how as a child she had hated teachers who shouted. She was very frightened of them, and of one in particular, and remembered very well her early wishes to have a teacher who did not shout. This anecdote opened a discussion for her and other group members of the pain and disappointment inherent in fulfilling one's own early ideal, only to find that it is not necessarily appreciated. Such bitterness is hard to get into perspective. If one is unaware of how early experiences as a child affect one's teaching, it is easy to feel negative toward some children—for instance, the ones, whether they are green, purple, or puce, who sit at the back of the room and squeal, "I can't hear you, I can't hear you."

Another issue which arose consistently, unless the leader was so active or so inactive as to prevent it, was whether someone was "in the group" or out, that is, an outsider, a stranger. One could be different, a stranger, either by being an outside person or institution so designated by the group (e.g., a principal by a group of teachers) or by being an outsider within the group (e.g., the leader or a member espousing an unpopular cause or position). The extent to which this "stranger" came to represent an irrational threat to the group members, who could only be comfortable if all were like them, is a lesson in the dynamics of prejudice. Because our groups were convened under the aegis of METCO, it was inevitable that this "discovery" of how easy it was to arouse fear and hatred through what Freud (1914) called "the narcissism of small differences" was made explicit in terms of the METCO program.[1] It was the observation of the project team—and one of the basic reasons that led us to doubt the researchability of attitude change in these groups—that, when the group attacked a group member who, for instance, had defended the leader's reticence and when the group recognized how excessive the anxiety was that prompted the attack, there was an alive, electric atmosphere in the room. Then some clever group member would make the connection between this and how some people might feel about the METCO children. The other members would seize upon this and dutifully intone some comments about prejudice in themselves and others. It was as if the teachers who volunteered for a METCO group knew that it was foreordained for them to discover their "prejudice." Now, in doing so, they

---

[1] One element in prejudice (Allport 1954)—though certainly not the only component of this complex social and psychological phenomenon—is *difference*. If someone looks different from oneself or, as far as one can tell, thinks differently, he may be disapproving and hence an enemy. Prejudice reverses this procedure by striking first.

came together, which obscured their fully noticing their preoccupation with each other's differences: the very essence of prejudice.

The issue of what and who was prejudiced took a similar turn in so many of the groups that it seemed to represent a pattern, one that was extremely difficult for the leaders to handle. There would be one teacher (occasionally more than one) who was the best of the liberal element as far as the METCO kids were concerned. He or she was the one who, in his home school, had taken his own after-school time to set up mixed groups of kids to go to the theater or a sporting match or develop into teams. He had gone to great trouble to see that transportation back to the inner city, always a serious problem with bussed kids, was arranged. In short, he had done good. One respected and admired his efforts and knew that the development of METCO into an integrated program rather than just integrated classes depended on such people. And yet, once the members got over their initial admiration for his accomplishments, any one of them would have described him as a pain in the ass. Invariably, this good person was nowhere near good enough to suit himself. He detected evidence of prejudice in himself and asked to be punished for it, particularly by black group members. His insistence on that theme combined with his prestige seemed to leave the group with but two alternatives. They could try to join him by finding prejudice in themselves and worrying it endlessly, which they could never do to his satisfaction, or they could find themselves, oddly enough, defending prejudice and even racial bias. In either case, they became increasingly angry with Mr. Good.

The group leader's dilemma paralleled that of the group. Were he to point out, no matter how discreetly or tactfully, that this liberal member, in the course of fighting and punishing himself for evil, was managing to control and even to torment his peers, it would hurt that member's feelings. And the leaders each felt that whatever purpose this man's functioning with METCO kids might serve in his own psychic economy, it needed to be preserved. We must note parenthetically how heavy the aegis of METCO was, not just on the group members. If the leader supported this teacher's prejudice against prejudice, what chance had the group to think about and accept the concern about differences, which has been called the essence of prejudice? The leader would have as much as said that there was a clear place which we must strive to reach where we will be prejudice-free and thus without differences. Such a comment would certainly be against the entire principle of the group, although it must be reported that one group leader did just that.

Silence was not useful. The groups generally either broke into small warring subgroups who invented topics to fight about because they were so angry with Mr. Good and couldn't express it directly or became depressed or apathetic. Usually the leader said something or other about how splendid these accomplishments were, but how hard it was for the group to consider the necessity of different people doing things differently. To a certain extent this always meant directly disagreeing with Mr. Good, who didn't for a second believe that there was room for anything other than exposing and fighting every shred of prejudice. Sometimes the leader's comment made it possible for the group to join Mr. Good by attacking the leader for his usual nonspecific comments. Sometimes it allowed the group to move on to a different way of handling prejudice such as recognizing the pain in it for both parties and the extent of the conflict it evoked in any person who, although prejudicial, was willing to join a group like this one. Sometimes they took up an entirely different (at the conscious level) topic. Either way, a few sessions later some members were usually able to talk, without hurting the liberal teacher's feelings, about their frustration at being told how to be unprejudiced; these discussions would often be about some other issue so that the comments were less personal.

One way of looking at the groups (one which the project team resisted) was to think about them as having specific phases. There are many articles and books (Bales 1951; Bennis 1964; Corsini and Rosenberg, 1955; Durkin 1964; Homans 1950; Stock 1964) which show groups struggling with authority and intimacy or fight-flight and the like. We could not totally resist this concept, but our theoretical thinking (Chapter 21) looks toward underlying motivations in groups rather than behavioral manifestations. Our preoccupation with motive leads us to describe the group as now moved by hope or now by desire, which at the behavioral level might still be described by saying that the group now struggles with the authority question, now with the intimacy one. Probably many different students of groups end up finding different ways of looking at groups that yet have a certain similarity, because there is so much that is the same in groups. Yet each group is different and has individual characteristics based on its members, the leader's personality and choice of technique, the reasons for its coming together, and its relationship to events in social institutions (schools, hospitals, and so on) and in the larger society. But certain aspects of what happens in different groups seem similar and appear again and again. All our groups had important similarities, as they were made up of teachers who came together under the aegis of METCO, from schools that have METCO programs, all of which struggle with the overriding social significance of school integration; and so it is not surprising that the leader becomes for us a key variable in the ways in which the groups differ.

Leader importance is particularly striking when one looks more deeply at the groups' similarities (Bass 1960; Bell and French 1965; White and Lippit 1962; Yalom 1970). Most of the teachers were intensely identified with METCO kids and the METCO program but not with the leaders, whose psychological distance and objectivity were resented. Many of them thus shared the wish for the leader to *make* them super-teachers or to allow them to feel like *good* people: the first by a magical participating in what he has, his answers or wisdom, and the second by acceptance and love of them. This is what Part II is about. The teachers could see themselves identifying with the leader's activity, but they rejected his substantive position. For instance, many members began to ask other members searching questions, which they saw as counterparts to the leader's questions. Usually, at least in the early phases, these questions led toward discussion of how the member in question could have handled a particular real-life incident better, i.e., could have applied a more useful technique, could have known where to go for assistance, could have attempted to reform himself, to avoid difficulty, conflict, or disappointment. And, if the leader pointed this out, as he often did, such a comment too was experienced at first as a criticism and, what was perhaps worse, as condescension.

It took considerable time for most participants to recognize that their expectation that they share the benign objectivity of the leader was prototypical of their excessive expectations of themselves, was the very essence of their hope to be super-teachers or their desire to feel in a state of grace. For the leader has one job in the group, and the group member has a very different one. The leader's objectivity permits him the distance to be in touch with his feelings, to observe them and the group, and to make the separations that allow him to respond as much as possible in terms of the group. This capacity is not a personal one, but rests basically on the role definition of leader. He is charged with that responsibility, and it is accepted by him and the members simply by their turning up. Group members take turns at "leading" the group and, at times, are objective and helpful—more so than many leaders—but they have then usurped a role, and by doing so have created a group situation in which they must defend the aggression involved or explain why they have given up membership and taken on the leadership of other members. It is not their prerogative. Hence, when the leader points out members' efforts at identifying with him, he is not putting them down but is attempting to advance an understanding of their conviction that "things" can and should be going better than they have so far in the group. They can and should be taught better in the group, just as they should be better teachers. No doubt each of our group leaders wished for more experience, more ease, more understanding so that he could lead more surely and effectively, just as every teacher in the groups knew of mistakes in the classroom that kept lessons from going as smoothly as they might have.

To note that the hope to be better, to be super-teacher, created a problem for group members is not to call for bland self-satisfaction. It is to say that people must first know and accept what they are, what it means to be an imperfect, fallible human being who can be loved and respected as he is. On the basis of that kind of knowing and accepting of oneself, the acquisition of new knowledge or teaching techniques might be useful. If one recognized how much one did *not* want to acquire new knowledge, one might actually permit a somewhat different perception or perspective to emerge. The group members had little awareness of this view. They saw themselves as wide open to be improved, and only the niggling, frustrating distance and manner of the leader prevented it. When they were aware of powerful, mixed feelings about topics that should lead to improvement, they saw this as only the final evidence of their imperfection. Better to try to be like the leader and conceal such conflicting feelings, which can only lead to being unloved, criticized, exposed as unworthy, and even despised.

This view of the groups' functioning puts considerable responsibility on the leaders' maintaining neutrality. A leader who indicates that he is more interested in the members' being less prejudiced than he is in *how* they struggle with their prejudice appeals to a powerful hope in them; the leader who lectured and exhorted his group to be better was popular. Likewise a leader who promotes conflict—"Let's stir things up and get them out into the open"—minimizes the concept of a never-ending struggle within each of us. He agrees with the members' fear that all that hostility and anger is *the* real basic part of them, but that if it is painfully, ruthlessly brought out into the open, it can be changed, reformed, repressed, or even expunged. The leader who accepts the group's view that better techniques or more facts about black children are needed conveys the message that the human struggle is unnecessary. If one can plug into this or that better way, then all will come smooth and clean.

One way or another, these leaders offered "better ways." Neutral leaders don't. The benevolently neutral leader permits the member to see that his conviction that a better way is expected of him represents his projection onto the leader. No one expects better of the member, nay demands it, than he does himself. No one is as condemnatory of his humanity as he is. No one is as impatient with where the group is getting substantively—that is, as endlessly concerned that it is getting no-where—by noticing blocks, inhibitions, struggles, and conflicts than he is. Once some of his concern to be better becomes clear to him as a sign of his unwillingness to accept himself as he is, he as a teacher and as a group member is more likely to accept as a shared value the leader's description about what is going on. But like most of the basic human struggles, his fear that someone else expects this perfection of him still comes and goes. For, after all, can one know that the desire to be a better teacher will come, after one has accepted the desire not to change? How hard it is for each group member and for all of us to accept the human struggle as never-ending.

Several post-group interviews were conducted. The participants were asked why they had joined the groups and what they thought of the sessions. Motives given were a better understanding of (1) METCO and black kids and a wish to learn more about the METCO program; (2) those responsible for the program and how to improve it; (3) available information for teaching black children; (4) how other teachers handle black and white children together; (5) how black children misconstrue you so that I can present myself better; (6) prejudice in self and schools and how other schools have overcome it; (7) what my feelings are about these kids so I can feel more comfortable. Of these seven reasons, three can be catalogued as desires for information, three as desires for techniques, and only one as a wish for self-study.

Data like these led the project team to a greater interest in how each individual processed the group experience. The data showed that people were selecting an experience to try to get something that those offering the experience explicitly said was not available. How would people deal with such an inherently frustrating situation? How had they made that choice, by not noticing what was offered or by concealing from themselves motives other than those stated?

The only direct data we have about the teachers' responses to the groups came from the post-group interviews: 74 answers to questionnaires mailed to 103 participants after the 1968–69 sessions and post-group report forms given to 106 participants in the 1969–70 groups. In addition some indirect data were garnered from Mrs. Batson. She asked the METCO representatives at each school to find out what they could about what participating and nonparticipating teachers said about the groups at their schools. The excerpts given in Appendix B to this chapter were chosen because they were typical and brief. They include both positive and negative comments. The more-or-less positive outweighed the more-or-less negative about three to one, with almost no opinion 100 percent in one direction or another, not even those of the teachers who had dropped out of the groups.

APPENDIX A: SPLITTING AND PROJECTION IN GROUPS

To give a brief example of splitting and projection, let us look at an excerpt from one of our teachers' groups. The second meeting is just beginning.

Mr. R: With regard to the number of people, I'm surprised at so many. I would have guessed half as many. It seems curious. I think what brought people also stirred them to come back to see who had left.

Group leader: Why did you expect that?

Mr. R: There seemed to be failure in their faces, attitudes of dissatisfaction. They felt doing that fourteen more times would depress most of the people.

Group leader: What was a failure?

Mr. R: Not failure but that expectations had not been met. I felt they would not come when they saw what we would do.

Mrs. J: I expected everyone because I couldn't wait to come back. I was amazed at how much you think about people when you don't say anything. So—

[Silence]

If we look closely at this brief interchange, we see some curious things. On one level, we can say that two views of expectations are expressed: Mr. R is critical, and Mrs. J is pleased. Mr. R and Mrs. J, voicing opposing views, appear to be at the brink of an argument. Then everything trails off in silence.

What Mr. R and Mrs. J have done is to split the "good" expectations and the "bad" expectations between them, so that neither consciously has to experience both at once. Let us hypothesize that each feels that the group experience will be more wonderful and more terrible than one can imagine. To keep such a two-edged feeling within is intolerable; yet part of the essence of the experience is its two sides. To conserve both sides, if we assume "conservation" matters, Mr. R and Mrs. J split them, and each reposes in the other what he wishes to maintain but not to hold within. Mr. R and Mrs. J, then, make use of *projection* as a way of keeping alive, instead of renouncing, what are felt to be valued but intolerable feelings.

Projection is generally understood as a mechanism of defense used by the individual's ego when faced with an intolerable impulse. It takes place in three phases: first, the individual is aware of a forbidden impulse, e.g., *I hate him*; second, he unconsciously projects this impulse onto someone else, thus freeing himself of it, *I do not hate him*; but third, he then automatically perceives the repressed impulse directed back at him from the reciprocal, *he hates me*. We came to understand that projection as a means of defense fails in these groups unless those onto whom the projections fall are willing to assimilate them and act as if they were not imaginings, but matters of fact. This reciprocation is a dynamic element in groups. As long as the group in some way lends countenance or approval to these projections, as long as it sanctions them, then they can serve the simple principle that nothing should be lost or wholly renounced. We find that in a curious way when two people, or two sides, have split the conflict between them they are, underneath, sharing a common assumption.

Projection might be parsed as follows:

Mr. R: I'm surprised at so many . . . They felt doing that fourteen more times would depress most of the people . . . I felt they would not come when they saw what we would do.

[Intolerable feeling:] I was dying to come to the second meeting.

[Feeling is repressed and denied:] I didn't want to come to the second meeting at all. The thought of wanting to come so much was depressing.

[Repressed feeling is projected:] The others must have wanted not to come when they saw what we would do. They only came to see who wouldn't come.

[Projection sanctioned by the group:] Either silence or assent would reinforce Mr. R's projection. Facial expressions that could be interpreted as dissatisfaction, or the absence of even a few group members from the second meeting would keep his projected position firm.

Mrs. J: I expected everyone because I couldn't wait to come back. I was amazed at how much you think about people when you don't say anything. So—

[Intolerable feeling] I had bad thoughts and feelings about people at the first meeting.

[Feeling is repressed and denied:] I didn't have bad thoughts. I had nothing but good thoughts about everyone.

[Repressed feeling is projected:] They probably thought that my silence meant that I had bad thoughts, and I can't bear for them to think that.

[Projection is sanctioned:] The group conveys, in one way or another: "We are glad that you told us, because we now know that you didn't have bad thoughts."

APPENDIX B: DATA FROM POST-GROUP INTERVIEWS

From teacher interviews, questionnaires, and report forms:

I [a white teacher] reassessed my own objections to the unfair advantages of blacks in the job market.

I had wanted to change the aloof attitudes of others, but found that some of my attitudes changed.

I learned how ambitious I was.

I thought I would learn new teaching techniques and didn't, but was not too disappointed.

I learned a lot about racial imbalance and what others hoped to achieve in bussing.

The discussion never got into the black/white situation that I was most interested in.

The leader was not enough interested in METCO, which was why I joined the group.

I learned a lot about how METCO kids fitted into the school.

I became more inner-directed as a teacher as a result of the experience.

I learned to see myself through the eyes of the students.

Talking about problems and frustrations has made my experience in teaching more relevant.

I became less defensive about other people's ideas.

From Mrs. Batson:

Many of the teachers thought they got a lot out of it.

Some groups continued informally into the following year because they found they wanted to continue to talk over their problems.

White teachers said, "I had no idea what black people were like before I joined this group."

Many teachers said it helped them particularly with discipline. A kindergarten teacher said that after the group she could discipline black kids without falling apart.

Several teachers thought the leaders should have been more active and told them more about black kids.

The leaders didn't seem to know enough about METCO.

All in all, the comments were nondescript. Some liked the program, some didn't. Some said they liked it but, in our opinion, didn't. Some said they didn't, but we thought they would remember the experience later and that its meaning would grow and change in their minds slowly. Just what the project meant to these people, how their attitudes did or did not change as a result, was not easy to pin down using our data. And we certainly had no way of delineating how the teachers participating conveyed to their students whatever the experience had meant to them.

The urge for the need to discharge in activity was far greater than in the adult groups. "Freedom" in the student groups meant freedom to *do* something you ordinarily shouldn't. Homework was done, books read, friends brought in; there were silences, latenesses, sleeping, whispering, and refusals to repeat dirty words if asked. In the junior high groups, all the mechanisms of childhood appeared: giggling to the point of physical helplessness, punching on the arm, kicking, spitballs, paper airplanes, dirty words repeated to no purpose, nonsense talks, and above all no coherent response to anything the leader asked. You won't talk to us the way we want, we won't talk to you. No one is doing much talking or listening.

This mechanism will be discussed at length in Part II. It stirred up the leaders, and was probably intended to do so. As a consequence, we have to ask whether children of this age, even though they volunteer, are too young to be asked to participate in a discussion group, whether this leader is adequate to the task of conducting such a group, whether youngsters of this age can verbally communicate their preoccupations, and whether they raised some of the more important issues in their discussions.

Some of the questions are easily answered. We know that children have the vocabulary for discussing their feelings (Piaget 1962); human preoccupations can be expressed in the simplest language. More ornate and complex language is required to obscure or dress up one's basic concerns. These children had already demonstrated their capacity to participate in a discussion group by the time they reached an impasse. Even the seventh-graders talked about things that concerned them, raised pertinent questions, and expressed their feelings, although those feelings were chiefly ones of frustration, anxiety, and fear (direct or indirect) of criticism. But is that not to be expected, given their usual relationships to adults—to parents and teachers?

The question about adequate leadership is harder to answer. The teacher/leaders were inexperienced and subjected to unusually provocative group experiences. The great social distance between leader and member required a lessening of psychological distance, so that the leaders were asked to be benignly objective and neutral, and yet to be human and convey some feeling of what they were like as people. Let us take a look at some of the teacher/leaders' experiences.

Each teacher had his own style, strengths and weaknesses, and concerns. Such differences were often the crucial factor in his relations to the members of his group, the project researcher and supervisor, his colleagues, and the authorities in the school. All the high school teachers shared a fascination with the exciting and mysterious world of today's adolescents that frequently interfered with their ability to discern covert meanings in the groups' interaction and to share this knowledge with the participants. Although apprised of the consequences of this preoccupation in many general meetings, all the teachers (in varying degrees) still frequently allowed themselves to be so titillated by the private earful they were getting that their third ear was sadly neglected. Consequently, useful material was often passed over unanalyzed.

The junior high school leaders encountered many of the same problems as those in the high school. If they were less entranced by their glimpse into the world of their students, they were more eager to create a successful group experience and thus more susceptible to discouragement and withdrawal. They were most like the high school teachers in their reluctance to disturb their students with interpretive interventions.

The teachers displayed various capacities for "eschewing all authoritarian comments" and enacting the role of the nondirective leader effectively. This capacity seemed to be a function of how threatened the individual teachers felt in their relations with the students.

MRS. V

Mrs. V, a group leader in the pilot project and one of the high school leaders, was an English teacher in late middle age with older children of her own. She seemed to be struggling with the difficult issue of sexuality in persons of declining age. Interestingly enough, this was the primary preoccupation of her group the first year she participated. As the observer reported,

Mrs. V's group's response to her proved to me once and for all the extraordinary sensitivity groups can have. None of its members were her regular students, yet in the first session they chose as testing ground a subject that could be characterized as why don't adults give up, they are old and dried up, anyway! This subject for this woman, whose children were nearly grown, was obviously one of immense concern. She just kept quiet in the first session and in the second, when they continued, successfully showed them how curious they were about what made adults tick.

Dating behavior and the generation gap were clearly the topics which "turned her on." (Mrs. V taught sex education at the school in addition to English.) Thus, sometimes her keen interest in such issues prevented her and her students from being able to see how and why they were using the discussion to express personal concerns. In the fourth meeting of the year, for example, Mrs. V had every reason to be preoccupied with two issues: (1) one of the original members had announced his intention to leave the previous week and, despite some coaxing on the part of her and the group, did not attend this session, and (2) the only girl in her group of ten has thus far been excluded from the discussion. Mrs. V may have sensed that the girl might leave soon also; she did so just one week later. Mrs. V elected to deal with her own concerns by persistently maneuvering the members into a discussion of the responsibility boys had on a date. In the general meeting for leaders, Mrs. V said she "goofed" in conducting her meeting, but "got satisfaction out of knowing how the boys felt on things."

Although her supervisor warned her that getting involved and excited in the group discussion made her a silent participant and not an observer, the following week she closed her meeting with a short lecture on hermaphrodites. Two weeks later she found herself admitting in the general teachers' session that she introduced a discussion of sex into her group because she "didn't want another week of silence." She said she "broke every rule in the book but it was a good discussion." Again the supervisor and the researcher pointed out to all the teachers their tendency to concentrate on individual students rather than the group and on social topics rather than group issues. Even as the group began drawing to a close in May, Mrs. V still managed to engage her group for three sessions in a discussion of the proper behavior and apparel for old people and kids (she had worn a short skirt to a school function recently and drew comment about her dress). In indirect ways the group told Mrs. V to "act her age," while Mrs. V countered that there was some "selfishness" in the group and that maybe they didn't want to admit that older people still had sex drives.

Mrs. V genuinely liked students and often volunteered for extra duty—shepherding girls to a home economics convention, setting up and supervising a temporary nursery school, and so forth. With three sons of her own, however, the temptation to treat the group as "my boys" was too much. In addition to the flirtatious undertones of her remarks, there was a motherly, nurturing quality to her relationship with her group members which allowed the students occasionally to indulge their needs for attention and dependency without having to address themselves to that issue very squarely. For example, Mrs. V quickly fell into the ritual of writing out passes excusing the students for being late to their next class because the group met at some distance from where the other classes were held. Even when it became evident that although none of the other teachers issued passes their students didn't have any difficulty making their next classes on time, Mrs. V continued to write out the passes.

Like the other leaders, but to an even greater extent, Mrs. V found it very difficult to retain the detachment necessary to serve as a focal point for group issues and as a model for how members might relate themselves to each other. Although she exhibited acute sensitivity and insight in her written summaries of the group meetings, she could only rarely bring herself to share these observations with the youngsters. Halfway through the year, Mrs. V was able to admit in the general meeting that when the supervisor had interpreted some of her remarks for her in the past, she was defiant and it bothered her. She said she would have to go home and think about what was said before she decided that the interpretations were accurate. She said that she had refrained from making interpretations in her group because she didn't want to bother them in the same way. Toward the end of the year, she was still sufficiently ambivalent about the issue to say to her youngsters' group, "I don't think any of you should feel psychoanalyzed in here. I guarantee you I don't know anything about psychoanalysis." After she reported these comments in her teachers' group, her nemesis, the supervisor, replied, "That's obvious." She said, "Thank you," in a nonsarcastic tone and dropped the matter completely.

Like some other leaders, Mrs. V was very preoccupied with the presence of the research observer. The observer made her feel vulnerable and self-conscious. More important, his constant presence thwarted her desires to indulge at least occasionally in her impulses to teach didactically or to ask pointed questions about things in which she was interested. The researcher reminded her of the painful things she should be doing —like interpreting and being open—and the pleasurable things she shouldn't—like flirting with or nurturing "her boys." When she allowed herself to indulge such impulses, she felt guilty and would reproach her students for taking advantage of her when she had to appease such dangerous authorities as the principal and the English Department head. Mrs. V was quite preoccupied with her relations to these authorities in some general meetings as well. Although there was some substance to her concerns, the observer noted that they were usually expressed at times when Mrs. V felt most guilty about cheating in her group. One tactic occasionally used to cope with her feelings toward the observer was to manipulate her students into expressing her displeasure over his presence. An excerpt from a meeting in mid-November will illustrate:

Mrs. V asked the group why they waited for her to cue them to start talking, but there was no response. John suggested the researcher read the minutes and Mrs. V asked the group if it bothered them that he was taking notes. John said, "Yeah," and there was some laughter. Mrs. V asked if they knew why he was here and then asked if they wanted to hear what he had written down. John said, "Yes," and George said, "No." There was some noise and confusion. John said, "Who wants all your words written down?" Manny asked Mrs. V to give them something to talk about. This request was not answered and the conversation temporarily lapsed.

The crisis point in Mrs. V's relationship with the researcher occurred in April (Starr 1970). In the meeting of April 8, with the supervisor's approval, the researcher expressed some of the feelings of frustration that had been building in him regarding Mrs. V's performance in the group. He indicated that he felt she had sort of given up. He made reference to some caustic remarks she had recently made as well as some lengthy silences she had endured without intervention as reflections of that impatience and/or resignation. She complained that she was still learning and didn't know that much about leading groups. The researcher replied that it was not so much a question of information, but of feelings; that she had demonstrated her insight in the written summaries, but appeared discouraged and resigned in the group setting. The researcher said he felt Mrs. V's disclaimer that she was too stupid was an excuse. Discussion turned to the leader's attitudes toward making interpretations in the group, and there was some agreement that such activity was still considered somewhat illicit and something to be careful of lest it disturb or alienate the students.

Mrs. V took heart and finished the year off with more enthusiasm. Once her apathy abated, she tended to return to her previous method of stimulating the group with provocative remarks but with more restraint than formerly. She ended the year feeling positively toward the experience and led social education groups the following two years. With each year she gained in experience and comfort in the group situation and never found herself again quite so much at odds either with her group or with her colleagues.

MR. D

Mr. D, another high school leader/teacher, was under the initial impression that the object of the group was to get the kids to see both sides of issues discussed. The members of his group often gravitated to the same theme—the police. The researcher said of Mr. D's first group that they "went after authority and policemen, a subject clearly not to his taste, like a jaguar to the jugular. They were the least verbal group, more silent and restless, but even they could partially see this behavior as the concrete representation of what they were feeling about him."

Judging by his remarks and written summaries, Mr. D made a sincere effort to stick by his guns and not give in to his group's request for direction. The students reciprocated by clamming up, and, after a month, Mr. D began to show signs of severe frustration. He complained about his group's stubborn silence and denial of his interpretations. The supervisor explained that his group was angry at him for not directing them and was giving him a taste of his own medicine. He added that their silence could only mean that they wanted to talk about themselves but felt at the same time that they couldn't or shouldn't talk about themselves. In late November, the supervisor pointed out that Mr. D tended to ask questions when he didn't like what was happening, or not happening. He said that questions from him appeared to them as policeman signals and they felt criticized. He said you want the group to do what they want, but you also want them to do it your way. He pointed out how Mr. D reprimanded one member and supported another in his last session. He said he had the feeling that it would be better for Mr. D to take specific issues and generalize them.

Throughout December Mr. D continued to express feelings of discouragement and annoyance. The fact that conversation in his group often centered on the police suggested to the supervisor that the members felt that whatever they had on their minds to do was forbidden and they were going to get caught. In January Mr. D's group continued feeling that he was judging them and expressed it in discussions of guilty dreams and police harassment. At the same time Mr. D admitted that he felt a sense of being inhibited from saying certain things or participating in certain ways in the group. The supervisor explained that as long as the leaders themselves felt threatened or discouraged, the members of the group would feel this way also. He encouraged them to express themselves when appropriate. Still, Mr. D's frustration carried into February when he began to express particular annoyance at one boy's domination of the group. He said he had become a little aggravated that the other kids hadn't started to put him down yet. The researcher asked him why he thought this was, and he said that perhaps they didn't feel strong enough yet. The supervisor said, "And you wish they would." He asked him why he felt it was his problem, and Mr. D pointed out that he himself had conceded the boy's dominance on one occasion.

Near the end of the session the supervisor said that progress in the groups depended on how much the leaders cared and how willing they were to show the students their sadness and hurt. He said anger is the easiest thing to show, as there is a quality of righteousness to it. Anger, however, was really the reaction to his feeling of loss of control, disappointment, and sadness.

In April all the trends in Mr. D's group converged. In a highly emotional rendering he described his most recent group session in which the group—especially one previously silent girl—rose up to put the boy down. The supervisor led the adult group into a long and fruitful analysis of the situation, pointing out that the intense envy all the teachers were expressing of the boy in question had to do with the boy's aggressive efforts to command attention and their own feelings of frustration due to the restraints imposed upon them by the supervisor's advocacy of the nondirective role. Mr. D's ability to acknowledge his own desires to dominate the group and to understand his antipathy toward the boy in this light somehow seemed to set him free. His perception and leadership skill, like that of the others but in an even more marked way, greatly improved as the year drew to a close.

MRS. G

Mrs. G, a math teacher for the seventh grade with peripheral responsibilities for girls' athletics, conveyed an aura of firmness that seemed to border on the authoritarian. Her own education had included convent school, and at one period of her life she was a novitiate; even now, in her middle twenties, she seemed unusually certain of the rights and wrongs of most issues. She had spent recent summers working in day-camp programs with the mentally retarded, which suggested a sense of compassionate mission for young people, at least when their need for special concern was evident. She seemed to possess an almost dogmatically equalitarian approach to things. She also was less easily discouraged than the men. The deeper she got into the complications that developed in her group, the harder she fought. She had unquestionably the most eventful and productive group experience of them all.

In the first session she looked to her group only to find that they were no less looking to her. Mrs. G discovered herself at a loss. Her expectation had been that the twelve- and thirteen-year-old boys and girls who were in her group had things in mind. In this she was, of course, entirely correct, as time was to prove. But in that first meeting, as in those that followed it for a while, there did not seem to be anything much to talk about, certainly nothing to discuss. An acute and clearly painful sense of self-consciousness pervaded the atmosphere. It was all Mrs. G could do not to introduce topics and require "class" discussion.

That she did not was in part a result of her belief that the project directors knew that they were about. The directors had urged that the leaders withstand the pressure from their groups to re-establish the familiar pattern of the classroom, whereby the teacher proposes and the students dispose. But what was to occur, Mrs. G demanded, when the kids weren't discussing anything, when they were either sitting around in moody silence or whispering and giggling? Mrs. G, like her colleagues, had seen this happen before, and it always presaged trouble. The usual antidote was to come in hard, with directive leadership and firm discipline if idle hands were not to do the devil's work. Despite the fact that the supervisor's counsel went against Mrs. G's sense of the fitness of things, she struggled to put his suggestions into effect.

In subsequent meetings she focused continually on the difficulty the youngsters were having getting started, and half in response to her attention to the problem and half to escape it, the youngsters began to talk.

These early sessions were in their way crucial. The students sorely missed the constraints of the classroom and were much afraid of the sudden freedom they were given. They felt the risk of irrelevance and inappropriateness, and the stretch of time seemed an endless expanse of desert to cross before the familiar oasis of the classroom could once more be attained. Moreover, it was clear to them that Mrs. G, whom they were coming to like for the gift of freedom she was giving them, was struggling with disappointment in herself and in them, and this at once worried and angered them. Their task, accordingly, was a difficult one. They had to find a way of expressing what was on their minds in a form that was acceptable to the group, to Mrs. G, and to themselves; they wanted to talk freely, but not too freely, and they had to find a way of learning what such an optimum condition would be. At the same time, the difficulty of this task discouraged and irritated them, and they were tempted to say to hell with it, and either subside into indifference or act out their own annoyance by being annoying.

In focusing on these difficulties and making them something that could be talked about, Mrs. G provided the group with a leg up on the problems. The first real sign that the group was coming to feel that the struggle was worth the candle came when the youngster who had been using much of the session to recount the "Laugh-In" program of that week was firmly shushed. Even those who had previously been using those narratives, both to fill time and to insinuate the program's salacious overtones into the group, joined in. Now, with the conviction developing that to talk about how hard it is to talk is a good and useful thing to do, those who had taken the early lead in avoiding the issue were no longer valuable. In the fifth session that same youngster was called by another in the group a "retard." Other members, fortified with greater generosity as a result of their burgeoning confidence that they and the group would surmount temporary setbacks, protested. Retardation became the topic, and the discussion took place on two levels. On the manifest level it was an effort to learn about this mystifying and terrifying phenomenon, its cause, condition, and mutability. Indirectly—latently, as it were—there was at work a sorting out of acceptance and rejection, of compassion and fear about differences in competence, articulateness, brains, and the like. When it became evident that Mrs. G worked with mentally retarded children in the summers, the group felt both prized and safe. She could accept them at any level of competence, and in her eyes there was hope.

After that session, Mrs. G received a note of thanks from one member of the group. Others chipped in together to bring cookies to the following session. The group had become a place to be invested in, a nest to be feathered.

Gradually the meaning of the early constraint became clearer. Secure now in the reciprocal acceptance that all would and could offer each, more and more personal concerns began to emerge. The kids talked of home and school, of dating and parties, admitting to their worries, their strivings, their hatreds. And then came a session when, taking off from the phrase "blowing someone to a treat," the group came to a dead pause. Mrs. G later said it was as if everyone but she knew what was coming next. She wondered whether it was planned. More likely it was not; rather, the group members sensed that they might now be ready to take a further step, drew back, and then took the plunge.

One boy said that "blow" has another meaning and that it is funny when you think about that other meaning in the phrase. Several boys laughed. One girl demanded to know what was so funny. Those who had laughed laughed louder. Another girl hazarded that it was probably something dirty and that the boys should be ignored. A third girl asked the second if she knew what the boys were talking about. The second said she didn't. The third girl asked Mrs. G. Mrs. G hesitated. She had the feeling at that moment that the groups were all a bad mistake, that she wouldn't ever be caught dead leading a group again, and that the project director was a dangerous person. Still, honesty is precious to Mrs. G and she nodded. "Tell us," cried the boys. Mrs. G refused. "If you want to talk about it, O.K.," she told them, "but don't ask me to give you a cheap thrill."

Her interpretation was not well received. It was, however, not only accurate but useful. The boys tried to complain that she wasn't holding up her end of the discussion. Mrs. G remained adamant. She went on to inquire why they were not getting on with talking about the subject, since it ostensibly interested them. The girls took this as a taunt and echoed it. The boys then laboriously began to piece together their information on the subject. One girl became visibly uncomfortable. Mrs. G noticed this and asked her to speak. The girl said she had never heard anything so disgusting in her life, and that her mother would kill her if her mother ever found out what she had been hearing. Shame and guilt entered the discussion to counterbalance the issue. At first, those who disapproved were made villains by those who approved, and vice versa. But in time it became recognized that the disapproval of others had an effect only when linked with self-disapproval. This allowed the group to reunite in its acknowledgment that each shared with the other an awful sense of conflict. At this juncture "blowing" exited from the discussion and masturbation, the more basic issue, entered. But since masturbation was so basic, no one could talk of it personally; it was too real. The group then became a forum for a more factual exploration of the issue; and when Mrs. G was called upon to contribute what she knew, she acceded. The youngsters left the session both shaken and relieved.

One could see from that session what all the difficulty in the beginning was all about. It was as if the group members had dimly surmised that given the freedom of the group, it would sooner or later come to that. But at the beginning there was no groundwork of confidence, controls, and comfort upon which such exploration could be based. Now there was, and more: the groundwork had been strengthened by the test the issue posited.

Still, the sessions subsequent to that one were tame and careful for a while. Neither Mrs. G nor the youngsters were anxious for an early reprise. The issue of guilt became much more the focus than what the guilt was about. The youngsters were considering and together working through the problems of defying grownups because of the latter's capacity to induce guilt, or of submitting to grownups out of guilt. Some of the youngsters tried to project their guilt onto the adult world and then put distance and rebelliousness between themselves and it. Others felt such guilt over that solution and over particular issues that they chose to burden themselves with a continual sense that they were bad and must become good by meeting every parental and teacherly wish. There were, inevitably, flareups between the two factions. Each faction showed signs of approaching the other and thereby finding less extreme solutions.

Then Mrs. G made an error. One of the boys in the group had been caught shoplifting, had been rather severely punished for it, and had come to the group furious with everyone but (seemingly) himself. He launched into a tirade which, in its one-sided insistence and length, annoyed Mrs. G. Finally she interjected the question of whether it had ever occurred to the boy that had he not been punished he might next time have committed a more serious offense.

It was an unfortunate question, as Mrs. G soon realized. Just as important, it was a question that revealed to Mrs. G the degree to which she had been in conflict about the role of the group leader. For she really did hold the belief, far more than she realized, that transgressions must be stamped out immediately—today a venial act, tomorrow a mortal one. Inspecting that belief in the context of the group leaders' meeting, she came to recognize that she had been moving given acts from the bad category to the tolerable and understandable one, but that the categories hadn't much changed. She set out to think that discovery through, but, as it turned out, her wish to do so was severely tried by the behavior of the boy in question.

He and the group all realized that Mrs. G had violated a kind of implicit pact with them by her judgment of his potential. Not only did her comment scare the boy badly, but it broke faith with him and the group. He spent several sessions blazing at her, and each time, though the other group members eventually told him to shut up—that Mrs. G didn't deserve all that—they didn't really act to help him stop.

Finally it fell to Mrs. G to stop the boy, and she did it in the most helpful way possible. In the session of moment, the boy began to say over and over, "fuck you, fuck you, fuck you. . . ." As Mrs. G later put it, "You know, I felt that in saying it that way, he was sort of doing it, in his mind, pushing the words into me. So I said to him, 'You'd really like to do it, wouldn't you?' Well, he gulped, turned red, and muttered in a surprised sort of way, 'Yeah.'"

The impact on the rest of the group was just as striking. The fact that Mrs. G could see the love and want beneath the outraged hatred was deeply reassuring. The fact that she could tolerate, even in imagination, the idea that students might have such wishes toward a teacher was profoundly relieving. The fact that it could be said without guilt or compunction, and yet without the need to act on it, was moving and helpful. It was as if now the worst and best were out and, in coming out, became facts of love and life; and now the group could go back to being a discussion group in which a teacher meets weekly with students to help them see what the issues of life and times and people mean to them. Still, when the same boy told Mrs. G, but this time outside the group, when they chanced to meet leaving school, to "go suck," she had him suspended for three days.

All in all, the project team answered the question about the leaders' adequacy in the affirmative. It was a frustrating job, but most of the teachers caught on. Once they understood certain basic aspects of the youngsters' behavior, the pressure was off. When they could hear that all those unrelenting questions simply meant, at one level, "What I am saying must not be worth anything or I would get an answer from a grownup," the leaders visibly relaxed. Up till then the teacher/leaders were so used to making what they knew directly available to kids that they could not bear holding back, even though they recognized that they did not know what the youngsters were asking them.

The youngsters' motives for joining the groups were less complex than the teachers'. As the groups settled down toward the end, some members acting as spokesmen for the groups were able to make their feelings explicit. Children know less about grownups than grownups about kids. Though they see a great deal of their parents, those relationships are so highly charged that they cannot let themselves know what sorts of people their parents are. Their relationship with teachers generally takes place in a highly structured situation with minimal free interaction. When they cannot permit themselves to get this information from the horse's mouth, they turn to their peers. Their friends help in providing comfort, support, and information exchange with much less fear of criticism and judging. In the groups, they came to recognize that their deep hopes to be changed and to be made better and more comfortable were essentially irrational and more or less conscious. But they also recognized in the reality of the groups a protective situation which might still be open enough to get evidence—material—so that they might learn how to go about growing up. Young people want to learn how to get on in an adult world, not just in their peer group world; and, like the teacher groups, they want to learn this without exposing their feelings, conflicts, and expectations. They compare themselves with the leaders, the omniscient grownups, more than with their peers. This leads to obvious frustration and to a less obvious intensification of hopes and desires, with a resulting fear of exposure and criticism. They are not really surprised when the teacher/ leaders don't answer their questions because their projected conviction is that what they have to say is not worth much. Underneath, they fear that what they want to say is bad and, if said, would only result in attack.

As the groups draw to a close, many of the members overtly state that what has been going on is so chaotic that it is *incomprehensible* to them and, they fear, to others. They have tried to conceal this incomprehensibility by clinging to tried-and-true stereotyped and provocative presentations of themselves. They express relief when they find out that they can be understood by group leaders and peers (Tryon 1939). Then they can conceive of substantive identification with the group leader by way of mutuality. There is an effort to see which general perceptions they share with adults, how they each use rules of evidence, how many of the problems between them are real and *not* projections because they are problems for both (Hartmann 1950). The adults, too, suffer, struggle, worry about the right way, are uncertain, and find their feelings hurt just as youngsters do. It doesn't mean that you, a young person, cannot accept yourself if they don't accept you, or that acceptance by adults automatically includes self-acceptance. Each has a high degree of psychosocial autonomy.

Generally speaking, the youngsters' groups ended on a higher note than the teachers' groups. As the weather got warm, there were insistent demands to hold the groups outdoors and then to have a party at the end. Several of the teacher/leaders, despite what they thought would be the disapproval of the project team, brought a cake or soda for the last session.

What did they get out of it? We have fewer data (hence fewer unreliable data) on the children's groups than we do on the teachers'. There are only twenty-three post-group interviews for direct data, an indirect report by Dr. Roens, and the record of a later meeting held with most of the teacher/leaders.

The post-group interviews showed little strong positive or negative feeling about the groups; the usual response was that they were "O.K." or "interesting." Compared with a control group, interviews with group participants were consistently longer, showed greater in-depth exploration of issues, and were more personally oriented. We have the impression that the youngsters who participated seemed to *notice* more. A girl just out of the eighth grade and beginning to date told us casually about how her mother talks to her dates. "You know," she said, "I've noticed that she is a little jealous of me." Not many fourteen-year-olds notice motivation on their own.

Those interviewed were principally participants in senior high school; we have less information about the factual sexual or drug knowledge of the younger participants. The older participants were well schooled, wherever they got it, in contraception, varieties of sexual activities, and abortion (Coombs 1968). They also had absorbed much sexual mythology, such as the stories about saltpeter, sex as addictive, and the destructive aspects of sexuality. They also knew what the different drugs in common usage were and the chief differences between them. They greatly exaggerated the potential dangers of drugs—which seemed to deter no one (Lewis 1970). The group participants knew no more or less than the control group, but seemed to have a greater interest in what might make someone look at something this or that way. "Jason took acid, or at least they told him it was acid, and got terribly sick. He told me he was going to try it again tomorrow and wants me to take it with him. I'm really scared but I think I'm going to. Do you think that's strange?" Comments such as these seem to us to indicate not only an interest in motivation, but also a somewhat greater tolerance of ambiguity. There is no evidence that the participants leave the groups more self-confident than when they came or that they have an easier time resolving social conflicts. Generally speaking, the interview material, if it did nothing else, seemed to support one of the original ideas behind the project. Information—the stock-in-trade of schools—loses value and hence effectiveness to the degree to which it comes into conflict with powerful feelings, as exemplified in Chapter 1.

The children in the groups do seem to have more interest in differentiating myth from reality. "I heard my parents talk about kids my age getting pregnant but I didn't believe it. In the group Joan said a doctor told her that she was too small to have a baby and I knew right there that she was making it up. She felt just like I did that she just didn't want to think about such things and so she believed some story." They wanted just as much to set the factual record straight about drugs and what adults are like as they did about sex, in the opinion of the interviewers.

Dr. Roens, in an informal and unstandardized manner, followed up a number of the youngsters. It was his habit to speak to as many departing seniors as possible, and he had used the opportunity to ask those who had participated what they thought about the groups in retrospect. First of all, he reported that many who had not been in the groups spontaneously mentioned them as one of the things they were sorry they missed. He also said that an unprecedented number of teachers had asked for an opportunity to teach a social education course. Roens is the major proponent of the sleeper effect of this project. He specifically reports that almost all of the students he spoke to told him that it was "a great experience," that they "wouldn't have missed it for the world," and the like. They were not apparently particularly specific about what made it so important or interesting in retrospect, but their later enthusaism was in marked contrast to their guarded replies just after the groups finished. Above all, they obviously remembered it.

One other group deserves mention, and that is the teacher/leaders who met as a group with their supervisor. In general, this group went much like a longer ordinary teachers' group, except that they spent a lot of time sharing their experiences in their social education groups. They also spent more time directly noticing parallels between what went on in the teacher/leaders' group and what was going on with their students' group. This helped to increase their inner options, their choices when acting as leaders.

The teachers had difficulty in criticizing (however gently and constructively) each other's performance. This reflected a deep-seated sense of inferiority that Zinberg noted during the pilot year:

Above all, what the teachers didn't say directly but what was clear to us was how much common cause they had with the students. As teachers they felt little attention was paid to them and many demands were made on them. They felt caught between what they regarded as an unsympathetic administration, unrelenting parents, and troubled children. All this resulted in a concept of themselves as inadequate in their jobs, with a fear that they knew too little to be sure what was "good" teaching. They had been exposed to and had accepted a value that a good teacher should be aware of his subject and a complex correlation of knowledge about the motor, cognitive, and emotional potential of his students that spanned neurophysiology, sociology, and psychology. It is just too much to expect of anyone. In these last few years of working with teachers nothing has impressed me as much as their mass feeling of inferiority. After a time I realized that my initial view of supervision that I had to keep the teachers from isolating themselves from the group by holding onto their position as teachers, had to be balanced by my helping them not to identify too wholeheartedly with the excessive expectations from students, and giving up their positions as group leaders (Zinberg and Boris 1968).

The teachers did, to a very great extent, identify with their groups. They found themselves constantly tempted to spare their group members from disturbing interventions, and they often indulged these temptations. They were encouraged in this enterprise by the students' own sense that uninhibited discussion was an illicit activity and their frequent denial of the validity of the leader's clarifications. On the other hand, the teachers felt "thwarted" or "inhibited" from resorting to their traditional teaching role (Shmuck 1971; White 1959). This was especially true for the teachers under observation. Mrs. V expressed some of this feeling through her attacks on the boy who served as the unofficial leader of her group. After two or three months her annoyance with Tom, the boy who "never shuts up," began shifting to the research observer who, it could be said, "never lets up." The resentful feelings she and Mrs. G felt toward the researcher persisted until the meetings in April, when they were expressed and examined. These feelings were more or less resolved in early May, when the supervisor indicated that he thought they had been displaced from him onto the researcher. The supervisor said that the presence of a researcher apparently did make the leaders uncomfortable, but that he really thought the researcher had become a lightning rod for criticism that would otherwise be directed at him.

Like the students, the teachers were relatively noncommittal about how much they liked their groups. All of the teachers who served in the first two years of the project and stayed in the school system volunteered for the next year. However, the most important thing the teachers brought up in discussing their group experiences, both the teacher/leaders' group and the students' groups, was their effect on their teaching. To a man and woman they said that, although they would *never* think of running the classroom in a group fashion—and their vehemence on that point spoke volumes as to the negative part of their feelings about the experience—the experience had changed their teaching. They had become aware of group activity within the classroom; they noticed scapegoating, subgroup formation, splitting, projection, provocation, transference, and the like, and were able to use these occurrences to further the discussion, to observe and sometimes prevent inhibitions or breakdowns in discussions, or sometimes to head off disruptions that they would not have noticed earlier.

Group members in all these groups may or may not have got "something" in terms of their hopes for answers, gratifications, rules, self-importance, greater understanding and tolerance of ambiguity, more choices, or even knowing more about how people worked in groups. But they had the experience of living through the struggle with one's inhibitions, with others' inhibitions, with what they made of others, and what others made of them, under conditions which permitted them to experience that struggle, notice it, know that they were seeing it going on at the same time: they needed the group for nothing except what they could learn from it. *No* secondary benefits, of which life is so full, were available, not even small ones, and their difficulty, reluctance, and even pain at attempting this knowledge, their efforts during this process to return to the internal and external status quo, to avoid knowing what they found themselves learning, to begin noticing the process, and vaguely, inchoately becoming aware of wondering about it, were all there was.

CHAPTER FIVE

THE SHIFT IN RESEARCH DIRECTION

In his original memorandum recommending the grant, Mitchell Sviridoff listed the following "research objectives" for the Group Consultation Program for Teachers: "to measure (1) the extent of attitude change within the groups; (2) the dynamics of that change; (3) the degree of individual internalization; and (4) the effect on the children." He indicated that the research on the Arlington youngsters' program might tell something about (1) the transfer of attitudes into and out of the group; (2) the value of the course in shaping adolescents' personal growth and at what ages that might best be done; (3) the transfer of group leader behavior of the teachers and their consciousness of group process into the classroom. Incorporating all the above, he believed, research might produce a "how to" procedure for other school systems, professional psychologists, and psychiatrists.

These large aims as presented by Sviridoff accurately represented the *original* position of the applicants. However, even then we had begun to have considerable concern about our capacity to achieve even the rough quantifications of an empirical value that would lead toward the kind of social change that both Ford and we had hoped to attain. We began to focus on our *own* interests, legitimate, we believe, in pure research on group process as such.

In the end any efforts at quantification began to seem an interference with the social process we wanted to learn about, so that our viewpoint and Ford's grew ever farther apart. What was probably more to the point was that, from the time the project had actually gotten under way, we had begun to see many pitfalls because our objectives were so various. The project would be working with people who themselves had high hopes that their social conflicts might be resolved. We were to work within social institutions—METCO, the town and school system of Arlington, Ford—which hoped that the project would offer a means of resolving conflicts within society at large. We were expected, we feared, to weigh,

70

measure, and evaluate these hopes and what came of them. All this needed to be done, although we were increasingly convinced that for group leaders to anticipate some change just because all of these researchers were going around looking for it was the equivalent of wanting something for and from the participants which led toward social engineering.

Doubts grew, but it was only very slowly that we relinquished the idea that we should be able to carry out a project that at once gave insight into groups as such and also afforded models for the empirical use of groups for social change. Our preoccupation by this time was with maintaining relative neutrality. This showed itself as a concern about not wanting things from people or for people. We found ourselves insisting that participants have a chance to think about what kept them from thinking about what they wanted for themselves, and this great care about not interfering with this process began to sound so damn pure, even to us. Was there something the matter with us? Each time we discussed our goals and someone like Ford's first research consultant talked about measuring variables like prejudice, hostility, openmindedness, tolerance for ambiguity, and even greater awareness of motivation, we found ourselves muttering darkly in our beards about form and substance, and how would you know it if you found it? Were we sinking into research misanthropy?

At this point, we received Ford's request for an evaluation of the project, a simple *pro forma* request. Whatever concern the foundation people may have felt about the research aspect of the project, Ford's interest and support continued throughout, and anything the foundation could do to assist in its success was forthcoming. As an evaluator Ford chose someone with experience and a deserved reputation for objectivity and competence. He was interested in the area to be studied, yet he had no axe to grind. The authors' regard for the research evaluator (and there is evidence of mutuality) as well as for the program and administrative staff at Ford has never wavered. But our positive bias toward Ford, which took the form of wanting to do what they wanted, seems important to report. The urge to come up with "findings," so as to supply what Ford wanted out of the project, our fear that the non-quantification portion of the research represented inadequacy, obstinacy, or simply foolishness, plagued us throughout. The reader should have that knowledge with him as he traverses this report. (Erik Erikson found it important for the reader to know that a bias existed in his report on Gandhi [1969]. He wrote a letter to Gandhi when the book was half-written acknowledging that they might not have liked each other and that, unquestionably, Gandhi would have resented this scrutiny of his life; but, armed by knowledge of his bias, Erikson said that he would maintain an objective stance.) Also, despite the evaluator's clear misgivings about the research and evaluation arm of the project, he recommended that Ford continue and even extend their support.

In January 1970 the program officers asked the evaluator, James Laue, to assess, first, the general approach "as a theory for social change or social conflict resolution." More specifically, Laue was asked, in regard to the Group Consultation Program for Teachers, to think about the following questions. "(1) Is the approach effective in changing, or helping teachers to deal with, their racial attitudes, especially for white teachers, as they affect black students newly integrated into their classrooms? (2) Would such changes favorably affect the performances of their students, particularly the METCO students? (3) Does the approach affect the teachers' view of themselves in teaching in a positive way?" And about Arlington: "Does the approach make a significant difference (1) in the participants' self-confidence? (2) in their ability to resolve social conflict within themselves? (3) in their ability to live with ambiguity? (4) in their ability to perceive more clearly myth versus reality?"

These questions are somewhat different from those in the original memorandum from Sviridoff, which probably reflects the program officer's sensitive reading of the research team's position. We were beginning to shift our point of view from "what happened?", which implies "what changed?", to "how is the group experienced?" Hence, the questions Laue was asked to report on were intended to fit more closely with what we had in mind. In the Arlington project, we were concerned with what happened inside the psyche of the participants and less interested in what the individuals did with it, such as using more or less drugs. The third question pertaining to the teachers' project also reflects this approach, although two questions resolutely hope that these teachers would do "better" by their black students as a result of the group experience. That is, Ford (and hence the evaluator) assumed that there was something "wrong" with teachers, especially in white teachers' attitudes toward their new black pupils. They assumed that these attitudes should be changed for the better, that the groups would do it, and that when such changes occurred the students would "benefit" from this and their school and human performances improve. These assumptions amount to a firm statement that we can get a hold on these attitudes, that they can be shifted toward what we know to be better, and that, as a result, specific behavioral changes will come about not only in the teachers but also in the children.

From the vantage point of the present, the implicit assumptions outlined above seem untestable, particularly in the complex social and personal milieus of a school which is itself in the midst of social and educational upheaval. How does one *define*, let alone test, an ability to differentiate myth from reality? In what areas? At what times? For what reasons? To what degree? The same questions arise about living with ambiguity, resolving social conflict, or acquiring self-confidence. What about changing racial attitudes? At what level of personality does one change attitudes, and how is this reflected in behavior? Certainly when people leave a situation in which there has been great social pressure, they can be heard spouting a new line. They are sometimes even "convinced" consciously. But if these persons still experience certain conflicts, less consciously, won't the conflicts emerge anyhow, appearing, though perhaps subtly, in the individual's "changed" behavior?

At the time, however, both Laue and the project team took the evaluation questions seriously. It was as if we agreed on something like the following: "Yes, the groups can't resolve any personal conflicts in depth; they are not a thoroughgoing psychoanalysis, you know. And just to let them have the experience and study that, why, where will that get anyone? No, let us researchers set a goal of less prejudice on the conscious level and accept that at face value. If the individual retains a complex conflict about prejudice, let him take it out on someone else, let him kick his kids more often or what have you, just so long as he behaves better in school. That would be a desirable social change, and it could be measured." This, of course, is an argument for social engineering, and it indicates a belief that some control of individuals' responses is consistently possible and that their responses in a complex social situation are directable. The authors do not share that belief now, and, in retrospect, we realize that we really did not share it then.

In any case, whatever one thinks now of the mandate, Laue accepted it; and there was no protest from the project team (we were still laboring under the concern that we were delinquent by reason of our lack of faith in quantification). A full-scale evaluation of the project thus got under way.

On the Group Consultation Program for Teachers, there were four final suggestions from Laue in 1970. (1) Recruit, orient, and train group leaders, particularly black leaders, who would be more knowledgeable and oriented to content questions; in turn they could better orient the groups away from studying process and toward achieving substantive change in racial bias. (2) Do a systematic comparison of all-white groups with mixed groups. (3) Have the program built into the school curriculum rather than holding meetings after school; meet in homes and lounges, not classrooms, in black areas; try for broader involvement of administrators in preparatory work and evaluation. (4) Develop a more specific focus on white racism and problems of white children.

As to the first suggestion, it must be abundantly clear to every reader who has come this far that the project team was moving ever farther away from empirical content to an ever-greater emphasis on overall process. The team had pointed out to Laue that, except during the pilot program, black leaders had found it very difficult to remain neutral and had tended to exhort and lecture group members. Ruth Batson, the METCO director, had specifically reported feedback on this as a problem for group members. She had been active in asking the project team not to rehire such leaders. Further, with reference to Laue's second suggestion, Batson had explicitly requested that we stop the practice of trying to arrange group member representation in the groups. When you deliberately arranged to have black leaders or black members in the group, she argued, then the group simply used them as resource people to tell about the black experience, which was no good for anyone. She strongly suggested natural groups, that is, take members as they come, either numerically or geographically, and let that *modus operandi* be clear to everyone. But in his final evaluation report Laue argues that "lack of *factual* data on race and racism and the [project team's] unwillingness to make direct data statements will allow the groups to proceed with false assumptions on race and racial prejudice" (Laue 1970).

In all four of those suggestions, Laue did not recognize two cardinal principles of the whole project. One, the issue was *not* the acquisition of factual knowledge but rather information concerning the process by which people selectively perceive, misperceive, repress, and generally inhibit the acquisition of accurate information and maintain this process in themselves. Two, the project team did not conceive of working with prejudice in the usual direct sense; that is, a teacher who had a hostile response to blacks would bring up that prejudice in the group, be persuaded to recognize it as irrational, and would then change. Rather the team thought that in the groups participants might come to recognize the extent to which people insisted on being prejudiced. If the members used this special opportunity, where no one was likely to be hurt by the prejudice, to study how it worked, we thought this indirect approach might be, somehow, more useful. No one who looked at the project ever bought this argument (sad to relate), despite our pointing out how in the pilot project our search for symmetry was used by the group members as a means of avoiding any more affectful response to prejudice.

Everyone agreed completely on the value of Laue's third suggestion (that the groups be built into the curriculum), but no school superintendent was willing to accept the scheduling hassle this would require.

Laue's suggestions for the Arlington project were similar. He thought the project should more actively recruit and select teacher/leaders, circulate news about the project to various other schools so that they might know of its existence and perhaps build it into their curriculum, and specifically "shift the focus from process to goals. The project should establish prior criteria for evaluation of solutions . . . to the problems to be encountered in a social education approach" (Laue 1970).

Again, Laue clearly disagreed with the process-oriented approach and asked for goals and solutions without defining what they might be. He did not consider whether, if you aimed for "less prejudice," for example, anyone knew what "less prejudice" really was. Also—and this is the nub of our discussion of the difference between a social change project and a research project—in his interest in getting "better" leaders in both projects and getting the projects more securely fixed in more schools, Laue saw the project as a tool for social change. It was the impression of the project team that what Ford wanted was more and better (i.e., more quantifiable) research, and at the same time more and better use of the project to bring about social change as quickly as possible. Our conviction was that the groups were not crisis intervention techniques, that they could not be hurried into a particular direction, and that *how* they worked ought to be thought about and even studied. These convictions were pretty much at odds with Laue's recommendations.

These differences can also be seen in another area. Laue strongly supported the hiring of a research director. In Laue's words, this director would not be concerned with the groups and their processes, but only

with data to be collected and analyzed in a systematic fashion which will lead to some useful answers about the research questions posed by The Ford Foundation. Zinberg and Boris are not trained in, oriented toward, nor sympathetic towards scientific research as it relates to the kind of groups they are running in these projects. As is common with psychiatrists and psychologists, they view groups in a process-oriented rather than a goal-oriented context. Without established goals, it is impossible to evaluate output, for there is nothing to measure against.

Laue's two misperceptions of cardinal principles of the project become important here. For he goes on to state the need for testing the attitudes of participants before and after, in order to know what happens within the groups. He states that Zinberg and Boris resist such measures because of their fear that the groups might not be as "free" in their behavior as they would have been without a researcher present. And, indeed, this problem was mentioned and discussed both with Laue during his evaluation and then with the Ford program officer. But the team, with our self-conscious concern that it was our inadequacy at research that got in the way, allowed that to resist testing of the groups on such grounds was too picky. Laue neglects anywhere to mention a basic argument advanced by the project team about the extent to which group members reach for what they believe they are supposed to be doing.

There are actually two issues here. The first is the influence of the fact that the participants were being tested, and the second is the influence of the content of the tests on the subsequent behavior of people in the groups. The second issue reflects the first, because the willingness to test indicates that the testers will ask things that they fear they could not otherwise trust themselves to know. If a group member felt that group membership was a good idea for him because he was, let us say, too hostile a person, which of the following (and here is a test item for the reader) would be true or false?

(a) His test score would reflect the actuality of his hostility
(b) It would reflect the severity of his conscience
(c) It would reflect his docility in the face of his expectation that the group (leader) would change him
(d) It would reflect an extreme in order to secure a big change
(e) It would reflect the disguise he makes for his hostility, because he feels hostility is bad
(f) All of the above
(g) None of the above

One is hard put to find the correct answer. There is probably no one correct answer. Rather, different people would respond to the same test in different ways. We would have to know each person in order to know what his test scores reflect. When we do not figure out in what spirit a man takes his test, we do not know what his score says about him. Totaling everyone's scores compounds the confusion and magnifies the uncertainty.

The next step in a testing procedure is to garner "after" scores to compare with the "before" ones. Assuming each person takes the test afterward in the same spirit in which he took it previously, we would still not know what his scores say about him, but we would, at least, know how much he has changed (or not) on a certain item. That is, we would not know for a certainty his Hostility Quotient, since we may not, in fact, be measuring that; but we would know his X Quotient. But what if the spirit in which he takes the test changes? This will possibly be reflected in his score; but how will we know what has changed? If he was docile at first and then became bold, yet his level of hostility remained the same, his test score would change; yet what would we know?

We would have to delude ourselves rather insistently in order finally to imagine that the tests measure anything we can know about. If, on the other hand, we do not delude ourselves, then what we have is a group of numbers which, with whatever statistical craft they are maneuvered, might as well have been taken at random from a telephone directory.

No responsible research scientist would knowingly delude the larger community with whom he shares his findings. He would not fudge his figures or his statistical treatments. But self-delusion is quite another matter. Is there not every reason to suspect that test-taking behavior is so variable among people that to take a score as responsive only to the test items and not to the meaning the test holds for the subject in his larger context is to share the tester's unrealized delusion?

Our position is probably obvious. We have to regard the taking of a test as an act of communication from subject to tester; to make such a communication the subject will fortify himself with certain assumptions about the tester. These will likely be based partly on what he can learn of the tester from the circumstances of the testing, from the tester's person and manner, and from the tester himself. Then the subject may well consider to what use and by whom his communication will be put. Where there are unknowns or ambiguities, the testing situation itself will be like a projective test. The subject will read in some mixture of hope and previous experience to fill in the gaps. If, moreover, he takes the test in a group situation, he will be influenced by what he can make of the attitudes of his cohorts. When, finally, he checks an item, all of this will have gone into it. The specific issue posed in the item will have only partial weight in this assembly of factors.

The tester, then, cannot be viewed as an antiseptic person in the halls of science. What he is doing has its parallels in the behavior of the members of our groups. He too, for example, is hoping to split off pure cultures from the admixture. He hopes, also, to know only that which does not jeopardize other hopes, whose preservation actually depends on his *not* knowing. His faith in numbers is akin to the group members' preoccupation with the numbers present or absent, the number of sessions, or the number of times the leader spoke or used a given word. From our perspective, then, we must suffer the loss of an illusion in return for what the perspective enables us to know. We must sacrifice one form of knowing—of knowing through testing—for another, of knowing what one cannot know through testing. To know that one can't know seems scant consolation for the illusion of feeling one can, but have we really a choice?

The other of Laue's essential misperceptions is not quite as clear-cut, but it is equally important. He sums up what he sees as the Zinberg-Boris approach by saying that the project "assumes that if they [group participants] can be freed up to clearly see themselves and the seas of value ambiguity in which they live, positive behavioral consequences will follow—*but it does not insist on this as a test*" (italics his). To the degree that we allowed that we had no negative responses should a teacher feel that the groups alleviated his direct feelings of racial bias by allowing him to recognize their irrationality, Laue is correct. But he is not correct in implying that we believe that behavioral consequences follow from the groups and insist only that they not be used as a test. He goes on in his report to quote Allan Winker, who found that fewer than 10 percent of groups tested showed "behavioral counterparts of changes in attitudes." Laue, then, was saying that if Zinberg and Boris believed that their groups would change the participants' attitudes, which in turn would change their behavior, Zinberg and Boris would jolly well have to prove it, for there was evidence against it.

Here for the project team was a perfect example of the morass of misunderstanding that we saw so often in the groups and that we eventually came to believe plagued many social action projects (see Chapter 21). We thought that we had tried to make our position about attitude change and behavioral change clear; yet it seemed terribly hard for people to abandon even for a time the concept of improvement, of a goal that will improve oneself or society, in order to study how a person is *using* this hope to be better. In our research evaluation, as in our groups, people found that concept hard to assimilate, and the team didn't have fifteen sessions with Laue.

Laue's recommendations raised certain questions and "results," quantification that we felt could not be answered readily by the means at our disposal, and indeed should not be the main area of our concern. We felt we were being asked to give credence to certain "tests" of the groups—certain numerical measures of their performance—that would not be meaningful. We also felt that the nature of these tests would force us to ignore or overlook the subjective nature of what had occurred in the groups—the involvement of leaders with members, and the like. In short, the entire process of being evaluated by Laue was a traumatic experience for the researchers, primarily because his narrowly focused goals were difficult for the researchers to absorb.

Following our experience in being evaluated, the project was focused more clearly on how individuals in the group metabolized their experience. This led to thinking of each individual as coping with an internal group of his own. No schema for looking at the groups could lend itself less to quantification or be less directly connected with issues of social change. Obviously, the project team was aware of the many conscious concerns about social educational issues and of the implications to society at large of any project concerned with how people metabolize their feelings about things like prejudice, sex, and drugs. This is the subject of Chapter 21. The keystone of the project's view of groups follows in Part II. We use the "inner group" as a window on the interaction within the larger group, stressing particularly the member-leader relationship.

One other phenomenon deserves mention. Zinberg and Boris, going along with Laue's suggestion, hired a research director who prepared forms of all sorts for the participants and group observer to fill out. These forms were considered positively splendid by Laue, who saw them as a breakthrough in the research and the first collection of data considered "hard" and appropriate for systematization and analysis (see Appendix II). Data was collected and collected; and nothing could be made from any of it. Every attempt to analyze it fell afoul of what has been pointed out again and again: how could you *really*—really, mind you, not going by just what a person says—find out if someone is "less prejudiced"? The research director played with it and played with it, then discreetly folded his tent, moved to London with all the data so as to continue searching for a coherent scheme of analysis, and, despite written entreaty after written entreaty, has not been heard from since.

Part II

This book, we have said, represents the failure of a research project. Failing increasingly to strive to produce certain results, we increasingly failed to apply ourselves to the measurement of results. As an exercise in applied research, our project fails absolutely.

Still, as we abandoned applied efforts, we began more and more to do basic sorts of research. If basic research involves attempts to understand the nature of things or events without a closely connected concern about doing anything with or about what one learns, except to communicate one's findings to others, that rather accurately describes what we did within the groups and what we are about to do in the pages that follow.

The criterion of success for basic research is different from that for applied research. Applied research is undertaken to try to make things work and then to see if they do. Basic research is undertaken to learn what is so and to try and say what one thinks one has discovered. People may wish to take the findings of basic research and apply them: participants in our project groups often did so; the reader may do so also. Others may wish simply to know what we think we learned and have no urge whatsoever to do anything with or about it. This option was also used by our participants, and may be so used by the reader. In both cases, the research might seem to be a success, neither the one case more than the other. The only issue is whether what we think we have discovered is in fact an accurate rendering of the events we studied.

For that reason we have tried to show from what data and by what process of inference we drew our findings, much as we might have done with participants in our groups.

CHAPTER SIX

THE GROUPS BEGIN

In what follows, we shall try to answer a single question: what happens when people are invited to come together to talk of matters of general concern and mutual interest? Over the course of two and a half years, we invited people to gather in small groups lasting from twelve to thirty weeks to discuss matters of interest. The times and places and number of meetings were arranged for them, the groupings were made in advance and consisted either of fellow high school or junior high school students or of fellow teachers. All the participants had to do was present themselves and get down to the conversation.

THE PROBLEM OF WHAT IS "SUPPOSED TO HAPPEN" IS ENCOUNTERED.

Although it is not perhaps a common event for students to be allowed out of classes for such occasions, or for teachers to be reimbursed for their transportation expenses, the matter of people coming together is by no means uncommon. At almost every social gathering—a dinner party, for example—people (many or most of whom are strangers to one another) gather, introduce themselves or are introduced, and with little ado fall to talking. Not everyone, of course, is equally at home with words; but surely teachers are, and the prospect of a good exchange of experiences or information would seem both pleasant and, it is conceivable, helpful. But let us look at what in fact does happen. Let us look at the beginnings of four groups.

Group I, Session 1. METCO Group

Leader: Is the group waiting for me to start something?
H: In a class we are used to sitting and listening. You're not telling us what you want.

Leader:	What do *you* want?
H:	I don't know.
R:	I want to know who you are.
Leader:	What about the others?
B:	I came because I'm not too sure of myself. I act and think later.
G:	I wonder if the longer day has any effect on the METCO child. What do you do with a child that is sick and has to go home?
Leader:	Is it communication with and curiosity about the black kids, then, that drew people to this group?
Everyone:	No.
Leader:	Is there something else then?
[Silence]	
Leader:	I wonder why the silence.
L:	We don't know what we're supposed to be thinking of; we don't know what we're supposed to be talking about.
F:	[To the observer] If you are expecting any profound statements from this, you are not going to get any.

Group I, Session 2. METCO Group

Leader:	Is everyone waiting for something?
F:	This reminds me of a classroom.
Leader:	People seem at loose ends to talk. People seem to be sizing up the group, seeing who's here—who's not, what I am going to do.
[Silence]	
Leader:	I get the impression that some kinds of assumptions are getting checked out.
[Silence]	
[Member enters late.]	
D:	[Referring to latecomer] He just saved us; we're all here.
H:	I'm surprised so many people returned. Last time there seemed to be failure in everyone's face. They felt doing this fourteen more times would be too depressing.
L:	I expected everyone because I couldn't wait to come back. I was amazed at how much you think about people when you don't say anything.
[Silence]	
F:	It takes time for security to build up. I feel like you're going to get sick by the awkwardness in here.
E:	I think it's too warm in here; I think she [nodding to F] thinks so too.
H:	There are 49 stars in the flag here—we can discuss that. It might be interesting to check the rest of the school.

Group II, Session 1. METCO Group

Leader:	My name is _____ .
K:	What was the point of that [referring to research measurements]?

Leader:	I haven't seen it. . . . Has everyone come here with something in mind?
C:	Perhaps we are part of an experiment.
K:	Yes.
C:	An experiment of teacher attitudes to the METCO program.
M:	Have any of you had any experience with people who have come to the groups before? The three of us [indicating] just finished a group.
C:	Perhaps it's not too good to be tied to structure.
K:	It was deliberately kept wide open?
G:	I'm not leaving because I'm angry and upset.
C:	[To leader] You are not going to lead us?
Leader:	What would you like me to lead?
C:	We have to begin somewhere.
Leader:	It seems we have begun.
L:	We've tried experiments in school when kids were put in an ambiguous situation, and they just floundered. It seems we have the same trouble.
Y:	I had experience in a sensitivity laboratory. At least we were told to say what we liked and didn't like about people in the group. At least we had a starting point.

[Silence]

Group II, Session 2. METCO Group

M:	Is it the purpose of the meeting to set up a topic for each meeting?
Leader:	I feel you don't like this.
R:	It makes me uncomfortable and uneasy. It seems like a waste of time sitting here trying to get ideas.
F:	What would you suggest?
R:	I had no specific topic.
K:	I agree. Forty minutes of dead silence *is* difficult.
Leader:	My memory wasn't of long blocks of silence. Did people feel that?
[Group members nod and murmur: people felt the silence like that.]	
K:	It's because of a lack of structure. If we adopt structure, we can go there.
F:	What if we didn't want to go?
M:	Should we indicate again who we are?
Leader:	How would this be helpful?
M:	Couldn't you relate better to people if you know them? For example, not a soul here knows you.
Leader:	This is similar to what came up last time—what does METCO want, what do I expect?
F:	Honestly, it looks like we're trying to fish out what we can say and what we can't. It's like a teacher having an answer and asking the kid to find out.
K:	I could comment better if I knew what work people were doing.
B:	And more about their background.

Leader: How would that help?
F: I feel people should talk about themselves if they want to.
K: O.K., you start.
[Round robin of identifications by place taught, specialty, etc., then silence.]
L: I don't see how this helps.
M: [With suspicion] Do you think it was planned to include a cross-section grade-wise?
K: It could very well have been planned to.
Leader: A greater plan? [Looks around, inquiring]
[Silence]
P: You're right, F, it wasn't really useful to give names.
L: Maybe they're trying to get people to communicate with each other and themselves.

The reader will have noticed a number of differences between these two groups of teachers and the guests at a dinner party, in addition to the fact that no food or drink was served.

1. In these two groups, the session was preceded by certain tests and measures.

2. A person was present who, following the conventional term, is designated in the transcription as a "leader."

It would be naive to suppose that the presence of these factors had no impact on the participants. But let us look at the first meeting of two groups where preliminary tests had not been given.

Group III, Session 1. Arlington Group

Leader: My name is _____ .
[Others introduce themselves. Short silence. Noise comes from the hall.]
T: What's that? We're being invaded.
[Everyone shifts restlessly. Silence]
B: What do they usually talk about here?
Leader: I've never heard them talk before. What would you talk about if I weren't here?
R: Paul McCartney—is he really dead?
B: I don't know.
[Silence]
M: That was an interesting subject. Let's try another.
Leader: What is it about me that makes it hard to talk about Paul McCartney?
J: [Looking at observer] What bothers me is she is writing but we're not saying anything.
K: What bothers *me* is you two do all the talking.
R: Lots of kids talk but no one listens.
J: You should talk.
[Silence]

J: If we talked we wouldn't be staring.
S: It's hard to talk without knowing anyone, or their grade or any-
            thing; you don't know what's interesting to them.
B: It gets too quiet.

Group III, Session 2. Arlington Group

C: It's so quiet. What did everyone talk about last week?
B: That girl told this guy that he annoys her.
C: It's even more quiet now. How come everyone is so shy?
P: You have to get to know each other.
Leader: Can you help us to get to know each other?
B: That's stupid, like last week. You just have to start talking.
L: When you talk here, it's like everyone is very, very quiet and
            there's just one single voice.

Group IV, Session 1. Arlington Group

Leader: My name is ⸺ .
[The rest of the group give names, and a few start anecdotes about parties
involving others who are not in the group. Only a few present talk.]
V: Let's hear something from *them*.
N: Yeah; some people keep their mouths shut all the time.
[The silent members remain silent.]
B: [To the leader] You're the head of this. *You* should bring up subjects.
M: What's the other group like? They started last week.
P: I hear they're all going to quit.
B: Are we going to be doing this all *year*? Why don't we write down
            topics on a piece of paper and hand them in each time?
[No response from others.]

Group IV, Session 2. Arlington Group

P: This time I'm not talking. I want other people to.
L: Maybe there's *nothing* we can all talk about.
P: Actually, there are *lots* of things to talk about but no one will start.
W: [To leader] Won't *you* start a topic? I think you ought to because no
            one else will.
L: Everybody's afraid to talk. After school it's easy to talk.
M: If girls are together, they talk about boys. And I bet if boys are together
            they talk about girls. But girls can't talk about boys in *front* of boys,
            not in a group like this.
Leader: Maybe there's a topic for both groups.

There does not seem to be much difference between these groups and
those in which all three factors—leader, tests, and observer—were
present. We cannot, of course, provide transcriptions of a group where

neither tests nor observer was present, for of these groups we have only
the record provided by the leader himself. But our impression is that, like
the omission of tests, the absence of an observer does not make a
significant difference in how the groups behave in the opening sessions.

To evaluate the presence of the leader, let us imagine him the
counterpart of the host. This is a poor comparison, of course, since it is
already clear that he (or she) does not know the people present from
previous acquaintance and so cannot steer the interaction in any pre-
knowledgeable way. But perhaps the comparison will hold insofar as
there is a person present with a designated status different from those held
by the other people present. Thus in all four examples so far presented,
the "leader" starts the proceedings.

But what then happens? A rude answer would be: relatively little. The
guests for the most part neither do much about nor seem to want to get
much from the discussions for which the situation was created in the first
place. To the contrary, conversation is desultory and strained, as if
everyone not only feels that something very necessary is missing from the
proceedings but also feels that until it is supplied nothing good can come
of the experience. Nor is the nominal leader unaware of this. He too is
searching for the missing ingredient.

Let us, the readers, do so as well. The authors' experience in listening
in on group proceedings has indicated that there are generally two ways to
learn what people in a group are concerned with. One way is obvious.
People say what they want—"Pass the salt, please." The other way
involves not so much speech as sign language. One must guess what is
wanted much as one does the title of a charade. A fist, thumb side down,
shaking over a plate implies a wish for the salt or pepper. A reading of the
excerpts of these first group sessions reveals a high degree of preoccupation with the matter of "supposed to." We infer that the groups are
intensely feeling the absence of a sense of what is "supposed to" happen or
what they are "supposed to" do. Far from cherishing the freedom of
opportunity invited by the absence of supposed-to's, the guests at the
meeting are keenly feeling their absence.

That preoccupation with what group members or leaders are supposed to do and with what is supposed to happen seems at first quite
reasonable, and, as one can see, it was, for the most part, put forth in
quite a reasonable spirit. Members felt that since someone had brought
these groups together, that person must have had something in mind in
the way of procedures and results. But though that expectation seemed
quite reasonable to the participants, it was not, in fact, our (the authors')
position on the matter. For us, the groups were an opportunity for people
to work with matters of general concern in a different way from ordinarily
available methods. It was our intention, indeed, to subtract from the
experience what is usually the most characteristic, even urgent, feature of

the more ordinary procedures—to subtract, that is, the element of supposition.

That those who came to participate in the groups immediately and ardently sought to find out what they were supposed to accomplish can thus be regarded as an attempt to put into motion their suppositions that this new experience was to be an ordinary one—new, but not really different. But, in the persistence and intensity of the question, one can see that something more than an ordinary assumption is at work. The participants seemed to feel that by subtracting expectation from the enterprise, we had done something to cause upheaval and distress. It began to look as if what we did—which was to observe, notice, describe, and clarify the members' experiences with the issues of general concern —was poor practice and poorer policy, so long as a prescriptive factor was not provided. All those participating as leaders were made by their groups to feel that the omission of prescriptions was not an omission or subtraction, but an introduction of a malevolent element into the cordial possibilities of the relationship.

We persisted, even though we did not know, and were not willing to invent or pretend to know, what was "supposed to" happen. All that we knew or felt we knew was that if things did happen and if we quite carefully described to the groups what was happening, people could choose, according to their own expectations, whether they wanted things to happen that way or not.

If one knows what is supposed to result from an undertaking, one can devise a strategy by which to affect the course in the direction one wants. The strategy may or may not work, but at least one has both it and a goal. If the strategy pleases one and the goal seems valuable, one can have quite good feelings as one first awaits and then begins the task.

Our colleagues, the leaders, however, were without such security. As they awaited the first meetings with their groups of junior high or high school youngsters or of teachers and the occasional principal, they had neither goals nor strategy, only the function of observing, noticing, describing, with special attention to the goals the participants might have and to what, if anything, impeded the participants from attaining these goals. Though this seemed simple enough as a general procedure, experience with previous groups had taught them as leaders or had taught us as supervisors that the members of the groups might find it hard to say what their goals were.

The reasons for this difficulty were several. A strong expectation that we would have things in mind—a lesson plan, so to speak—meant that the participants would simply put themselves at the disposal of the leader, much as an audience will grow silent when a performer arrives on stage. An individual's fear that his own goals may be questionable in some way can also persuade him to put himself in someone else's hands. Then, too, to ask for something which may seem inappropriate in the circumstances may strike one as a source of embarrassment to oneself or the other person. Asking for something also implies need for affection, and one may be reluctant to expose oneself to the possibilities of humiliation or rejection. Too, to want something may be felt to be greedy and selfish, and hence another source for distressing feelings. Any one of these viewpoints can exist or prevail by itself and, in so doing, can inhibit one from declaring his goals; equally, several goals can coexist in the same person with the same effect of marked inhibition. Indeed, just to feel exposed to these *potential* feelings or to the inhibition which is their outgrowth may make one angry enough to withhold participation in a situation that stimulates them. With so much preventing the group leader from learning of the participants' goals, no group leader could feel sanguine upon approaching the first meeting with his group. Our teacher/leaders have told us in no uncertain terms that teaching any class—even as a substitute teacher—was nothing compared with the prospect of meeting the students who were to constitute their groups.

Ideology is some help in situations like these (Maslow 1963), and it was not uncommon for all of us in the project to seek its comforts at various times. Thus a leader driving through the streets to an unfamiliar school where he is to meet with his group might well feel that he is about to do something "better" than just meeting with these teachers for a dozen weekly periods during which he will describe to them what he notices. He may feel that he can bring psychology into their lives, expose them to deep personal encounters, or help the black children in their classrooms and, by extension, the blacks of the nation. Should he preserve these intentions beyond the time when he needs them for their solacing value, he will prove quite a popular group leader, as he will satisfy his group's needs for guidance. Yet to the extent that he brings in his own ideology, he will be unable to perform the more pedestrian task of describing and clarifying what the group members find of concern. Similarly, the schoolteacher who is to lead a group of youngsters may wish to feel that at least he is doing the kind of teaching, unencumbered by curriculum or assignments, which he has always believed in. This sense of being a good person in a good project may ease his entry to the task, but he will probably discover his ability to perform his actual duties decreased by the steady necessity of finding confirmation for this image.

Some of our leaders found the first meetings dismaying because the only familiar face they saw was that of the graduate student who was present to observe and take notes. Then the teachers or young people who were to participate began to arrive. Some already knew one another and occupied the waiting time with familiar conversation. Others were without such security and had to confront their own feelings of being a stranger among strangers on the threshold of an unfamiliar experience. But chances were that all were sizing up the others.

If we could know in what dimension and to what degree these mutual appraisals are taking place, we could know each individual's chief preoccupation in life. In that preoccupation could be found both aspiration and impediment, striving and conflict, hope and despair. But no one will speak of that centermost aspect; indeed, few will recognize it as of any interest and importance. Such interest and importance as there is lies *within* the preoccupation; the fact that the preoccupation itself exists will not strike them as any more noteworthy than the fact that they breathe. So they operate from the source of their most intense preoccupations in the initial phases of the meeting and, when done (momentarily) with this, go on to await some activity from the leader.

Our question, as we have said, is, what happens then? In answering, we shall be, like the members and leaders and observers of the groups, viewing and attending from within our own particular preoccupations. This is inescapable. Objectivity would not help; it too expresses a preoccupation and, as such, partially represents what happens through its particular prismatic view. The quest for one right and good way is admirable but is no more likely to succeed of its purposes than any less admirable hope. In presenting and discussing our experience, we have focused on *our* preoccupation, excerpting material from the sessions as seemed appropriate with it in mind. But we have left in enough other material so that readers with different preoccupations can form their own conclusions.

In working with groups the authors have observed that people in groups *enact* the matters with which they are preoccupied. Consequently, the best, and perhaps the only, way of knowing what they have in mind is to study not what they do or say but what results from it. If their behavior is designed to have a result, an impact, the most accurate understanding of the meaning or function of that will come from noticing not the behavior itself but what it elicits in oneself. All of us must, therefore, allow that behavior to affect us—to wash over or into, to bombard, to tickle or tingle, to warm or frighten, to enrage or bore, to inform or confuse us. And then we must notice what we want to do. With that, with noticing what response and urge to action that behavior elicits in ourselves, we come to understand what that behavior is motivated by and what its design and intent are.

Being so open, so susceptible, to what, after all, may be quite unpleasant stimulation and noxious elicitation is not always a welcome position to adopt. At such times, we may wish to use our senses and so head off impact by watching and listening to the group. Our heads are also good for "heading off"; we can become quite adept at interpreting words and actions without experiencing them. If, for example, we hear someone intently controverting something he said previously, we can infer that at the least he has mixed feelings and probably is trying to deny the truth of what he said before. This inference may be entirely true, as far as it goes. But what we miss is why he now wishes to mislead us, how he now intends for us to feel, what he wishes us to do as a result of that feeling, and what or who our response makes us feel like. These are the vital data and can only come from within us.

This way of "listening" to groups has influenced this report in two ways. It has influenced what we include (and exclude) from the excerpts of the groups' meetings, for we include those portions of the sessions that seem to us to be the key elements in the elicitation that results. And it has influenced our commentary on what we experience the sessions as being about. Our subsequent "portraits" of these sessions are, therefore, far from photographic. They are more like the relationship between an abstract painting and its subject than like an academy portrait. The reader who, nevertheless, tries to spot an eye or chin or curve of brow in the abstraction will have a somewhat frustrating time of it. In the commentary, relatively little reference is made to what people say, however important what they say may be as a stimulus. The greater reference is made to what the "sitter" evokes in us, for in that lies not the eye or chin in itself, but the meaning of that feature.

To return once more to the groups, we have noted the difficulty the participants experienced with getting on with the purposes with which, variously, they had come. One might think that had someone in authority come right out and said that there was no larger purpose or grand design, matters might have been made easier. But in fact somewhere between 30 and 50 percent of the teachers in Groups I and II attended an orientation meeting at which they were alerted to that very fact. That meeting was held because our previous experiences with groups showed us they were profoundly preoccupied with the notices of the meetings. Members brought them along, read them aloud, and looked for the supposition concealed in them; two and three sessions passed before the members decided that they had, as it were, to believe their own eyes. One can see that the situation is much the same in the present groups. One must conclude that members may disbelieve what they hear as readily as what they read.

So intense is the wish first to believe and then to discover the missing ingredient making up what is "supposed to" happen that it suggests more is afoot than a wish simply to be told what to do or be. Even when members "figure it out" and conclude that they may do as they like, they act as though there must be more to it than that. Perhaps they would prefer to feel that something is missing from the experience, rather than realizing that all they encounter in it is all there is to it.

CHAPTER SEVEN

"THIS CAN'T BE ALL THERE IS TO IT"

The group members, involved in the group experience here-and-now, try to manipulate the situation and hold out for their highest hopes, treasuring the dissatisfactions thus incurred. Hence they postpone fruitful, immediate sharing.

In the next sessions, the theme "this can't be all there is to it" still occupies the groups, and, in most instances, the leaders as well. Periodically, the groups get beyond their preoccupation with the here-and-now. Group I, in time, talks of ways of helping children learn; Group II gets past the number of people present and talks of parent-teacher conferences, and Groups III and IV find other topics. The topics seem to bring considerable relief, suggesting that discussing specific subjects is an appropriate thing for groups to do—that this constitutes a good part of what the experience is all about.

By talking about topics, the group manages to subdue its preoccupation with the here-and-now experience—to "sublimate" this preoccupation, as it were. Thus Group II talks of the leader as teacher and themselves as parents and thereby airs its preoccupations without dwelling explicitly on them or being inhibited by them. And Group III discusses reactions to its leader's little speeches in the form of responses to a recent speech by President Nixon. But this strategy of containment proves only partly successful. After a bit, it comes apart to reveal the group's core preoccupations once again. The here-and-now returns.

Group I, Session 3

Leader: [Looks around a quiet, expectant group; his glance stops at O, and he asks with quiet moderation] I wonder whether you would find it useful to share your impressions of what we've been doing so far?

O: [Apologetically] I really forget.

[Silence]

F: [Turns to the leader] Why isn't your tape recorder here?
Leader: I forgot it.
[Silence]
O: [With a slight moan] I didn't think we were going to start again like *this.*
Leader: How would you want to start?
O: Like we ended last week.
F: [Apologetically] *I* forgot the question we ended with last week.
O: [Begins to muse] I guess it's that you keep thinking you *have* to start with very superficial things. We always start out talking about things with no relevance.
F: As we were coming here, I was thinking how great it would be with food . . . if we could smoke and drink coffee. But [regretfully] that would be postponement.
O: No one wants to say things like "How's the weather?" So no one says anything.
L: You don't want to talk about you, it may be boring to somebody else.
E: Maybe some of us are afraid to listen. We may hear some pretty bad things. Sad things maybe. The way some of these children have to live and yet they come to school each day, and *we* expect them to learn.
[Everyone looks long and hard at the leader. The group goes on to discuss ways to enable difficult students to learn.]

Group II, Session 3

[A smaller group than last time has assembled. Everyone keeps glancing at the door.]
Y: I forget where we stopped last time. [Turning to leader with a half-hearted apologetic note] You made some attempts to sum it up nicely and I *wanted* to remember, but I went home and promptly forgot.
[Everyone looks at Y as though this is exactly the case for all.]
F: [Has continued to glance at the door] Looks like we've dwindled.
Leader: Is that why it's hard to get started?
F: Oh, no. Heavens, no. It's hard to get started because it was a hard day at school. [F goes on to describe a fight between children.] I felt I had to do something so I called their parents and got into a mess of bringing out their feelings—the way they felt about their children, school, and everything.
Leader: You refer to it as a "mess."
F: I'm glad that I did it: we got our feelings *out* rather than shut them off. But I'm *exhausted.*
[The group slowly, and then with more animation, picks up on the subject of parent conferences. Some describe them as a battle; some as "pure and utter apathy." More group members come in and join the discussion, which turns to battles with or apathy from students. Everyone talks about whether to try to change children or to change one's own attitudes toward children or to change the institutions. R tries to sum it all up.]

R: The institution is really people, and when *people* have decisions to make, they can be very cautious. For instance, I would like to figure out how to work with *this* group so people are willing to take a chance and do what other people want them to do. *Let's* be willing to give it a try.

F (to R): I think you're trying to change our attitudes about things. [Nonchalantly] I don't mind that.

S: [With relief] Today the group is much more *open*.

Y: That's because we weren't talking about our feelings but about our experiences with the kids. We have a better handle.

R: Maybe it's our method of talking together that's changed.

F: [Not quite sure] Maybe . . . [Turns to leader] I feel much better about you and *your* role now. Before you were taking what people said and restating it in a sarcastic way. *That* was turning people off.

S: Isn't that a technique of group leaders—to shake the group up?

F: Maybe, but I didn't think it was working. [With a very reasonable tone] Although you *were* getting people to talk to each other.

[Everyone nods.]

Group III, Session 3

[Everyone has assembled. There is a long silence.]

N: [Throws a question out to the air] What did you think of the President's speech last night?

[L responds and they talk about it, but most other group members seem bored and look away. Another long silence.]

Leader: A, how would you compare today and last week with the first week?

A: [Glumly] There is more talk but it's not better. N is really the only one talking.

N: [To the leader] Why was the room changed from the first week? It seemed so comfy. Who decided?

Leader: Who do you think?

N: Some supervisor?

Leader: Are you angry because we moved without asking you? I decided.

N: How *come*?

Leader: Can anyone here answer for me? Why do you think?

L: [Tentatively] There wasn't enough room?

A: [Sullenly] I don't know why. The other room seemed more comfortable.

E: [To the leader] *You're* the one who did it. *You* tell *us*. *I* can't read your mind.

M: I don't know why we're discussing this. It's like discussing the discussion table at the Paris peace talks.

E: This room is so cold, like a classroom. I feel awful in this room.

Leader: Is it important to go back?

N: [Firmly] Yes.

[Silence]

M: Maybe if there was a good discussion, we wouldn't notice it.

L: Let's talk about something good.

[O suggests that they talk about suspension from school and then launches into a story about himself. Everyone asks him questions, prods him on, laughs with him.]

Leader: Does this group seem like academic suspension?

O: Yeah. We just sit here doing nothing.

[But the group continues to ask O questions about his experience until it is time to stop. After everyone else has left, N and O talk briefly.]

N: What do you think of this group?

O: I thought he [leader] was a psychiatrist, saying things like, "How do *you* feel?"

N: It's not his fault; he's not sup*pos*ed to talk; but if *he* doesn't talk how is anyone *else* supposed to talk? We need a topic each time.

[They both leave, nodding their heads in perplexed agreement.]

Group IV, Session 3

Leader: So what's new?

[Silence. Some group members are playing with shells that someone brought; others are writing notes.]

Leader: L, how do you feel about the group, or are you more interested in these objects?

L: Yah, they're more interesting.

[As the shells are being passed around, the group talks among itself about the leader, how in science class she doesn't let them do anything.]

Leader: Why do these objects let you talk?

[An uncomfortable shifting]

P: Maybe if *you* weren't here we could talk. Even if you're not taking the role of one, you still *are* a teacher.

Leader: If it's true that if I weren't here you could talk, why not pretend I'm not?

L: No, we can't. The boys would talk to the boys, the girls to the girls.

[There is a brief, more comfortable silence.]

N: [Looking around the group, with an informative, neutral air] Yesterday my mother was mad at me. She told my brother and me she was kicking us out. She started hitting us with a belt. She's *crazy.*

F: My mother doesn't hit us—we just walk out.

[Another silence]

Leader: What do *you* think of this, Y? Compared to last time?

Y: [Glumly] It's the same thing; no one talked.

O: [Reasonably] We should be able to do what we want. Like switch our seats around. It's too formal this way. Boys may be talking about one thing; us another.

Leader: The problem is not seating; it's the fact that you're boys and girls.

[Large laugh]

P: Why don't you let us walk around?

[The leader agrees. One group member gets up. A girl moves her chair. The group breaks into small units: girls who have never talked together are now talking together.]

Leader: Is it better to have small groups than no talking?
P: Well, it sounds better. You might join into another's discussion.
[People get up and move around.]
Leader: Being able to walk around helps you talk?
N: No, but it makes it more exciting.
[The group makes more noise. There is deliberate talk about teachers—who's the best.]
T: [Referring to another teacher] *She's* not boring at all; *she* gets so excited.
[There is more talk and giggling in small groups. But one subject slowly comes to prevail: movies and TV programs one has seen, and the people with whom one saw them.]
Leader: For people who don't talk, you're doing O.K.
Group: Now you're going to stop us. You're going to slow us down.
[But the subject emerges again.]

If, in reading these excerpts, we did not once again actively remind ourselves that the members of the groups came to the meetings to discuss issues of general interest and social concern, we would have forgotten that this was their purpose in attending the meetings. It is as if the real purpose, the ostensible agenda, has been replaced by another purpose; a new agenda seems to have come forth and taken precedence. In comparison to the formal agenda, which was to *discuss* issues, the informal, but now ascendent, agenda has become *how to* discuss issues. In a related way, issues concerning matters external to the here-and-now of the group situation have given way to preoccupation with the immediacy of the group situation itself. A centripetal movement seems to have taken place, as if the people present have acquired a new set of priorities in which former first things have been shoved back and new first things have come to the forefront.

These new first things have to do with one another and the leader. Most of the activity taking place seems to reflect this preoccupation. It is as if the others have a great deal to do with whether or not the hopes of each person in the group are being achieved.

The parties are acting, too, as if everyone else needs to be altered in some way. The strategies are various, with people attempting to earn, win, lure, exact, extract, or force others to change. The objects of each party's hopes likewise are various. For some it is something in themselves; for others it is their fellows; for others still, it is the leader of the group. But judging from the way that, in the end, everything falters and a vacuum replaces previous activity, we sense that all the previous attempts were diversions from the leader, deflections, moreover, which failed. The failure, we sense, was due either to the fact that self and fellows were poor substitutes or that the very use of them as substitutes was part of a strategy designed to induce the leader to give something other or more than it turned out that he provided. In the end, then, one feels that the hopes still adhere to the leader, and all else is shadow play.

The conviction is that matters could be made better at any given moment by the leader. The strategy is that one must concentrate on stimulating the leader to make matters better. Interestingly enough, the leaders themselves are by no means immune from either the conviction or the strategy. The degree to which they share these with the other members of the groups can be roughly measured by the extent to which they abandon their function of attending, noticing, and describing, and turn to other activities—as if to say that these are insufficient for the group they would like to have come to be.

Put in slightly different terms it is as if each of the people present envisions a more perfect group experience (Boris 1970b) than the one he or she discovers, and as if each in one way or another (and tactics differ, though the strategy remains constant) is busy trying either to discourage the continuation of what he encounters or to stimulate the realization of what he envisions, or both. Indeed, so ardent is the pursuit of the potential everyone seems to see, that attempts to make the most of what *is* possible from moment to moment are notably short-lived.

One cannot mistake the frustration members feel at their inability to keep something going. What impedes them from doing so? Partly one can sense that the very implication that all and sundry have learned their lesson suggests that, in fact, they have not—else why the need to proclaim they have? But more fundamentally still, one senses that more than such a "we have seen the light and will mend our ways" tactic is involved. It is as though frustration is better than satisfaction, as though hope is better than realization, as though, indeed, worldly satisfactions and realizations tempt them from hoping finer, better hopes. One feels, then, that for the members of the groups, at least at this time, it is better to hope hopes than find satisfaction, for present satisfaction is the enemy of future hopes.

In this sense, one can begin to understand that a major part of the strategy being exercised in each of the groups is devoted to shifting, interrupting, quelling the development of a here-and-now satisfying experience. Further, the groups maintain the fictitious belief that not this but its opposite is taking place. For no one says: "I am reluctant to have and especially continue a good experience, because it may be good enough to outweigh my highest hopes for a still better one, whereas frustration fuels both my hopes and my resolve." To the contrary, the theme is: "I should be content with and grateful for the good-enough experience." Here, one surmises, is a tactical move based on the suspicion that to say "We are so unappeasible as to refuse even to be appeased" would place in great jeopardy the chances of realizing the more utopian hopes. In saying, "I should be content with . . . ," it is as if the "should" expressed a statement of conscience—not "would be" but "ought to be" (but am not, hence the conditional). Conscience makes cowards.

But why? Why not say in so many words: you shall not satisfy me so cheaply! Why do the group members not speak their wishes outright and make known the disparity between the good-enough experience and these wishes? Help with these questions will come as we continue to study the group sessions.

CHAPTER EIGHT

THE SEARCH FOR AGREEMENT

> As the group members attempt to deny the existence of or to hide from inner antagonisms, they seek empty commonalities with others in the group.

What we see in the next sessions is *not* the members' harsh judgment that someone (the leader or the architects of the group meetings) is getting away with fraud. At least, that judgment is not made straight out. To the contrary, the group members seem as ready to accuse themselves as to judge others. Though this self-accusation may be designed to set the leader an example, still the members are wary of speaking out on the criticism they appear to hold.

Something, it seems, must happen first, if criticisms are to be leveled with force and conviction. And that something appears to be the other matter of absorbing interest in these sessions: the degree to which the members share views (Frank 1957; Yalom and Rand 1966). One receives the impression that commonalities are warmly received, whenever they can be obtained, while differences in views are frowned upon, even ignored. For Group I the shared common experience is that of manipulating or being manipulated; the common theme is what people can do to others—students to teachers, teachers to students. But the experience to be avoided is that of disagreement: to disagree would be to criticize and finally to sit in judgment on another.

Group II, like Group I, has become less concerned with how to talk in the group and more interested in issues of general interest or social concern. But the issues must be those on which all can agree—"greater solidarity" between teacher and student is a stance approved of by all. One concern is that students be able to express what is on their minds and still feel that they are not being judged. Is there a message here for the group leader as well?

For Groups III and IV the difficulty of finding and keeping to "something in common" is painful. In Group III two group members try to find a common topic—lounges, jukeboxes—a shared experience, but to others clearly an innocuous one. The others wonder what it means to have two people in the group who don't join in, the leader and the observer. It is awful; it is like the story one group member tells of some people whose expensive new purchases were stolen—it is like being "taken." On that everyone can agree: it is awful; teachers are awful; group leaders who leave you dangling in an experience in which they do not tell you what you are supposed to do are awful. Group IV seems determined to make the leader experience the difficulty of the situation. Their message seems to go like this: we cannot talk because we have nothing in common. We have nothing in common because we are not friends. We cannot become friends because we have nothing in common because we cannot talk to each other.

What we must ask as we read through these excerpts is what makes it so necessary to share common views, and what makes it so painful when group members suspect they may not be able to do so?

Group I, Session 4

[K begins a discussion of why teachers go into teaching and whether they "manipulate students" to suit their own "grim needs."]

E: [Counters] Youngsters are doing their share of manipulating, too.

L: That doesn't give us a right as teachers to do it.

H: [Nodding vigorously to L] I agree.

N: What does it mean when you say kids manipulate teachers?

K: [Joining H and   L] Oh, like kids want to smoke so they say they want to go to the john.

[A lively discussion follows on who manipulates whom, and on how one mixes kindness with discipline. Some care is taken not to disagree too greatly. When two group members begin to disagree, the leader suggests: "Let's talk about this kind of disagreement. I think it's quite a common experience." At this, talk falters; people glance at one another.]

F: [Zealously] *I* think we've taken so long to develop rapport in this group. We care about each other here so we're not going to damage each other. Before long we can say anything here.

Leader: But what is it that makes one think that what one will say might damage someone?

R: Sometimes when you were in school and gave wrong answers, someone laughed. Or I've had the experience of having an idea shot down and not being able to defend myself because my emotions were wrapped up in it.

[The group ends with a discussion of whether one can criticize students and make demands on them and still have them feel good about themselves. Everyone offers ideas on this with politeness and moderate good fellowship.]

Group II, Session 4

[After a desultory beginning, with people wondering "what to say," the group starts to consider how one treats students, to what extent to make demands on them.]

F: Kids usually turn off when they're not interested in what you ask them.

R: But, F, don't you think it helps when you say, "I know you don't like to do this but . . ."

F: [Not quite sure but trying to agree] Ye . . . es.

N: I think one of the biggest hangups for teachers is—how well do we really know the kids we have? How do we know how they feel? Or do we ever tell them about ourselves—they think we live in the walls.

[Everyone agrees and joins in by telling how he has talked directly with a child or a whole class or how "time pressure for getting things done" prevents him from doing this.]

S: [Regretfully] It *should* happen more.

Leader: Why?

W: [Answers for S] For far greater solidarity between teacher and student and because then the teacher can be more effective.

[Everyone murmurs in approval of W's statement.]

N: What's fun to try if you have 10 or 15 extra minutes in your class is to have the kids write down what they like most or least. They can write it down without signing their names.

Leader: What's wrong with signing their names?

N: Not signing their names will help them think they won't be judged.

S: [Hastens to add] Just speaking out clears the air: the fact that you can express something that's on your mind is instructive and healthy.

[Everyone murmurs in approval of this statement, but for the rest of the session people can think of little to say.]

Group III, Session 4

[N and L are discussing how other high schools have better facilities—lounges, jukeboxes—or worse facilities. They are the only ones talking for a long time.]

M: [Finally breaks in] I was wondering how everyone felt about having her [nodding to observer] sit there. Having her write things down, doesn't it do anything to you?

L: [Shrugging] I don't care.

N: It is weird. You ask her something and she doesn't say anything. I ask him [nodding to leader] and he doesn't say anything. It's awful.

Leader: How would you describe "awful"?

N: Not awful, just unnatural. It's like when someone doesn't recognize you and just walks by.

[There is a long silence in which no one looks at anyone else.]

N: [Hopefully] Is anyone going any place for vacation?

Leader: I guess I'm not surprised at the expression of the weirdness or awfulness of something not coming from me or the observer. Do you feel that when I don't say anything or the observer doesn't say anything that *no one* has said anything?

O: I can tell you something *awful* that happened. A man and his wife spent three hundred dollars on skis and a ski rack, left them in the Lechmere parking lot, and they were stolen fifteen minutes later.

[Everyone looks more alert, but no one adds to O's story.]

O: [Starts another topic] Does anyone here know Mr. Y in math and he's a coach too? He calls us Birds. He said, O.K., you Birds, sit down. He told us how to play football—anything but math. It wasn't too bad. After that I had Miss X for math—anyone had her? She's the worst.

L: Every math teacher in high school is the worst.

[S agrees heartily.]

N: Every coach I have who's a teacher is nice but they stink as teachers.

O: How about driving school? I paid sixty-five *dollars* and boy, was I taken. They don't even tell you what you're doing wrong.

[There is a lot of commiserating laughter about the fact that teachers and courses are terrible.]

Leader: I wonder if the question is—what did I let myself get into this time? Did I let myself be taken for a sucker?

[There is more laughter among the group as though the leader were referring to himself.]

Leader: [Persists] Is that what we were talking about: what have we let ourselves in for here? Are we suckers? Are we being taken?

[Long silence]

L: [Angrily] We have to talk about stuff we all know about, not just what *he* [looking at O] is talking about.

Leader: What do you think O is talking about?

L: [Gruffly] I don't know.

T: So far I think we've just talked for the sake of talking because we can't stand the silence. We're not interested in subjects.

N: I think it's because we have nothing in common. That's why books would help: everyone would read the same thing.

M: We have a lot in common—people, feelings, being human.

N: O.K., we all have experience in common.

M: No, not our experiences, our feelings.

T: We're afraid to talk about those.

N: I'm not.

M: We have to be aware of how everyone is feeling each time we meet.

Group IV, Session 4

[The leader begins when everyone has settled down and stopped talking to a neighbor.]

Leader: Last week we broke up and spoke in twos. You looked at me to see if I'd act like a teacher and stop you. People tested that out, too, by walking around. I'm not a teacher here and you're not here to be graded. Why do you think you're here?

P: It's an experiment to see if it'll work out for other classes.

N: To discuss things—it's a seminar.

T: It's to see what the students would talk about. It's a survey on students' feelings about topics.

V: [Turning to T with some exasperation] Yes, but you don't talk like that unless you're with your friends.

P: Maybe that's the purpose: to see how you talk, whom you talk to, what you talk about.

Leader: Why is it difficult to talk?

B: Because you're not with your friends.

Leader: Maybe you share common feelings, thoughts, even though he's a boy and you're a girl, or these are not your friends.

V: We haven't *talked* enough to see if we have common thoughts.

[All heads swivel toward the leader. Everyone looks as though he cannot possibly think of anything more to say.]

Despite more substantial excursions into exchanging ideas upon issues, the groups are clearly concerned with keeping views shared rather than differing. This may be due, we sense, to some enemy within, in the form of self-criticism and brooding doubt. The affirmation of other members of the groups to the member's own position may stave off these undermining hidden fears and antagonisms.

We have then a situation in which the members of the groups feel quite divided within themselves. A member's assertion that he is "good" provides some further evidence supporting our premise that the enemy lurks within; for only then would a member gain possession of the evidence of badness, which is felt and then resoundingly refuted.

Our excerpts here are in the nature of a stop-time photograph. If we let the time-projector run forward, we may expect to see that the alliance-building activity is in anticipation of a struggle with an external giant, namely, the leader. But at this point the members of the groups are not yet ready. It may be that they still hope to have the leader as an ally against the inner fearsome part of self. If, however, he does not come over to help, he too will be identified as part of that feared inner self, and the alliance between members now being wrought with such energy will be used to overmaster the leader. These intentions, dimly felt, are what, we imagine, are stirring the inner preoccupations. The leader, then, is coming in for it because "those who are not for me are ag'in me." The group may speak of acceptance, but what they mean is ratification. Such an intemperate requirement for endorsement is not adequately explained by the fear of disapproval in return for feeling disapproving. The question left over is: why do people feel so disapproving (hence disapproved of, hence in need of approval)? How this question will be developed we cannot know at this point: we can only surmise that there is something more to know. Perhaps the following sessions will tell us.

CHAPTER NINE

THE GROUP MEMBERS AGREE

The leader must be put to "good" work.

In these next sessions the leaders' non-approval thus far—their neither approving nor disapproving stance—is becoming more and more the object of focus. The groups are trying to put the leaders to work. As usual, they feel the leaders are potentially very valuable quantities. The only difficulty seems to be in determining the function the leader will agree to perform. In the eyes of the members, the leader might be compared to a talented but finicky individual who comes to an employment agency. The question is less what the leader *can* do than what he *will* do.

A number of suggestions are made, explicitly or through trial and error, as though the members wished to enlist the leader in various functions. Of these functions, the following are most easily distinguishable.

Leader in the Fight against External Evils

[Group II, for instance, has been discussing again the question of what the group is supposed to accomplish in its sessions.]

R: Why is this group sponsored by METCO? Since it was sponsored by them, I thought it would deal with problems about METCO students.

Leader: That's what you hoped to find here?

F: Maybe they are trying to get people to communicate with each other and themselves. If we're concerned with what METCO wants, maybe it's like this: they feel that if you can deal with your own feelings, you can deal better in class with all kids, METCO kids and other kids.

E: I honestly admit that I can't see METCO kids like our own children. Last week a teacher right here said that. And then she said she was "surprised" to find out later that they were "just like our own."

[Everyone in the group now joins in the discussion about whether being "surprised" in this way was an offensive remark, some defending the teacher who spoke "from her own background" and some attacking her. The topic moves to what METCO people want to be called—colored, Negro, or black. Many views of identity are proffered. The leader then speaks.]

Leader: The suggestion I made last time is that since students are not here, what could be studied is yourselves in relation to the students—how you feel, what you do with your feelings, how you feel about what others say, and so on.

Y: How could we do that? Take examples of our relationships with kids?

Leader: That's one way. But we also have a group here that can be used as an example. We have experiences as a group that we can look at.

L: [Turns to F with the back of his head to the leader] According to you, F, METCO kids are no different.

F: They are not completely different. They're all children and in that sense, they are all the same.

[F, L, and a few others continue discussing, as before, the question of METCO kids and other kids.]

Leader: I feel no one listened to me a few minutes ago.

R: [Sums it up] We listened; but we're not ready to deal with each other.

The conviction of the group here seems to be that the leader's motivation to conduct the group arises from his hatred of external evils. Here the external evils are prejudice and the difficulty for "other" teachers to teach students who are "different." The strategy seems to be that if the leader can be employed in this function as leader against external evils, he may both satisfy the group's dilemma over what it is "supposed to" do and (not incidentally) not go combatively looking for these evils within the group. Indeed, when the leader here suggests that the group might look within, at itself as a group, no one listens.

Leader in the Fight against Internal Evils

Group I

[After a slow, hesitant start with desultory conversation and moments of silence, K looks around at everyone.]

K: I don't know if this is pertinent, but I don't feel emotionally involved with anyone in this room, and I can't get or give very much if I don't. It's too bad because if I felt differently, I would try [to F] gently to help you not be so uptight—which you are. I feel

bad at the moment that I can't. I'm interested, but I don't really feel
emotionally involved with you as a human being. I think there's a lot
of that going on in the room.

Leader: Can you tell us why that is? Is it something about the group, or
something about me?

K: Well . . . [reluctantly] there's too much going on toward *you* and
away from *you*, and not enough among members of the group: there's
almost a reluctance to touch each other.

Leader: Would that help people, if they touched each other?

K: [Hastily] I was thinking figuratively.

F: I think a big part of getting to know other people is looking at them.
If someone talks to people and doesn't look at them, that puts up a
wall. [Turning to K] That may be part of *your* problem.

K: [Somewhat annoyed] I don't think *anyone* is reaching out to anyone
else any more than I am. It's a problem with the group.

F: Maybe we can't look at ourselves as a group because *some* of us don't
feel the isolation you feel.

N: [Thoughtfully] Isn't it hard to feel anything about people you don't
know . . .?

R: I felt in a different mood last week. We felt freed up to move somewhere. Today the whole sense of tightness upsets me.

K: Can you share with us what you mean by "moving" somewhere?
Because I didn't feel you were involved last week.

R: I didn't say much or bug anyone, but I felt like we were together
last week. I just felt myself feeling better about everyone and I felt
we were talking about things that mattered.

E: [In defense of R] She could've been very involved without saying anything—but just showing it by her expressions.

N: Last week I felt everyone was on the same wave length, but this week
[puzzled] everyone has different feelings.

The conviction here is much the same as for what we just saw in
Group II, namely, that the leader has agreed to conduct this group because he hates certain evils. But here the feeling is not that he can be
induced to lead the crusade against external forces, but that he is determined to rout the wrongdoings among the membership. The group members are prepared to comply—partly, it seems, out of a wish to be improved; partly because it may be less painful to submit willingly, since
there is already "too much" going on toward the leader and away
from him, as though the group is magnetized. Accordingly, the group is
discovering subversive qualities in itself—uptightness, a wish to be uninvolved, a sense of isolation and of feeling bad—and offering these for
the leader's delectation. If only, indeed, they could return to the good
they had, and the good they exemplified, last week!

Leader as Source of Good Benefits

[Group III begins its next session with silence. Someone has moved all the chairs into a circle instead of the usual rows. Then T turns to the leader and says, as though jokingly]

T: Aren't you going to say what's new? Aren't you going to make our day complete?

Leader: I know what's new.

N: What's that?

Leader: The chairs are put together.

N: Yes, we decided to do it last week.

[Silence falls again]

Leader: I wonder if you wait for me to say what's new?

N: It's funny, because you do say it usually. And yet after you say it, no one talks.

[Silence again]

Leader: My impression is that the group waits for an opening from me, and then we wait for N or O to start a topic. Does it seem that way to you?

T: It's difficult . . .

Leader: Do you feel pressure from me?

T: Well, it's just the fact that we're here . . . I mean, I think the pressure is on *you* too.

[Silence falls again, but everyone seems to lean forward.]

The pressure is indeed *on* the leader in the group here, pressure to be what the group hopes him to be. The hope here, if we think about it in broader terms for a moment, is not for a leader like Moses, for example, who leads people away from evil outside or from temptations within. It is rather for a leader more in the image of Jesus Christ, a person who *embodies* goodness and benefit and from whom these qualities can be assimilated, as in the ceremony of communion. In the first two functions, the leader's qualities are considered like but superior in effectiveness to the members' own, so that leader and group are all on the same side, against either evils without or evils within. Here the leader is experienced as both separate and different: he possesses qualities reciprocal to the members' needs, and need him they do. Hence, the circle is made but he must tell them "what's new."

Source of Demoniac Powers

[Group IV begins with the leader asking]

Leader: What were we talking about last time?

Group: Why we didn't talk.

Leader: What was decided?

Group:	We're afraid to.
Leader:	What conclusions did we draw before?
Group:	We were trying to test you . . . Like, people were talking to people next to them but wouldn't talk to the rest of the kids.
Leader:	The next step would have been someone jumping out the window to see if I'd stop you.
P:	Would you?
Leader:	What do you think?
T:	What is the purpose? What do they want us to talk about?
Leader:	What we did talk about—we can talk about anything as a group.
T:	Why does somebody try to get us to talk in a group?
V:	Maybe it helps make you communicate with people you don't know.
T:	[With disbelief] It can't be to talk about just anything because we were talking about anything—and those things were stupid.
Leader:	Well, maybe those stupid things have meaning—that people are really nervous, for instance. So I wouldn't say those things are a waste.
Group:	[Everyone turning to the leader and talking at once] Last week you asked different questions—*you* started to talk, *you* kept it going.
I adds:	It seems as though when *you* start talking we all shut up.
Leader:	Why's that?
T:	I guess because you're still the teacher.
Leader:	When is that going to stop?
Group:	As teacher, you don't express your feelings in the group as we all do.

This is in one way the antithesis of the leader as the source of good things, but related also to the thought that the leader's strengths might be directed at, not for, the group. As such it represents a most fearful hope that the leader may install in the members substances that will dissolve their constraints and hence lead them to excesses and indulgences, even to jumping out the window! The group here is noting the leader's permissive characteristics, and this is putting into question their assumption that the leader, like them, is in the group for socially worthy purposes. Confession and acceptance have previously been understood to be a means to a worthy end—appeasing the leader, opening oneself to his fight against one's evils, winning his goods and benefits. Now confessions and acceptance begin to look unnecessary. Can it be that the leader is sympathetic with one's evil motives and wishes? If one takes in the leader's attitudes and position, will one lose one's inhibitions and restraints? Can one use him as such an exemplar—will he stand for it? Again and again the leader is tested with just these questions in mind.

As one notices these alternative possibilities, one is bound to notice, too, the heavy lading of moral preoccupations. The absence of supposed-to's, which, as we noted earlier, was a veritable affliction for the group members, is still a major concern. It is as if the groups feel the relative de-emphasis of oughts and shoulds to be a shame and a delusion, the devil's guileful work. They cannot, therefore, trust the absence of these moral constraints. Insofar as the supposed-to's are absent, the group members must supply them for themselves. But the belief is that moral constraints must be only temporarily in abeyance—that sooner or later the supposed-to's will be made manifest in stunning form. It is impossible, it would seem, for the group members to feel that someone can want nothing of them or for them. Trial balloon after trial balloon is sent aloft to lure the leader out of hiding.

We can guess that it would be a relief to the members if the leader declared himself, if he accepted employment, so to speak, even of the most "demoniac" sort. A known enemy is preferable to an unknown friend. The leaders' seeming indifference to wanting things for or from the groups makes the group members all too keenly aware of how little they can reciprocate this hands-off position. In the silence of the leader's lack of demands, their demands on him ring with a crashing din.

CHAPTER TEN

SILENCE IN GROUPS

Silence is an absence that is felt as a presence. Silence is expressive of a variety of emotions. The dynamic evolution of emotions during silence.

Silence plays no small part in the group experience. For the group members silence is not simply the absence of speech; rather, it takes on various shapes and forms; silence becomes the presence of absence. Such a presence can be neither ignored nor dismissed, much as the groups might like to do so. Like the leaders' "indifference," it must be reckoned with. The leaders themselves seem to feel that silence is something else to be noticed, described, and clarified. Yet when the leaders in Group II and Group III ask what the silence the groups just endured was about, it is not that question but the question of what should be done about it that occupies the groups.

"Endured" or even "suffered" is what silence is for the groups. It is difficult to convey in these next excerpts the painfully felt quality of the silences. The reader must imagine for himself a roomful of people who have now met together for a number of sessions, people who have talked together, laughed together, who share the common experience of being either teachers or students. And yet they are people who, with all this, are aware of each other as complete strangers. When B, in Group I, tries to articulate this, K tries to help, but both find it difficult: one feels "among friends" but "ill-at-ease" about saying things; one goes home upset yet feels one can't "not come back"; one cares what people will think even though after (ten) more weeks one may never see these people again. But even then, "you never know," says B mysteriously, as though the group has somehow taken on a life of its own that will persist.

A few group members have been able to "not come back." The presence of their absence is felt too. Both Groups I and II appear to feel that until the entire group is assembled, nothing but silence can happen. Yet for Groups III and IV, who have no absent members, the experience is much the same.

Group I, Session 6

[Some of the group has assembled. It is time to begin. People fall silent and look at the door, waiting.]

O: [Says with a little laugh] We don't want anyone to miss anything.

K: [Adds ruefully] They ought to know that if they come late, they miss the silence.

Leader: They have to go through suffering to get benefits?

N: [Quickly, with a jolly tone] My husband doesn't believe that I can sit so quietly, as I tell him I do here. I tell him: It's so strange; I can't think of anything to say.

[Everyone remains silent, as though that were indeed the truth.]

K: [Gloomily] This is really bad news.

[E appears at the door and walks in briskly.]

E: I'm missing an important meeting today, so I hope this is worthwhile. That sounded nasty. I didn't mean it to sound nasty. I didn't mean to interrupt. Someone was talking when I came in.

[Everyone bursts into giggles at the very notion that someone was talking. This is followed by silence.]

B: [Starts out tentatively] You know, this is really awful. I've thought of not coming, but that would make me feel worse. I always talk myself into coming back, yet I wonder why I do come. I seem to be slowing things up.

Leader: You do? How do you do that?

B: I have trouble talking. I see that as detrimental to the group. I get something, but I don't give anything. That makes me feel bad.

K: [With interest] What do you get here?

B: Well, I feel part of *the* group, as though among friends. But [briskly] usually I'm not this kind of person, usually I talk and talk.

K: [Puzzled] You say you feel among friends and yet ill at ease about saying things—isn't that a bit incongruous?

B: Yes, it *is*. I go home upset, but I feel I can't not come. I feel that if I stayed away, you'd all think I couldn't handle it.

E: [Reassuringly] That's probably why a lot of us come back: everyone cares what people will think.

K: But the people in *this* group—if I walked out and didn't come back, I wouldn't expect to see these people again, so it wouldn't bother me.

B: [With musing uncertainty] You never know, do you?

E: [To K] It's funny you say that about this group, because I find a higher degree of intensity here than in a normal situation; and yet you say it doesn't bother you as much.

K: Maybe that's my way of handling it. I just say the group is unimportant.

E: It's funny you suggest that every time we meet!

[Everyone laughs at this teasing comment to K. The group then goes on to discuss kids who take drugs, drug education, and how to reach such kids.]

Group II, Session 6

[The group has spent the first part of the session in long silences, punctuated by awkward and self-conscious analysis of reasons for these long silences. After the next long silence, S speaks, as though musing to herself.]

S: Some situations can cause misunderstandings. I walked out on a speaker once—he could have thought I was rejecting him. Actually, I just had to go home.

I: I think this is ridiculous. I think we all have a lot to offer here.

Leader: Maybe one of the difficulties is that some of the group are not here today.

A: Let's pick a topic. You notice that was the longest silence; if we let it go on, it's like we're building up resistance—pretty soon we won't be able to talk at all!

W: [Agrees wholeheartedly] The longer the silence, the harder it is to speak. Why is that?

A: Then you have to think of something extra good to say.

Leader: What was the silence about? Why do people have to wait for something else?

F: We need something outside the group as an issue to talk about. We need a building block, something to start with; but whenever we get hold of one, "someone" [F looks pointedly at the leader] suggests it's a crutch.

I: I think people feel that what they have to say is not important enough.

Leader: Does it have to be important?

[At this, F turns to the leader.]

F: I find that *you* are not part of the group. It's partly the way you introduced yourself, partly the way you comment. You don't give me a feeling of empathy. You don't enter in as part of the group or as a facilitator. That makes everything seem harder.

Leader: The feeling is that I am critical.

F: I don't *care* if you're critical. It would be easier if you were part of the group and *were* critical. But like that last question: "Does it have to be important?" You didn't say anything about what *you* thought. And since you're not a part of the group, when you do say something, even something like that, I feel squelched—I can't talk.

I: [In some despair] We've discussed so many things that *aren't* important that maybe we should just not come.

Leader: Or, it could be you're labeling things as not important enough. My question was intended to consider if things have to be that important. Why isn't what you decide to talk about important enough?

A: Because it might be a crutch—just to get us talking.

Leader: But you don't know if it is until you talk.

F: [Turning to A, despair in her voice] If we feel we can't talk about something because it might be a crutch, we can't get anything off the ground.

[Everyone notes that by the clock it is time to end, and the session is over.]

Group III, Session 6

[The meeting opens with a long silence. Finally, N sighs.]

N: This time is being wasted.

Leader: Would it be useful to talk about what is going on during the silence?

N: [To everyone, with an imploring look] Isn't there something we can do to get together better?

O: What you need is something everyone is interested in, something everyone needs. You know the song Tom Jones sings—"Everyone Needs Love." How important is it for kids to have love, to have a boyfriend, or to go steady?

N: [Delighted with a topic at last] Right now boy-girl love can't be deep. But part of love is being accepted. Even in this room people want to be accepted, not outcast, and that's why people don't talk.

M: What about people just feeling indifferent to you?

N: Oh, that's *worse* than when they don't like me. It shows they don't care at all.

O: I'll tell you a story. Last year this guy said to me, "Who's that girl? I'm in love with her." So I told him that she always sits in the same seat and asks the person in front of her for gum. So he sat in front of her, and when she asked for gum, he was so nervous that he dropped the gum all over, and was he embarrassed! I said, "Do you still love her?" and he said, no, he didn't love her any more.

Leader: Why do you think he was nervous?

O: She was a senior and she was very cold.

Leader: Sounds like he had good reason to be nervous. Do we have good reason to be nervous here?

[No one responds.]

O: [Takes up a new tack] My English teacher wanted us to write an autobiography using events, no feelings.

Leader: What would happen here if we talked about more than events?

O: I don't know and we'll never find out!

M: Why not? That story you told of the boy with the gum is the same as in here: we're *all* afraid of not being accepted.

[The group falls into silence again.]

Group IV, Session 6

[The group begins by talking in small groups of two or three.]

Leader: Are we finished with the usual discussion of classes, teachers, tests? Are we ready for a discussion group?

[Silence]

Leader: It seems like my comment made everyone quiet.
R: It did—you told us to stop talking in little groups. You didn't say that but that's what you meant.
Leader: So now you find it hard talking in a large group; you find it painful.
[Someone giggles.]
Leader: Why are you giggling?
S: Cuz I know what we're going to talk about for the next ten minutes.
V: [Gloomily] Yeah. Why we can't talk.
[Silence descends.]
Leader: What's with this dead silence, hmm? How do you like sitting here for twenty minutes in dead silence?
R: We don't.
Leader: So why don't you do anything about it? Why don't you talk about why you don't care to talk?
[Silence, punctuated by giggles]
B: Does *anyone* want to do something useful during this period?
[No one responds.]
Leader: What do you think would be useful, B?
B: What we're supposed to be doing—talking to each other.
H: Yes, we're supposed to be talking about something that interests us all.
Leader: So why can't we?
H: No one tries.
R: We can't do it. Dress code—hunh, we beat that subject to death.
Leader: So why don't you say how you feel about not having anything to say?
S: We beat that to death too.
H: It's the other kids. You think the other kids will think things about you but they really don't.
[A long silence]
B: [Catching the leader's glance] Don't look at *me.*
T: [Finally says to the leader] I think this is killing you more than it's killing us.
Leader: I don't know how much it's killing you. I think I'm more willing to do something about it.
[Several group members get up and begin playing around.]
Leader: What's driving you to do that? Are you bored or something?
Several: Yes.
Leader: Why don't you say so?
H: [Joining the leader] How do you expect not to be bored if you don't talk?
Several: Dunno.
R: They're doing that instead of talking in order not to be bored. [Looking at the clock] Well, we got through this period.
H: No, the point is—we *didn't.*

In the sessions we have just examined, the silences intrude and ob-trude to such an extent that they almost become things in themselves, awful, lurking presences like the lion in the dark places in a five-year-old's bedroom. Like those dark pockets, they are not simply spaces empty of light, but spaces filled with the presence of something frightening. For the group, it seems, they are places filled with absence, places where something good and fulfilling used to be and has now gone.

In Group II, Session 2, we may remember, members of the group look back with horror at the silences of the first session. "Forty minutes of dead silence *is* difficult," says one member with heartfelt emphasis. The leader, on the other hand, does not remember things that way—for her there were silences, to be sure, but not the difficult, sometimes almost unbearable, spaces into which the group felt itself to have fallen.

But here we must pause to wonder—are these metaphors excessive? Do terms like hungry lions and empty holes describe what are really no more than periods of quiet? The answer would be no, except for the fact that the groups themselves offer ample testimony to the contrary. What accounts for the discrepancy between that simple notation on the record—"Silence"—and the experience of the group?

If we were to study the instances of "silence," we would see the silences as expressive of a message: "Perhaps there is not much use in talking," or, "If anything more than silence is wanted by you, leader, you had better get on the stick!" But even if the silences convey these views, this hardly accounts for the members' reactions to silence.

Let us, therefore, take matters further. Let us suppose that the initial moments of a silence do express the foregoing messages and that *nothing has happened.* The leader does not fill the vacuum. The vacuum and only the vacuum exists. When there was thought to be plenty, there suddenly was nothing. "The rest is silence."

Having come this far, the groups' reactions seem more plausible. Absence, nothingness, is dismaying and saddening, even frightening. But the extent and quality of the groups' unease about the periods of nonspeech suggest that something inhabits the emptiness, something fills the silence, and it is the wrong sort of something.

Nature is said to abhor a vacuum. Does human nature, too? If, as we imagined, the members of the group did say silently, "Nothing more from us unless or until you come forth," they were angry and demanding. Moments later they experienced great anxiety. Where did their anger and demandingness go? Let us see what happens if we suppose the demandingness to have increased during the initial moments of the silence and then, somehow, merged into the silence. The silence would abruptly have taken on consuming qualities, would have become the avaricious lion, the engulfing emptiness. The group, to complete the exchange, would suddenly become the object of the silence's intemperate desires. When people are in such straits, we expect them to speak rather quickly and desperately—to fill the void with anything. This is exactly what they do, and they do not forget their experiences at the brink. In the future, they are quite careful about how widely they allow the void to yawn.

As the groups go along, it develops that there are silences and *silences*. All are at once empty and filled with things. There are silences during which members are filled with anger. These occur when they contain their anger. They seethe, yet feel alive with it. And there are silences in which gloom pervades the room. During these, it is as if the members have swallowed their anger and the anger has cast a pall on any spark or lightness they may have previously felt. The feeling here is that something vital is missing, perhaps gone forever. "He just saved us," says a member about a latecomer in one of the groups. They had been alone with the leader, and it was gloomy. Now, there was a ray of hope.

The intensity of these reactions, of course, is just as odd as the explanations we have hazarded, particularly when, as usual, we juxtapose both to the ostensible fact that we are considering people who are experiencing all of this within a discussion group. What we must conclude from such reactions, it seems, is that the members cannot help feeling that discussion is the least that can be made of the opportunity.

This attitude may help to explain both the thirst they have for the leader and, sometimes, for one another, and the degree to which they must contain the bitter anger and disappointment they feel when that thirst is not quenched, for, after all, they know that they are not there to do more than discuss. This knowledge deprives their anger of the rightful quality it would have if they fully expressed it. And if they cannot sound their anger, how much less can they fall upon the leader with their wishes? So, as both wish and anger mount, so does compunction, until a terrible inner struggle takes place. Compunction proves the stronger. H says, "There won't be any fighting," and the aggressive wish gets thrown out into the empty hole of the silence. Would-be vanquishers suddenly become possible victims, and the silence becomes terrifying. For instance, B, in Group IV, says to the leader after the longest silence: "Don't look at *me*."

Experience with all of this, of course, gives the members of the group both the knowledge and opportunity to moderate the intensity of the experience. In time, they can begin to find words to express it—or at least an attenuated form of it. They can speak, that is, of their fear that they are not providing the leader with enough and of their anxiety lest he attack them. But words like these cannot express the inexpressible, and the commingling of experiences of horror and fear in the silences never quite gets considered by the group.

The leader may try to help the group articulate it, but to no avail. The group does not know—it happened both too quickly and too massively—that much of what it experiences of the leader's silence (not all, and this too complicates matters) was "put" there by the group itself. The silence of the leader makes them too anxious to go ahead and tempt fate by taking up the leader's cue and becoming angry. "If this can happen when we are no longer angry," they seem to say, "what could happen to us if we really became angry?"

To those who feel righteous in their anger, such a convoluted response will seem ludicrous. They may well wonder if this is the nature of what happens in a group. Or they may well wonder if what happens in these particular groups with these particular people is what evokes or receives such a response. Surely, if the descriptions we have provided have any accuracy, they may feel that the members of the groups are crackpots to begin with. Further, if they have any doubts about the quality of our schools, what they have read (if it doesn't indict the authors) will add to their suspicions.

But things do happen to people when the constraints they are used to are let down. Early in our investigation we spoke of the fervent wish all the participants felt to be told what they were supposed to do. Without that constraint, it was as if all bets were going to be off. Without that boundary, all hell might break loose. They asked to be helped to "escape from freedom." The absence of external expectations is at once a welcome invitation to expand and let loose and a breach in the containing wall at which their inner compunctions stand guard duty. Thus they let go their usually tamed wishes and at the same time feel vigilantly self-conscious and more than ordinarily inhibited. In short, they experience a heightened sense of conflict between openness and closedness, freedom and constraint, longing and inhibition.

In the silences, a considerable upheaval occurred. Subsequently, we noted, the tremors were milder and more attenuated. Adjustments between the irresistible and immovable were taking place as the members adapted to this new and different environment in which external constraints were reduced. As we witness this process, we see everyone in private. The public face is not on. In the classroom and elsewhere we would not immediately recognize the people we meet in the group.

CHAPTER ELEVEN

APPRAISAL OF SESSIONS ONE THROUGH SIX

The anatomy of anger in all groups. Two kinds of optimism.

We have seen the groups at work for six sessions thus far. We have noticed their struggles with the absence of explicit supposed-to's, their fascination with how to go about talking together, their need to find "something in common" before they can begin to talk together, their wishes to employ the leaders, and their painful endurance of silences. In Session 6 we heard one teacher in Group II lament: "We've discussed so many things that aren't important that maybe we should just not come"; a student put it this way: "Hunh; we beat that subject to death."

If we were to describe the attitude of the groups toward their leaders at this point, it would seem to approximate the following: if we were in his shoes, we would feel angry at our lack of achievement. Since he is angry, we must be watchful. We are best off putting our most vigilant persons forward, those who cannot be lulled by shows of innocent intentions, but who can discover the menace in the appearance of innocuous gestures. It is either that—waging a pre-emptive campaign—or being harmed.

The leaders are feeling something like this. The group blames me for its lack of achievement. As this is not wholly my fault, I feel unjustly criticized, hence angry. But I may not be angry with the group; to feel so is professionally irresponsible. Hence I must be quite careful. Still, if the group does not achieve more, the members will be angrier still. Thus I must either propitiate and disarm them or force them to work. As neither of these suits my intentions, I feel quite angry. Again, however, I may not be angry. Therefore, I must vigilantly watch my most innocuous response for signs of bellicosity.

On our part, at a comfortable distance from the fray, we can see that the group is angry at the leader but prefers not to experience that anger

120

for what it is. By reassigning their anger to the leader, they feel better than they would had they contained—and thus experienced—their anger (see Chapter 3, Appendix A). It is as if external menace is easier to cope with than internal menace, and as if believing the leader to be angry at lack of accomplishment is preferable to the fear of expressing their own anger in reply to his. The latter might imply a confrontation which the group wishes to avoid. Perhaps the group members fear that their superior numbers will do harm to the leader, or that his superior knowledge or skill will do harm to them. Perhaps they can deal more readily with external threat than with the results of swallowing their anger and having it threaten their own internal well-being. Within, the result is depression—those painful feelings of being unlovable and unwanted and of the sadness occasioned by the withdrawal of love and kindliness ("if that's the way you're going to be, don't expect me to be nice to you").

It seems, then, that the decision about where to place anger involves complex motives. The alternatives present the horns of a dilemma. If anger is assigned to the leader, the group feels endangered from without. Held within, anger may harm the leader or occasion retaliation. Held within, too, it may be turned by the self of each member against internalized parts, the leader's psychological forebears, or by these prototypes of the leader against the self. Inwardly or outwardly, it is a beggar's choice, with rapid switches among alternatives being the unsatisfactory way of searching for an equilibium.

Yet the members of the group have an alternative they are not using, perhaps not even seeing. It is to find everyone—oneself, one another, their psychological forebears, and the leader—both good and bad, and accordingly neither to love nor to hate but to like and tolerate indifferently. This amalgam achieved, everyone could get on about his business with dispatch, harvesting from the enterprise what its possibilities offer.

The teachers' groups seem readier to find this alternative than the children's groups. The teachers have an obligation to their pupils, the value of which offsets for them the destruction of their hopes for fulfillment from the group experience. This obligation decreases the enormity of their preoccupations with the group. But for the young people, it is as if (while they are in the group) the group and the leader are the be-all and end-all of their existence.

Is that too strong an interpretation? These youngsters, after all, have parents, friends, other teachers, and, doubtless, relatives too. On the face of it, the intensity of their frustration, anger, and difficulty seems unwarranted. If they have a disappointing hour in the group, why not shrug it off, the way they do a less than felicitous math period, and wander off a bit more philosophical about it? Yet the excerpts from the meetings suggest orphans locked into a "No Exit" circumstance. Does this not suggest that the children see the group as containing far more promise than all the other available sources of satisfaction put together? One may well imagine that the group experience was over-sold to the children, such is the ardor of their belief and their fury when their hopes are scorned.

Yet it was not, as we know. They were merely offered the opportunity to meet and talk about whatever they wished. If they were misled, they misled themselves, and—and here is the point of great moment—they continued to mislead themselves. They continued to hold high hopes and feel them unfulfilled, and thus were angry. They could not accept the possibility of simple discussion.

We are left, therefore, with the problem of understanding the wish that will not defer to the fact. Do these children have hopes which they have previously taken elsewhere—to their own parents, to friends, relatives, other teachers, siblings, perhaps even lovers—and which have not been fulfilled? Undaunted, are they not bringing these same hopes, still intact, to yet a new situation? Does not the very tenacity of these hopes suggest that the children feel they may be running out of other shops, as it were, in the marketplace of possibilities, so that rather than shrug and say, "Well, perhaps not here, still somewhere else," their behavior says, "It can't be that it is not here, for where else is there?"

The teachers, on the other hand, have moved on to say, "Ah, we had so hoped to find all of what is left on our hearts' shopping list here, all in one place, all at once; but perhaps we can find bits of what we want elsewhere, improvise for some of it, and need only find the remainder here, now." If this is so, how is it that these teachers, older, wiser, more experienced, and more disappointed than the youngsters, are at the same time more hopeful? Has experience taught them the world is a more fruitful place than those still wet behind the ears have found it?

The marketplace of possibilities no doubt expands somewhat (if only to narrow later) at the end of adolescence; home-bound and relatively immobile, young people have not seen the world and sampled its wares. The teachers have; some are married, all have been to college, some have been away from home, and so forth. But the sense of relative freedom implied above has an inner aspect, too. The teachers are freer from the incessant and imperious demands of pubescence. They move more easily amid their sensual desires. Part of this ease is due, no doubt, to their greater familiarity with these appetites. Part may be due to a reduction in the pressing demands of the appetites, whether because they are finding satisfaction for them, or have learned to style or apportion them, or both. This freedom, in turn, permits older people both to make more of less and to make do with less from more. The more readily satisfied one is, the more one is satisfied and the more optimistic one's expectations. Children have the harder existence, in this sense. For them, tomorrow is vague and its opportunities indefinite.

At the same time their hopes, as we have seen, are the more aspirant and ardent. This is optimism of a different sort. They are not yet stifled; they are not yet prepared to be sadder and wiser as the teachers perforce have become. Thus, when the teachers deflect their yet untrammeled expectancies, the children focus their hopes in all-or-nothing fashion, true and faithful servants of the imperious demands of their pubescence.

We are dealing, then, with two sorts of optimism—in the case of the teachers, that coming from experience; in the case of the children, that of tenacious desire. Accordingly, we are dealing with two sorts of suffering. The children suffer the thwarting of desire, the teachers the dashing of hopes. Somewhere desires metamorphose into hopes—"do not thwart me" turns into "do not treat me this way"; deprivation turns into despair, rage into outrage; injury into insult; love (and hate) of others into love (and hate) of self and its contents.

CHAPTER TWELVE

WHY PEOPLE DON'T
TALK IN GROUPS

The spoken and unspeakable. Two possible causes: social reality and each member's fantasy. The final hypothesis: the existence of public and private ideals, in "I-Thou" and "I-Me" relationships.

We have noticed the silences that the groups fall into and have speculated on how in wishing angrily for more from the leader the group members have experienced these angry demands as filling the silences. This metapsychotic state can rarely be consciously known in groups meeting for fifteen to thirty sessions. But the groups can begin to notice their concern that because they are not providing the leader with enough *he* will somehow attack *them*. Concomitantly (for most of the group experience happens over and over again, in cycles rather than in a linear arrangement), the groups behave in such ways as to show the leader that his or her "silence"—that is, his not insisting upon the supposed-to's and his lack of approval or disapproval—and his seeming imperviousness to their discomfort can be adopted as their own tactics. Whichever they undertake, silence or busy discussion, and whatever its tactical intention as behavior, it is clear that the concern with what is sayable and what is not persists.

Though the groups are, increasingly, finding things to say, much of what occurs to the members is dismissed, in the moment before the silence, for instance, as not worth saying. Things can be thought but not said, as if (as we have already noted) there are two standards: a more lenient private standard and a more stringent public one. If the public standard, as represented by the other members of the group, the observer or the leader, were in *fact* more stringent, we might try to solve the puzzle by looking at the empirical facts. But this is difficult to do, even from our remote vantage point. From time to time we hear of things too trivial to say, for example; yet "trivial" things are said and no derision greets them. At other times, quite sonorous statements are issued, only to find the most indifferent welcome. These facts are puzzling, and if we were to try to fashion the distinguishing characteristics of the appropriate (or inappropriate) statements on the basis of these empirical facts, we should be very hard put to do so.

Let us, therefore, cast further. If the facts, the social reality, do not provide the qualifiers, perhaps some sort of group "ideal" will do so. Can it be that the members have in mind an ideal sort of talk, compared with which much or most of what they are able to produce falls woefully short? This, it would seem, comes closer to the mark, for it explains why the "trivia" can be identified as such but cannot be replaced with "good" statements. The members do not know what a "good" statement is; all they know is that there is such a thing. Familiar, everyday-ish occurrences, *because* they are so prosaic, clearly do not fit the specifications of the Sunday-best ideal.

The private domain, then, is held by each group member to be rather more homely and informal than the public one. Each decides that the public atmosphere is probably more ideal than his own domain of thought. At times the group members resemble people who get together to decide the by-laws of a club and end up fashioning laws which exclude every one of those present. The old expression that the whole is more than the sum of its parts comes to mind, particularly if we read "better" for "more."

Yet how painful it must be to sit minute after minute finding that everything one comes up with is unspeakable. How can we account for such discomfort being suffered and sustained with common, truly unanimous consent when the alternative appears so simple: members need only voice what occurs to them?

One answer is obvious. If all group members, as it seems, maintain an ideal, any one member can expect disapprobation should he violate the canons. But that does not tell us why sanctions are not applied to errant statements. Is disapproval of un-ideal statements made by other members anticipated on a tit-for-tat basis? This may well be. But the feeling that inappropriate statements should be criticized because they ruin the group is also experienced internally.

We come then to surmise that the members believe it is better to suffer the pain of feeling inappropriate than to suffer the loss of a potentially ideal group experience. But we must go now back to a previous question: why does so much that is "not worth saying" continue to occur?

We have already touched upon one psssible answer to this question: though the members believe that there is an ideal, they do not know *what* it consists of and cannot therefore provide it. Yet one senses that a good deal of what they are thinking is not only less than ideal but far from ideal, and that, moreover, this less-than-ideal occurs with such forcefulness that its inhibition requires great mental strain. There is scarcely energy left over to replace the less-than-ideal with a thought-statement closer to the ideal.

Do we not need to account for this curious paradox—the existence of a grand ideal and the persistence of thoughts at a polar distance from it? One way to explain it is to assume that there is a strong, even stubborn opposition to the ideal which is manifested in the frequency and intensity of the "trivial," "irrelevant," and "foolish" thoughts that occur and yet cannot be spoken. If this were so, we could think of the groups as holding to two ideals: a grand, public ideal, which is palpably on the side of the angels, and a demonic, private ideal, which is anything but. In this sense, to speak trivially would be to reveal not the presence of this contrary ideal—for we know that such contrary thoughts occur—but to reveal its pleasurably idealized quality. And that, it seems, the members are not prepared either to acknowledge or reveal.

Such observations are not static. The members have time and again alluded to a wish to speak the currently unspeakable and have urged one another to do precisely that. But something frustrates this intention. The group is too public. The alternative ideal for the group would seem to be for it to fall into the private domain, in which what can be thought and what can be said are precisely congruent with one another.

One thinks here of a point made by R. D. Laing (1967), the British psychoanalyst. Laing observes how different is our response to the saliva in our mouths and to that identical saliva expectorated and to be re-drunk from a glass. Once what is inside and private crosses the boundary line of self, it enters into a different domain, a public realm, and becomes alien. In this sense, what the groups seem to hope is that the boundaries of self and the boundaries of group can become coextensive and congruent in order that each member's own saliva-thoughts can be expressed, reswallowed, and yet not have to cross that border which makes them alien and repugnant.

The saliva metaphor may help us go back, pick up, and juxtapose the conflicting ideal. Where is the wrongest place to spit? Why, in church, of course. We might think of the group's dilemma as one in which hopes of aspiring to the church-public group are in powerful conflict with hopes that the group may be a place with no "Thou's" but only "I's" and "Me's." Put another way, the group aspires both to perfection in an I-Thou relationship of purified man with an unblemished god and, at the same time, to a comfortable I-Me relationship in which all are homogenized in common if blemished parity. The group should be all church or all self.

It would follow, then, that it is the anomalous qualities of the other people present that so dismay each member. To each, the others are neither fish nor fowl nor good red herring. To the contrary, everyone is too similar to one's self to make a good god, yet too different to make a good döppelganger or "secret sharer," in Conrad's term.

In being different, the thought is, others have things to offer which I lack. In being similar, they have the very special possibilities of kindred souls to alleviate my loneliness, quash my doubts, and inspire my confidence in myself. But in being mixed quantities, neither me nor not-me, the others are something to crack or disassemble in order to get clear sailing in either one direction or the other.

I-and-Me and I-and-Thou are very different from one another, as we have seen. But different as they are in the one respect, they share something in another. They are twosomes. There is no third party to complicate matters. Inside a person, sometimes I and Me can get on famously. I can reverie, while Me watches the program with great pleasure. But I (or Me) is not always a steadfast alter ego. Sometimes I (or Me) comes under the influence of others in the environs of one's insides. I can suddenly think Me the most terrible fool—if he listens to the gods or duennas who also live within the compound. Similarly, I and Thou can make music or make merry in undistracted good fashion given the safe absence of any third wheel to queer the doings.

The sense of anomaly we have remarked in the group seems to us to reflect these issues. In being neither quite a Thou nor exactly a Me, I find You too like those gods and duennas who inhabit my innards and afflict my cordial relationship with myself with their whispering gossip and impossible standards. You are not Thou and not Me but not-me, a third class of folk whom psychological archeologists can recognize as having once been Thou's but who were subsequently captured and brought within a person's precincts to live and work there. The famous superego is one of these neither-Thou's-nor-Me's but not-thou's-not-me's.

Thus to speak of each member viewing the others as an anomaly is true only in the sense that the others are neither Me's nor Thou's. In another sense, the others are all too recognizable. They are, as it were, the personifications of all the not-me's that inhabit the member's innards, but not his self. In the problem of finding what to say, the groups are attempting, one can suspect, to cope with the problem of how to change the status of these personifications into divine or human representations, into Thou's and Me's.

CHAPTER THIRTEEN

RETALIATION/RESISTANCE

The groups ignore the leader. Motives for this tactic.

As we last looked at the groups, we noticed particularly their problems of what to do about the anger they feel at their lack of achievement thus far. The leaders, too, have been caught up in this dilemma of who and what is to blame for the lack of accomplishment, and what to do about it. Now, as we look in on the seventh session, we notice that the group members, while very much at work talking together, have chosen a particular way of showing the leader who is to blame and what is to be done.

Group I, Session 7

[As soon as everyone has arrived and sat down, E clears his throat and begins.]

E: I took a group of thirty-five kids, grades one to six, to the airport last week. They really had a good time.

B: How come grades one to six?

E: Because of the teachers' strike, that's all we have in the school: thirty-five kids and two teachers.

B: What do you *do* with just thirty-five kids?

E: Just babysitting—make sure they don't get hurt.

B: How have the kids reacted?

E: They're having a ball.

O: Do you think the thirty-five kids come to school because *they* want to or because their parents want them to?

[Everyone asks E questions about his school, the trip to the airport, the teachers. He describes in detail the interior of the 707 and the complications of the three-week-old strike. Slowly people stop talking and glance at the clock: half the group session is over. K turns to the leader.]

K: Is your experiment working?

Leader: [Puzzled] Which one?

K: I assume this is a nondirective one and a half hours?

Leader: Could you be more explicit?

K: I think we are suffering from your withdrawal, which I *assumed* was an experiment.

Leader: I wasn't aware of that intention on my part. I *was* aware of the choice of the group to discuss what it wished.

L: I'm glad you didn't interrupt. I kept waiting for you to, because *I* knew we weren't doing what we were supposed to do.

Leader: What were you supposed to do?

L: [Taken aback] Well, *you* know—get into deep issues, set goals for ourselves, be realistic and . . . [trails off].

Leader: Who said you had to do those things?

[Everyone stares at the leader in aggrieved amazement: it is quite clear, their looks seem to say, that he is experimenting with them.]

Leader: I'm puzzled by no mention of intentions on *your* part: how *you* want to spend the time, not how *I* do.

[The group begins slowly to talk about the previous session when they really had rapport and how they might recapture that better time.]

Group II, Session 7

[People come in, sit down, and look around with house-counting eyes; it is clear that several group members are absent. A begins by asking W a question.]

A: Have you felt tension in your school because of vacation coming?

W: Not yet. I expect I will.

A: Do you think the teachers are tired—getting ready for a vacation? If there weren't one, we'd get along without it, I think. But we're conditioned for it.

Y: Do you think people should take their sick days even if they're not sick?

F: You make it sound wrong. There must be a reason for taking sick days.

Y: I do it because there's no boss.

A: That's right; in a way a teacher is his own boss: you go into *your* room and shut *your* door.

Y: I chose the school system I'm in for that reason: they leave you alone.

[The group begins to discuss motives for teaching and what roles each of them sees him- or herself in as teacher. After a while the leader says]

Leader: I have a feeling there's something people aren't talking about.

F: [Offended] I was finding out his feelings about teaching to see how they fit with mine.

A: *I* didn't feel we were leaving some subject out and making it a difficult situation.

F: I felt we were getting something out of his discussion. At last we were talking about something *specific*.

R: I found it interesting. It helps you know your own thinking if you hear other people's.

[The group goes on to discuss whether teaching is a form of indoctrination or not.]

Group III, Session 7

[After some desultory searching about for a topic, the group settles on what it's like to be old.]

H: Being old is being like Mr. Powell, my math teacher. He is absolutely senile.

T: Can you think of any teacher *you're* completely satisfied with, H?

H: I can name four or five I really liked. I don't want to sit through a class and not be taught. It's disgusting.

T: Change teachers.

H: If I did I would have to leave Advanced Chemistry.

T: So there's nothing you can do. You should do something about it or shut up about it.

S: [Defending H] There's not one teacher in this school who hasn't been talked about. Not everyone likes everyone.

T: [Continuing to H] You have to consider his age. He'll retire soon. He probably *was* a good teacher. True, it's affecting you, but consider *his* life span. You have to have concern for others. You're being selfish.

H: You're insulting me, T. I haven't insulted you yet.

O: Let's change the subject. How many people here drink? Raise your hands.

[Since no one raises a hand, O continues.]

O: This buddy of mine and I used to dress up like old men and go to the liquor store. Or we'd get a "drag" to go buy liquor for us—they'd do anything for a drink. Sometimes the police dress up as drags, though. They're wise to kids. But I know another guy who used to ask for quarters, just beg, you know? He made $200 a week. It's like selling tickets you've bought up for more money than you paid for them.

R: Yeah, I heard that a young guy playing the violin in the street makes a lot of money.

O: And kids selling newspapers on the street can size people up before they ask them if they want to buy a paper. You size people up, what they look like; that's how things go. It's the same with a teacher. A teacher sizes the kids up too from the way *they* look—boots, funny hats, hippie clothes—and . . .

Leader: [Interrupting] Is that what's going on here?

O: [Startled and then annoyed] You mean, people looking at each other. *I* don't know.

[Everyone else looks blank.]

Group IV, Session 7

Group: Mrs. D, can we burn incense?

Leader: What for?

Group: It smells so good. *Let* us burn it. We have some.

Leader: Is this another test of whether I'm a regular teacher here?

Group: Yes. [They begin to ignore the leader and start to discuss where to put the incense stick.]

V: [To leader] *Can* we?
Group: What are you asking her for? She's not a teacher.
[Everyone clusters around and looks intent as the incense is lit. Then the group breaks up into smaller groups talking excitedly but not loudly among themselves.]

In the foregoing material, the members of the groups seem not only busily at work, but confidently at work. Despite all the previous confusion and obfuscation, they seem to have figured out what there is for them to do and are busy doing it. But to judge from the responses of the leaders, there is something else remarkable about the busyness: the groups are going on as if the leaders did not exist. Remarks to this or, for that matter, any other effect made by the leaders seem to cause barely a ripple. Yet, if we look more closely, we see that the groups greet the interjections offered by the leaders with a redoubled effort to do what they were doing.

Once we have surmised the nature of the group's activity, reference to the preceding sessions suggests its motivation. In previous sessions it was the leader who seemed impervious to the group's entreaties. The leader was to tell them explicitly what they were supposed to do. He was to lead them out of the wilderness of uncertainty and silence to some plenteous land. But by not wanting anything for or from the groups he has seemed indifferent and uncaring. Now the groups, as if they have agreed on the tactic, are turning the tables and giving the leaders a dose of their own medicine.

The leaders do not seem to like it very much. There is a querulous, aggrieved, and occasionally apologetic note to their comments; even more, one senses a note of helplessness. They hear the group saying: "You thought we could not do without you, that you could get away with your smug, self-satisfied self-containment—well, you're wrong! We can do without you very nicely, as now even you plainly see."

From our vantage point we may feel that the groups have rather overdrawn their newfound independence, that they do protest too much. Something more than independence is at work—the somewhat vindictive attempts to stimulate in the leaders what the members have experienced at the leaders' hands suggests that the earlier wounding of feelings still persists.

But if it is not wholly a newfound independence, it is not entirely vengeful either. There seems a tactical intention as well. Once the leader has suffered, it is intended that he should repent and, repenting, mend his ways. The dosage is designed to reduce his imperviousness and make him more responsive in the end. He may yet learn to care.

CHAPTER FOURTEEN

TENDENCIES OF THE MIND: SPLITTING AND FUSION, ALLOCATION AND COMPROMISE

After seven sessions we see that the people invited to come together to talk about matters of mutual concern still have difficulty in doing so. They cannot easily settle on a topic, keep a discussion going, as if more important than "a" choice for the groups is choice itself. The group insists that the focus on a goal is more vital than the content of "the choice" for the group. More valuable than focus is the maintenance of a proliferation of possibilities. Their failure to "stick" to something represents the conviction that whatever is worth "sticking with" has not yet come into being.

"Sticking with"! Has this expression a less conscious, latent meaning? Do people in or out of groups muse about phalluses and intercourse or accidents and murders? Certainly they do not do so manifestly: manifestly they are concerned with topics and discussions. Yet throughout our reflections on the groups' behavior, we have discovered that those "simple" matters, topics and discussions, are permeated with hopes and meanings of so different an order that they prove to be anything but as simple as they first appear.

We have already discussed the reason for duplicity of this sort. The members of Group II, for instance, in discussing for a whole session—punctuated by many pregnant silences—getting to "know" the leader, would probably be taken aback to be told that they, men and women alike, were unconsciously contemplating the possibility of a sexual relationship with the leader. Thus, even if what is inconceivable in these groups—that the leader is willing to accommodate such a sexual wish—were possible, the members would not avail themselves of the possibility, the absence of which they at the same time unconsciously regret, for convictions of wickedness undermine their high hopes of guilt-free and anxiety-free desire, rendering them abashed and constrained.

We understand, then, why this group makes no bold or explicit overtures to the leader or each other. But, on the other hand, they do not bandon such possibilities altogether. As a result, they must find a form that expresses their sexual interest even as that form conceals it. Indeed, the group was able to cunningly convey both ardor and constraint and yet conceal these under the sufficiently portentous rubric of getting to know each other. Here was one topic they could "stick" with.

Despite this considerable achievement, their sexual longings remain unrequited. Is it that the leader is incapable of reciprocating them, or is it that the leader holds someone else more dear? The first assumption can only lead to hopelessness and despair. The second, despite the jealousy and potential guilt it engenders, is the contruction the group is bound to prefer. But this construction now poses a new problem. How can the groups separate the leader from his presumptive chosen one?

Once more, heroic efforts are called for, and the groups must attempt to influence the leader without the attempts being clear even to the members. But this time the object is not the synthesis which blends ardor and constraint. This time the groups must sever and hold ardor and constraint separate. The device they arrive at for this object is in part one we have already remarked on. They set the leader an example.

By doing so, the groups show us something further of example-setting. We see it to be more than the charade of an inverted fist shaken to signal for salt. In fact, the groups use the mental equivalent of body English. Body English, of course, is used to influence the physical behavior of an object (frequently a miss-hit pinball) no longer under our direct control. "Mind English" works on the same principle and for related ends. The groups wish to sever the leaders from those the leaders are believed to prefer. The groups therefore split off from one another all the elements of their experience that normally are joined together— thought from thought, feeling from feeling, feeling from thought, in short, anything that might be fruitful and mutually enhancing if joined.

We cannot see this process at work, of course. But if this inference is correct, we can see the results. Little in the contents of the sessions fits together. The remarks of individual members fail, at those times when the device is at work, to engender "anything" from the others: "nothing" gets going.

The "nothing," of course, describes only the manifest experience. In fact, the lack of "happenings" is precisely what the "mind English" is designed to achieve. In keeping matters barren and sterile the groups are attempting, telekinetically, as it were, to influence the fate of the leader's relationships with others not in the group, and to do so not only magically but without knowing that they are doing so—or, indeed, that they believe in magic.

The need not to know what they are doing derives from the wish of the groups' members to avoid painful conflict. The melding of conflicting wishes into a compromise (a topic the group could "stick with") is another way of handling conflict. The attempt to "drive away" or split off the leader from whoever might be dearer to him than the group is a third. We cannot underestimate how deeply groups loathe conflictual situations.

But neither can we minimize how much groups dislike a compromise of conflicting wishes. Earlier, in Chapter 8, we referred to two such potentially conflicting desires held by members of the groups. One was that others should be such kindred souls that communication with them could be as though each were part of the same body. The second, held along with the first, was for others to be distinct, yet quite perfect, Others, Thou's, between whom nothing less than perfect communications would serve. But such conflictual hopes must either be compromised or "allocated" if they are not to result in still a third state of being—simple, inert inhibition.

Sometimes the group works by a method of allocation. The members assign one hope to the leader, the other to the group. With one another, for instance, the group members hope to fashion a replica of the self within which they can enjoy the domestic comforts of the kindred or I-Me relationship. However, this, to the extent to which they succeed, deprives them of the exchanges which are based on divisions of labor, specialization, and difference. For these exchanges, therefore, they turn to the leader, even developing, as we have seen, sexual longings for the leader: he becomes the Thou for them. Insofar as the plan succeeds in this direction, one may imagine that the group enjoys a utopian experience. From one another they receive the magnification and amplification of I-Me communion, and as no one is left over to comprise the anomalous shadows which are the negatives of the I-Me's, the community is without skeptic, doubter, critic, or object of envy. Selves combine into a kind of super-self. Then, from the leader, the community receives the specialized fulfillments it cannot produce for itself. The two sorts of satisfaction complement, indeed facilitate, one another quite magnificently, and the group wants for nothing.

However, when this ideal situation does not quite occur, the group must rethink its course of action. It must determine whether it is the principle or the practice that is at fault. If the principle, the group falls into an uneasy and gloomy inertia. If merely the application, the practice, the group tries a different deployment. There are three rough alternatives. The group and the leader may exchange functions. The leader, that is, may become the Me, fellow members the Thou. Or if the leader proves hopeless, as the members of Group III have been finding theirs, the group can subdivide. Cliques of an I-Me sort may form, the members of which go on to use the other clique or cliques as the Thou's, or differentiated objects of their hopes. The third alternative is for a new "leader" to be created from among the members of the group, in terms of whom the remainder of the group can coalesce into a self-community.

One may well wonder how these intricate designs and contrivances can be planned and effected while all the time ordinary sorts of discussion are absorbing the attention of the group members and perhaps the casual reader as well. Are we inputting our own fascinations with intricate processes to people who are simply having a discussion?

That is always a risk, even at this stage of our examination, when we have become accustomed to having to look for more than meets the eye, that it is more than likely that we have been reading all this cunning into the group—that is, if the cunning were as complex as it sounds. But it may not be quite so intricate as it seems, given one or two considerations derived from the group material.

The first of these considerations is that the blueprint for the utopian ideal of a group, a hope clung to increasingly by group members, is not drawn *de novo* by the members of each group. The second is that the members of each group are not unfamiliar, because of previous experiences, with the basic stratagems they need to (and, we have been supposing, do) employ. The ideal of the group members is that there should be not one and not three but two entities, and that these two entities should find and enjoy a meaningful and gratifying exchange (Lieberman, Whitaker, and Lakin 1967). The problem to be solved then is how to reduce the numbers of individuals involved to two, and then how to assure a meaningful and gratifying interchange. The principle is the same as that which quarrelsome couples use when they decide to take up common interests or have a baby. If there is something else separate and distinct, they can get together in terms of it. In politics it is similarly said that common enemies make common friends. Equally, in threesomes if two of the parties don't join each other, three becomes a crowd and two must fight or one must flee.

But there are certain circumstances in which the odd man out doesn't mind being the odd man out. One of these is when he is literally out but vicariously in. We don't generally feel jealous of lovers in a movie or play, though we may be of lovers in real life. In the drama we watch: though a mere member of the audience, we vicariously enjoy the good fortunes of the character in whose shoes we imagine ourselves to be. There is at least one other such circumstance. This is when two persons can do what we cannot, and we want the fruits of their activity. Thus, if we are the beneficiaries of a union, we may well wish it every success and happiness. Hasn't each of us at some meeting or another been delighted, and not jealous of the loss of the spotlight, when two others engage in an animated discussion of a topic about which we are supposed to know a lot but don't? Those two unite in talk and give us the benefit of inclusion—and a chance to collect our wits—at the price of but an occasional nod.

Despite these exceptions, the main aspiration is that the group condense into a twosome. The pair is to be composed of the formal leader or an ad hoc leader and the remainder of the group. Once this is accomplished, a relationship usual to a twosome can take place.

Like the breaking of a crystal, the "breaking" into twosomes appears to follow the most likely delineations. Since the leader is readily seen as distinct from the group, he or she easily becomes one of a pair. But when the leader fails to make a good partner, the search for a substitute tends to exploit other natural cleavages, for instance, age, sex, or social status. Whatever the choice, the principle of selection appears to be determined by the need to have present a quality that supplements or improves the leader's own absent or derelict qualities.

In this sense the membership of the groups may be likened to a repertory company. It embraces a host of specialized talents on which the company may draw to stage various dramatic dialogues. Those selected for the part of leader will vary with the drama to be performed. Sometimes the part of leader may require a harsh and scrupulous critic. If the leader himself fails to demonstrate this quality, the harshest and most critical of the members will be induced to come forward to do "his thing." Group members may similarly be auditioned and chosen for such other qualities as benignness, flirtatiousness, antic-ness, or cordiality.

With some of these observations and ideas in mind, let us turn again to our four groups, now in the eighth of their sessions.

CHAPTER FIFTEEN

THE HALFWAY POINT

How groups and leaders experience their work, and how the researchers feel in observing the work.

Group I, Session 8

[Some group members have brought food for all. People are munching on doughnuts. As the group begins, people look around at each other.]

R: How many more meetings do we have?

O: I know. I looked at a calendar: seven.

[Silence]

Leader: [Gently coaxing] Perhaps people have thoughts about the remainder of the meetings.

F: I can't imagine what will happen that hasn't emerged already.

A: Your expectations are lowered.

F: Yes. It seems like so little time. Sometimes I think we were closer at the beginning than we are now. I'm less enthusiastic about my expectations than I was five weeks ago.

Leader: People are backing off from their expectations. If I recall yours, it was for a group where people were open and communicating.

F: That's where they *were*. *Now* I've about given up. . . .

O: You want to save yourself from further discomfort.

F: [Still thinking] But that makes it seem worse. It would be *more* of a disappointment to give up.

Leader: My impression is that other people feel the same. Why did those expectations take center stage as opposed to simply learning about yourself?

F: I had high expectations in *addition* to learning about myself. The original idea was that the twelve of us would develop a rapport that was very unusual. That's what I wanted to have happen because I have faith in that kind of thing.

H: [With a sigh] At least we would be chipping away at alienation.

F: It's like an experiment—to see if twelve people can associate like a family. To make yourselves honest and sincere enough to work together like the spokes of a wheel. To give everyone satisfaction and security. I expect everyone to ultimately feel the same.

Leader: People have high expectations for their group and are a little leery of them now. Do people know what these feelings come from, what they wanted from the group?

R: I have a need to be closer to more people than time allows.

[Silence]

Leader: My impression is that people are having memories of other times and places, that there are secret wishes that come close to being told here. We wish for family relations to be re-created here. That secret is a very strong wish—everyone is trying to rebuild that kind of closeness.

[Silence]

Leader: People are embarrassed about their secret wishes.

[Silence]

Leader: People are to be left alone today, allowed the prerogative of silences, of secrets that cause alienation.

A: In a smaller group than this there's a better chance for everyone to express his feelings. I've heard that smaller groups get much more close. If you express precious feelings, there should be times to *see* them then.

[Silence]

B: I find myself thinking inside myself, like everyone is saying. But I don't feel that using experiences that mean something to me will mean that much to others.

O: You don't realize that others feel like you do *unless* you say them.

Leader: It's a frustrated, alienated group. No one can say what's important—it must be painful.

[Silence]

Leader: What does the silence have to do with since we're here to learn?

[Silence]

Leader: No thoughts about it?

A: Personal things are sacred things. So we all feel like it's taboo, which is too bad. Yet it's respect that we build up for each other—we respect other people's sacred feelings. Because you really don't know what one thing brings back to a person. A wooden floor can bring back different things to me than to others. It would take a long *time* to talk about it.

O: I don't see anything wrong with personal thoughts and feelings that you keep to yourself. It's healthy to keep them to yourself and work them out. It's only natural that we do these things—clam up, rationalize what we said, make ourselves appear different to others. It's a healthy way to be sometimes.

Leader: Is that a message?

O: [Looking at the clock] It's the end of this meeting.

A: But if we do what you said, O, it *is* alienating.

O: You have to know how to cope with things alone at times. So we *have* taboos in the group—we have to find a way of adjudicating that and getting goals. Also, we have to learn to deal with the hurt and disappointment that are part of those taboos.

Group II, Session 8

[Several group members are missing, among them Y. People begin to talk about the "other" groups in this project.]

I: I know someone in_____'s group. They always seem to have interesting discussions.

A: I heard they had some difficulties too, though.

Leader: Does this make you feel better, that others have some difficulties?

S: This is the second year of this project. Is there a way of finding what made the others succeed? *Some* have been able to tune into things that were important.

Leader: What would be important to you?

S: Anything that would make one better in their profession.

[Silence]

Leader: People seem lost in their own thoughts—looking down.

F: I feel I started out not so much to be a better teacher but to be a more honest person. Somehow that goal got lost.

A: At first there seemed to be a tendency to rely on stories or problems, to get to know each other. After that was over, we talked about a child in your class, S. Many of us had had that kind of experience. It's all helped but still it leaves me puzzled.

Leader: It's not exciting enough.

A: It's *been* exciting.

F: It's *not* a matter of excitement.

Leader: It sounds like one was expecting something special or exciting to come out. People have raised that as a possibility.

F: [Wistfully] It would have been nice if I could have gotten at feelings.

A: T–groups sound like they could be exciting. I've heard about some that go till three or four in the morning. There are teachers in our school connected with some. They talk about the experience in positive and negative ways.

[Silence]

Leader: It sounds like there was some such hope or expectation or fear of these group meetings. Maybe it would be like T–groups or some experience you have had. I wonder if this hasn't been what's in the back of people's minds: here we are with seven more meetings and we haven't started yet—with what?

F: With communication, with meaningful feelings and thoughts. Not necessarily issues.

Leader: People would like to be able to but they get here and there are so many obstacles.

F: It's hard to sit down and say how you feel when you're *not* talking about issues.

Leader: But that's your wish.

F: We would like feelings to come *out* in the process of talking of issues.
[The group goes on to talk about the missing members, especially Y.]

Group III, Session 8

T: I wonder how it is with the other groups. I bet they don't have as
                much trouble as we do. Even if we did find something we were all
                interested in, I wonder whether anyone would talk anyway and tell
                their opinions.

N: Most everyone has expressed an opinion some way. You know why
                it's so bad here—because it's not planned and everything turns out
                rotten when it's not planned.

T: That's rotten to say!

O: You know what it is? It's the mood. [Looking out at the rain] It's
                lousy outside.

Leader: Did anyone see the Peanuts cartoon, "It always rains on our genera-
                tion"? How did you feel, N, when T said, "That's rotten"?

[N looks at T but says nothing.]

T: [Does respond] It's that everything in our lives is so planned. I hate
                schedules. One day I just had tea and I fought with the cat.

H: What's the matter with schedules? Without them you'd get nothing
                done.

T: I was enjoying myself: that's the point. People can't *enjoy* doing
                nothing any more.

N: They call *that* laziness.

H: [Nods in heartfelt agreement] *You're* not kidding.

S: [Turning angrily to H] H, there's no reason to be like that. T likes to
                do nothing. The important thing to *you* is getting something done.
                Don't you want to enjoy yourself?

H: You can enjoy yourself *doing* something.

O: I think people can accomplish something by doing nothing. I play
                guitar for two hours sometimes.

H: That's doing *some*thing. [Intensely] *Some* people have a problem
                finding things to do when they have too much time. I know this girl
                who had nothing to do so she walked three miles to a store, put in a
                quarter, and got four pictures of herself. She waited two minutes for
                the pictures to come out. That was the most exciting part, the waiting.
                She looked at herself, and then went home.

[Everyone has listened quietly and intently to this story.]

T: H, what would you do if *you* had too much time—have you ever done
                something foolish?

H: Foolish to some people—like if I sat and planned an experiment,
                someone else might think that's foolish.

T: Do you do things like color zeros in a telephone book?

H: Yeah, when I have to wait for the operator.

T: No, *not* when you're waiting for the operator.

H: A transcendentalist said that a truly creative person is never con-
                stant—he doesn't want to do the same thing twice. Some jerk!

R: H, do you admire *any*one who doesn't agree with you? If he doesn't
            agree with you, do you think he's a jerk?
H: You don't accomplish things if you change every minute.
L: H, do you accomplish things if you *never* change?
H: Not to be able to change is no good, but having to change all the time
            is no good. Ruts are good if they work.
T: *No* ruts are good!
[Many group members glare at H.]
O: [Shifts restlessly] This is a draggy conversation.
Leader: What do you think they are talking about?
L: Fighting with a cat? Hunh. I've seen kids punching walls just to let
            out anxiety. For everything you do, you accomplish *some*thing.

Group IV, Session 8

[The group is quiet. Some boys are looking at a sign tacked to the wall, but quietly.]
Leader: What do you think about when it's quiet?
D: That we have to talk.
Leader: Why is it so difficult for a group of young people to talk that you
            have to think up topics?
B: We don't have the same interests.
Leader: The group feels nervous to me. Why do you get nervous when this
            happens?
R: Because it follows a certain pattern and this is part of it.
[Silence]
Leader: The silence is terrible, isn't it?
P: [Partly mocking] What should we talk about—why the silence is so
            terrible?
[Silence]
P: [To leader] What are you looking at *me* for?
Leader: I'm not. But does feeling I am make you nervous?
P: I feel I have to say something.
Leader: Do you always feel you have to say something?
P: Well, nobody else does.
Leader: Why don't you find out why?
P: Why doesn't anyone else talk? . . . [Turning to V] You have
            matching clothes on. Let's talk about the dress code, then.
D: Yeah. Let's.
P: Mr. N said he was going to ask if girls could wear pants. I don't think
            it makes any difference whether a girl wears pants or a dress.
V: You think more about school in pants than in dresses. In dresses,
            you think more about where your knees are.
D: The Establishment probably thinks it's too revolting. If they allow
            that, the next thing it will be sandals.
P: How do you feel about it? Would you girls want to wear pants?
D: [Obviously prevaricating] No—oo. Not.
P: [Surprised] Why . . . ?
Leader: [Shocked] Why don't you give your honest opinion, D?

D: O.K. If girls feel like wearing pants, they should.
R: [Sarcastically] It's a big worry.
Leader: Is it a big worry? Why?
P: [More seriously] You're afraid of what the other kids are going to say.
Leader: [Still puzzled, to D] What made you give a dishonest opinion? Would you have done it outside this room?
D: I thought people would laugh at my honest opinion.
P: How about the rest of you? Y, do you think girls should wear pants?
Y: No.
P: Why?
Y: Because I don't want to wear my honest opinion!
[The bell rings. The group members gather together their books and school supplies and walk out, some of them snickering.]

With these excerpts, we have reached mid-point in the formal history of our four groups—a useful time for review. In order to make this review, one must bear in mind the critical differences between the way the *group* experiences its midway point and how *we*, from our perspective observing four groups, see the experience. We, as researchers, know that each of the four groups is in vital respects experiencing matters in much the same way as the others (Bion 1961; Whitaker and Lieberman 1964). The members of given groups, on the other hand, are more likely to regard their experience as a function of their particular composition.

Of course, one may well ask why members of particular groups do not suppose or even guess that what they are encountering is similar to the experiences of other groups. If they did, they might be relieved to feel that what they are experiencing is, so to speak, normal. On the other hand, they might derive from such a universality of experience a sense of futility. Each might feel that he is a cog in a wheel, a card in a vast computer, a pawn in an unresponsive system. In either case, the members would have to choose between feeling one among many, all in the same boat, or feeling free from helplessness, unique, particular, the masters of their fate.

"All in the Same Boat"			Each Group Particular		
Feelings of Comfort	vs.	Feelings of Futility	Hope	vs.	Futility

As we contemplate the experiences of the several groups, now at mid-point, the strongest impression is that, whether they know of other groups or not, they are seized with a sense of futility. It is as if they have tried everything and nothing works. Some members, having so concluded, have left. Most remain, signifying by their presence some flickering hope.

But even then, the gloom describes their mood better than shine or glow. Still, since they have not yet left, their commingling of doggedness and hope suggests that though they have tried everything and nothing works, perhaps something yet will—though no one is in the least optimistic— since there are still some sessions to go.

Time, then, seems their greatest friend, and the time remaining is akin to the proverbial half-glass of water. The optimists, though there are precious few of these left, see it as half-full, the pessimists as half-empty; those who will not accept half a glass have decamped.

There are also other sources of hope, however dim. People have left the groups (or recently entered). Perhaps things will turn out as in some parties, where if one sticks it out to the end, when people draw together against the lateness of the hour and the loneliness of the night, something good happens to make it all worthwhile.

And yet these cheering thoughts sound hollow. The feeling one gets is that of survivors—is that speck a boat? that cloud a puff of smoke? If they were to know that other groups are like their own, we conclude, they would more likely feel futility than comfort. Therefore, what the members do not wish to give up, indeed, what they seem almost willing to purchase with the pain of this futility, is the feeling that something can be made of the particular ingredients present in their particular group. To believe that things must be the way they are is cold comfort compared with the feeling that something can be done. The motto of the group at this juncture seems to be: "It is better merely to feel helpless than actually to be helpless. He-I-We could if we would, but we-he-I won't." "Can't" is what no one will say, or even hint.

The leaders are in much the same position as the members. They, too, earnestly, even desperately, are denying the enormous strength of the forces that produce the sense of futility. They coax, they wheedle, they argue, they scold, they set examples, they explain, they harangue— and so give strength and substance to the members' hope to hope again. Thus the members go around trying this, that, and the other thing, and so do the leaders. If at first you don't succeed, try, try again—but try what? The same old things?

"What's there to try?" the members and leaders would likely ask in exasperation. "It's easy for you to talk, just sitting there on Olympus with your damned research," they could ruefully add.

But we must not let the accusation obscure the truth. It *is* easier to be outside the heat and struggle asking what is happening and why. Why then, figuratively speaking, do the others not come on up too?

The answer, of course, is because they are bent on making something work, while we in the project are content with merely learning what and why. They, quite understandably, wish to contrive or receive an experience, we only to understand the experience they have. Ours, no doubt, is the more pallid harvest, and we may feel wistful in respect to the fervent attempts to fight off apathy and *get* something the leaders and members are making. Curiously, however, the envy of our coolly aloof perch expressed in "it's easy for you to talk" is deceptive. It is envy without admiration. For there is on the parts of the groups something more than indifference to understanding. There is even a degree of hatred for knowledge.

We have touched upon this before. Knowledge of selves is not merely poor consolation for what the groups hope to experience; it is a hindrance to it—the bite into the apple of self-consciousness. To be aware of what is going on and why (as we are trying to be) is viewed not as a vehicle on the road toward the small harvests of possibility but as a roadblock on the (somewhat precarious) path toward potential. The members do not, then, wish to learn of and from their experience; they wish to *have* their experience.

Accordingly, they are witch-hunting. That there is a fly in the ointment they have no doubt; the only question is who the fly is. The groups, by the very definitions of their quest, need to find an enemy. They are, therefore, the souls of prejudice. Sometimes, with Pogo, they seem to announce: "We have found the enemy, and he is us!" Sometimes it is clear that the enemy is the leader, as in Group IV during Session 8. Sometimes it is a member of the group, as T and S turn on H in Group III. Sometimes it is the system. Sometimes, indeed, the enemy is people who are prejudiced.

Because this state of affairs in the group or in the individuals has to be *someone's* fault, things cannot simply be as they are. Fault implies not only wrongdoing but willfulness, and willfulness means that things could be changed. People differ on how they do treat or would treat the fly—the enemy—if they found him outside of themselves. The groups find the question absorbing both verbally and in action. Some forgive him and offer him someone to blame: if he accepted that someone, they would join with him in the blame. Some simply scold. Others make themselves targets. They confess and mend their ways. This is designed to set the enemy a good example; this is what he should do. Some fight him. But no matter the tactics, all show the conviction that things would be different, if only. . . .

Is our solution from Olympus—that one must come to know and respect what makes people in groups as they are—simply our own favored antidote for prejudice, for the enemy in each of us? Yes. At this halfway point, we too are impressed with the futility of the groups' attempts to realize those many hopes which are in such impossible conflict with one another. We see from our mountain top all too clearly the force of these unreconciled hopes. We know something of how helpless all concerned feel in response to the force of their hopes. Knowledge alone could not help. We have seen how most of what we have written here, were it communicated directly to the groups, would be received as jeopardizing their hopes. But perhaps it would be of some use at those times when the members' own solutions have run their course and just before total apathy sets in.

Yet we must remember too that the tides of time are not by any means all on knowledge's side. The groups are more than half over. Yet there is time for the resurrection of hope. The groups may not yet be ready to suffer learning.

CHAPTER SIXTEEN

A STUDY IN MANIPULATION

A closer look at Group IV.

Group IV appears to be going anything but well; one may feel this even while being unable to say what "well" consists of. The feeling may simply be that whatever Group IV is doing, nothing of any merit is happening. Indeed, if we ourselves may not view the group in this way, it is reasonably clear that their teacher/leader does. It may even be that the youngsters comprising the group feel this way too.

Such unanimity of feeling calls for further investigation. It reveals that the group holds ideals against which the actuality of the situation is being measured and found wanting. One option for us, therefore, is to try to infer what these ideals are and why the people involved are finding it impossible to live up to them. Such an investigation might reasonably start with the pre-eminent characteristic of this group: the fact that no one is doing either much talking or much listening.

If we were to look for causes of this fact, we would have to repeat several questions raised earlier. Are children of this age, even though they volunteer, too young to be asked to participate in a discussion group? Is the leader of this group adequate to the task of conducting such a group? Should something in the format or procedures of the group be changed?

An attempt to answer these questions would probably have to focus on the matter of communication. Can youngsters of this age verbally communicate their preoccupations? That they have the vocabulary, no one can doubt; human preoccupations can be expressed in the simplest language. But more ornate and complex language is required to obscure or dress up basic preoccupations (Piaget 1962). Thus the members of the teachers' groups have an advantage. They can make their preoccupations respectable by voicing demands for "more structure" and the like. Demands so euphemized can more readily pass the censors. The "censors" are, as we have previously discussed, those aspects of the members' inner "others" who constitute fearsome aspects of themselves and those aspects of the leader which are experienced as censorious. The children are not likely to forget that their leader is a teacher or that when not a leader she is a teacher like other teachers, and that teachers are censorious. Thus, if we were to pursue this line of thought, we would see that the problem of getting their messages across is rather more difficult for these youngsters than for the older ones, and more difficult for both groups of young people than for the teachers' groups (Kohlberg 1969).

If we carry out this line of investigation, we soon come to the conclusion that the only possible way the children could find that the group was a successful endeavor would be if the teacher complied with their wishes without knowing either what these wishes were or that the youngsters had made them (Blatt and Kohlberg 1973). The ordinary devices used by the other groups do not prove satisfactory for Group IV. If they encode their messages to the extent required to pass both censors—theirs and the leader's—the chances are that the message will be so cryptic as to be indecipherable. On the other hand, because clearing up the message may make it too plain, and so agitate the censors, the only way out of this dilemma would be to stimulate in the leader a wish to comply, which she will then regard not as coming from them but from desires of her own.

The success of such an illusion would depend on the leader's holding two false beliefs. The first delusion she must entertain is that everything she has so far attempted has been the wrong thing. The second is that everything she goes on to attempt, having had her change of heart and mind, is equally the wrong thing. She must feel her activities previous to her change to be wrong because the children did not like them. She must, therefore, conclude that the group is doing anything but well because, for example, children of this age cannot be expected to cope with such an experience or do not have the ability to sit down and hold group discussions. Having come to these conclusions, and changed her approach, she must continue to feel that the group is doing anything but well lest she suspect that the wish for this new approach has come from the children.

If we too had pursued the lines of thought that seemed so reasonable at the start, we would also have missed the point. Even now we may feel ashamed and incredulous at the conclusion we reached. Can children be so devious and Machiavellian? Are we not imputing to them stratagems and contrivances that can only be called aweful? In the face of these doubts, we begin to feel intolerably unreasonable. Accordingly, the very hypothesis we dismissed—that the group may simply be too much for these children—takes on a renewed appeal. To hold that hypothesis enables us to feel a good deal more reasonable.

But is this not precisely the pivot and pinion of the matter? Does not the success of the children's strategem depend on stimulating just such a conflict in us? Surely, only by inducing us to find unreasonable that which we believed reasonable can the children hope to have changed us. Only to the extent that we need to feel "reasonable" can we be hoist on our own petards.

The children need to take the conflict within themselves and convert it into a conflict between themselves and the leader. Then they need to take that conflict and move it inside the leader so that she experiences it as an inner conflict between hope and doubt. Once there, she must go on to find her previous hopes unreasonable and her unreasonable doubts quite reasonable. Since this is a procedure adults employ with children on a daily basis and since children learn not only from what we say but from what we do, the fact that they are adept at these manipulations cannot surprise us.

For ourselves, then, what becomes evident is that much of what people in groups do is to be seen less in the attempt than in the effect. By their fruits, so to speak, must one know them. In the preceding discussion, we saw that the group strove for effect not only on the leader, but *in* the leader. In striving for effect *on* the leader, the group counts upon the leader's knowing what the group is after. In striving for effects *in* the leader, the group must take every precaution to ensure the leader's *not* knowing what it is about. If the leader feels that he or she has lost control or been manipulated, the whole thing recommences. Children who don't wish to practice the piano, for instance, must convince their parents that they have no talent. Laziness, desire not to practice, etc., are provocative but continue the inner struggle within the child, at the same time as it is translated into an apparent struggle between parent and child. In our groups, the leader must feel his or her disappointment within, having arisen from a shift in the balance from hope to doubt. That means that the leader sees her reaction as a rational reassessment of the situation. She organizes her position as one opposed to getting angry at the little bastards because they aren't doing what they *should* and *can*. This decision within the leader takes the pressure off the group, while a provocation merely postpones it.

In Group IV, in the most recent excerpts we have looked at, the group—after much silence during which the leader appears to suffer as much as they—picks up on the topic of the dress code, draws the teacher/leader into the "seriousness" of the discussion, and essentially makes a mockery of the whole idea of discussion: "I don't want to wear my honest opinion!" The teacher/leader is puzzled: why this prevarication and mock-seriousness now?

The knowingness of the leader, as in this example, must be bypassed; the group seeks a direct pipeline into the leader. It is as if the head of the leader stands between them and the leader's body or its contents (Slater 1966). The group, as a result, wishes to practice a rather primal sort of medicine; it wishes to gain direct access to the machinery of the leader, turn the requisite spigots, switches or knobs, and all the while keep the leader's head asleep.

With this as their intention, it would follow that whatever the activity going on at the time—silence, play, talk, the presence and absence of people—its purpose and thrust is to instrument that design. If that is so, we cannot regard speech as speech, discussion as discussion. Rather, we must regard speech as an instrument, discussion as a mechanism. Both are akin to the word "Boo!" A sudden, shouted "Boo!" is designed to create in the serene and unwary a state of experience precisely opposite to the one they enjoyed previous to the exclamation. In its essence, "Boo!" is barely speech. It is a blast of noise, a blow struck. A different sound is made by a jagged sigh, but the sigh can have in common with the "Boo" the intent of altering the hearers' state of experience. In Group IV, again, D's "No—oo. Not" is a complete surprise to P and the leader, who obviously expected him to say yes to this innocuous question.

Thus, the form of the communication is not self-defining. The form must be considered in the light of its effect; the effect, in revealing the function, informs us of the speaker's motive. But since this formulation merely redescribes what we have been calling the message, we must shape it further so that it may specify the fashion by which communication attempts to bypass the listener, so that he will not know what is happening to him.

The "Boo!" counts on shock and surprise to achieve its effects. It is akin to a rifle shot. Being so simple an act, even very young children can manage it, and mostly quite young children use it. But it contains in it a rather important element. While still under the influence of the "Boo," the hearer doubts his senses. The heart pounds, adrenalin courses, the senses reel a moment until it is discovered that the cataclysmic danger is only a little child with a mixture of triumph and guilt on his face. This doubting of one's senses or sense of things seems to have to be part of the design, for on it depends the lulling or gulling of knowingness which the "Boo" achieves with the element of surprise.

The joke and the prank also rest on the unexpected. The listener is lulled with the familiar and suddenly, bang, comes the punch line. (A rapid-fire series of one-liners leaves him reeling.) The ordinary and the familiar lure his anticipation into somnolence, anesthetize his wariness; even the style and format are stylized: "Didya hear the one about the traveling salesman? Well, it seems there was this . . . " And, then, socko, the punch line goes in like a hot knife into butter. The shaggy-dog story both lulls and gulls: the punch line never comes. But it, too, contrives at one effect in order to achieve another. This it shares with illusion and stage magic, where the hand deludes the watchful eye.

The principle involved then seems to be that it is necessary for the recipient of these devices to either do without or to mistrust and become alienated from what he knows. He must be turned against the very aspect of himself which normally renders him immune to being so directly and unknowingly manipulated.

Those who enjoy hearing jokes eagerly relinquish this aspect of themselves in return for the pleasures the joke will afford them. And, as we saw in the previous discussion, people can come to abandon what they know if they can be induced to dislike it. In both cases, he who wishes to contrive his effects offers the potential recipient a Faustian bargain: I have something for you.

The "something better" in a group situation is what most immediately concerns us here. When a leader wants nothing for or from his group, he cannot be drawn into a bargain. The group has then to depend upon him or to catalyze something the leader may want. If the leader does want something from the group, like lots of participation, the group, once it learns this, can arrive with him at a *quid pro quo.* By the simple expedient of withholding and giving, they can condition his behavior with relative ease. If the leader has the stipulation that he is not to be corrupted in the course of gaining participation, the group can oblige by postponing their participation until it no longer looks like being responsive to the way he has proceeded.

But what if the leader is relatively self-contained and offers the group little purchase from which to gain leverage? The answer, of course, is that they must catalyze desires in the leader. But they must not be seen to do so. If, for example, they wish to get him to feel that his methods will not succeed, they must struggle valiantly to adopt his methods only in the end to fail of success with them.

Group IV does this clearly in the brief excerpt we have been examining. P takes up the teacher/leader's methods of asking questions and goes even further by defining a topic; group members say they want to talk about it, and then they resoundingly fail to do so, with P, seemingly innocent, leading the way.

In this manner, the leader is to be persuaded that the group loves his methods and, by extension, him, but simply cannot make use of them. The leader is accordingly programmed to begin to doubt his methods; they will seem to him impotent and useless. Perhaps he will begin to remember the vaunted merits of other methods used for encounter groups, where people touch and feel, undress and hug. Has he been wrong? Have the project leaders misled him? Can he go on obliging this eager and willing group of his to take yet another feckless turn on the treadmill of his procedures? Is he not too square and uptight in trying merely to notice and describe?

It is easy to see the similarities between this approach and the joke. The group tries and tries. This is the pre-punch-line part of the experience. The leader rests content. His vigilance is lulled. But having tried and tried, the group fails. The unwary leader is filled with alarm. He cannot now see that the group's attempts, in failing, made a mockery of his methods. If he could see that, he might smile at the prank. But the earnestness of the group beguiles him. Their hand has been quicker than his eye. Moreover, in trying as they have, in their facsimile of assiduousness, they have produced some tediously contrived sessions, sessions which the leader would doubtless be glad not to experience again. Tempted by this prospect of relief, prodded by what seems to be necessity, and secure in the knowledge that the group has long since abandoned all their negativism, massaging, and complaining, the leader snaps at the prospect of different methods.

When this is, as we see it here, the issue involving the groups and leaders, then the function of activity in the groups, no matter what its manifest form and substance, needs to be understood in terms of its effects. Let us look again briefly at Group I during the last excerpt from Session 8. The leader is trying to coax the group, prod it gently into self-knowledge by describing, asking questions, responding to the group's silences by describing more and asking more questions. In the end he is told that people would like to talk but they can't—there are taboos among the group. Now, as we turn next to the twelfth session, we will notice that at the beginning the leader is attempting to change his methods: he, too, says nothing, is silent during the silence. He notices, also, that at this session the group's usual questioning and looking toward him are "conspicuously absent." Here he is coming to understand that talk *or* silence is used by the group to effect something in him, whichever path he himself takes.

CHAPTER SEVENTEEN

THE GROUPS IN THE HOME STRETCH

Knowledge now experienced and seen as understanding.
Groups assign roles, disagree, and agree to disagree. This
agreement/disagreement experienced as loneliness.

Group I, Session 12

[People have brought food. R passes the food around. The group talks about
how each one of them gets home, which routes one can take. Some of those who
have been quieter members are more talkative than usual, swapping stories.
After twenty minutes the animated talk begins to wane and finally descends
into silence.]

R: Now I can't stand to chew because it wrecks the silence [smiles with
           food in one cheek].

[No one says anything.]

Leader: What is the silence about? Certainly it contrasts with the opulence
           of the table. People don't want to know what the silence is. It seems
           that the group is still dealing with the issue of four sessions ago of
           what people get from their parents—people are trying to get some-
           thing comparable from this group. But the issue was put under the
           rug.

F: The issue was the value of recognition, and we agreed that the first
           source of recognition is the parents. That's where the idea of the
           parents came up.

Leader: Talking of dependency on parents, the group sometimes looks to me
           for answers. I notice that the questions to me today are conspicuously
           absent.

K: I hate to deflate your ego but why should I ask you any questions?
           Every time I ask *you* [to F] a question, it's *he* [nodding to leader]
           who shuts me up.

[Silence]

Leader: The group doesn't like what I did, but they only tell me so by their
           silence and soulful looks.

[Giggles]

H: In a way, you've done to K what her administrator does: you've turned her off.

Leader: Turned the whole group. The group is using the episode with K to express something.

[Silence]

Leader: The group is more afraid of me now.

A: It's because we respect you. If you stop it . . .

F: Because no one else says, "Let's stop it."

Leader: I'm saying, let's really *hear* it.

R: You do what parents do to teachers.

K: [To the group members] So let's vote him out.

R: Or continue ourselves.

Leader: Why does the group have to vote me out?

F: It would make us stronger, maybe.

A: [Musingly] Do you think we're getting ourselves ready for a loss? Is that the need to get rid of unfinished business? We want *someone* to get things resolved.

[The group falls into silence again.]

Group II, Session 12

[After desultory talk the group falls silent.]

F: [Gloomily] We're back in the silences.

S: Sometimes one can accept the silence and enjoy it.

Leader: I have the feeling that it's hard to deal with disappointments, though. The suggestion has been that I haven't been helpful in this. Yet it isn't clear to me what the disappointment is.

A: I have a question. Why do you call us Miss and Mr. and Mrs. and we call each other by our first names?

Leader: Why do you think I do?

F: It makes you a bit removed and maybe that's necessary to your ob- jective remarks. For me, I can't talk to people unless I get feedback. It's as if we are not one whole.

A: Yes, when you are asked questions, you don't seem to have to answer them.

F: [Sadly] I'm not saying that because I don't know *you*, I can't com- municate with other members.

Leader: So you sound sad.

F: Yes, I'd *like* to get to know you.

[Brief silence. But W begins as though he'd been thinking it out during the silence.]

W: I'm going to try an experiment with my third grade class. I'll go into a class with a box of rhythm sticks, give each child a pair, and send him off alone for five minutes. The idea is to communicate; let each one say something with his sticks to the rest of the group. Then synthesize individual things into a group expression.

F & R: [Together] That's a good idea!

S: I get it. The idea is that people feel self-conscious. You try to get them to say something without their knowing it. Like if we were just all sitting around outside on the grass . . . you reveal yourselves without thinking about it.

Y: I've heard some of the most revealing conversations in locker rooms.

Leader: So the important element is saying things without knowing it.

F: It's also that you, like, ran the race the whole way together . . . a common experience.

Y: Like people who are caught in snowstorms together talk freely.

Leader: So you don't have a common experience here.

R: But I feel better about today's experience than ever before.

A: It's because we've all struggled together to evaluate what's happened.

R: Maybe this *is* our common experience.

A: The question is if we have been struggling together and felt puzzled, how are we going to feel at the end? You like to have things resolved at the end.

W: We'll have cokes at the end.

A: I don't see how it will be resolved at the last session.

W: What's to be resolved?

R: I have a feeling about groups I never had before. It never bothered me before whether I was in or out. It occurs to me that it bothers me today. I would like to gather *everyone* in. [Waving hand toward leader]

Leader: Are you including the people who aren't here?

F: Both. You kept asking how we felt about people who were absent, and all along, I felt that way about *you*.

Group III, Session 12

[The leader arrives a few minutes late.]

T: We were just writing you a note to tell you we were meeting outside today.

[T, N, and Y stand up.]

N: [To leader] Are you coming?

L: Gym teachers take their kids outside.

O: Yeah, become a gym teacher.

Leader: What's the issue?

O: Are you in charge of this group or not?

N: Are you a leader in this group?

Leader: Which is the issue? Am I a teacher? Can we go outside?

T: I just want to go outside because the sun is shining.

A: We're trying to accomplish something. We'll have a more relaxed atmosphere. They [nodding toward T and N] want to know if you're the authority figure in this class.

T and O: Who objects? No one. Let's go.

Y: Either all of us have to go out or stay. We can't split up.

T: It's a group.

A:	No, it never was a group.
T:	Right, but it should be. Can we act as a group?
Leader:	Someone told me groups don't make decisions. They share information and individuals make decisions.
N:	How do things get done?
H:	They discuss it and the leader makes the decision.
N:	O.K. Who will be the leader?
H:	We spend *all* our time discussing where we want to be. After the first week, we spent three weeks discussing the room.
N:	Here we are, after all this time, doing it again!
Leader:	What keeps us from being a group?
Y:	If *everyone* joined in, this *could* be a group.

[Everyone stands irresolutely, looking at the leader.]

Group IV, Session 12

B:	Can we go outside?
Leader:	Why do you keep asking me?
P:	Right out there, by the trees?
Leader:	Don't you think it would change the atmosphere?
R:	Yes, but we haven't got anything to lose. When you're at the bottom, there's only one place to go.
Leader:	We've been here all year.
E:	But the weather's affecting our discussion: it's very slow.

[Silence]

R:	There's another breeze outside.
D:	There's more oxygen out there.
B:	It's healthier for you out there.
R:	Gee, it does look nice out there.
E:	Why *can't* we go outside?
Y:	We just can't.
E:	[To leader] You're taking advantage of your power.
P:	Yeah. And you *said* not to treat you like a teacher because here you're not.
Leader:	Well, what do you think?
E:	We voted to go out. If *you* voted for it and *I* didn't, the group would go. But if *you* didn't . . .
Leader:	You're saying that you wouldn't go without me. It seems like you want to be anywhere but in this room.
E:	After fifty, teachers should be given full pay and not required to teach.
Leader:	When else should teachers be put out to pasture?
D:	When they can't teach.
E:	Those teachers who can change with the students, *they* should be kept.

In earlier sessions, we saw that knowledge induced self-consciousness; as the groups progressed, we saw that knowledge menaced certain hopes. As the groups enter the home stretch, one senses that knowledge continues to be an issue, but with a slightly different focus. This time it is as though knowledge represents growth. The position of the groups seems now to be: "We have at last found our metier. Some reasonably exciting things are taking place. Do not, leader, insist on talking about these, for thinking about them will take the joy out of what we are doing."

The leaders' attitudes seem, by and large, to be this: "But you came here to learn and not to have fun. For you to accomplish that, I will continue to pass on what I notice and observe that might lead to your goal of the development of insights and understandings." In Group I, for instance, the group is having a good time eating and talking until the leader's silence becomes too noticeable. When the group becomes silent, the leader tries to interest the group in considering the difference between the silence and the opulence of the table. The leader wants to talk about what is happening; the group wants to have a "happening."

In a pluralistic society, one might imagine room for a variety of pursuits and ideas. Were the groups able to adopt a pluralistic frame of mind, one could imagine the leaders getting their satisfactions by gaining and communicating insightful observations, while the members went ahead and had their experiences. Yet neither party seems to take this view. Rather, each acts as if the activity of the other interferes with his own pursuits. From our standpoint, no inherent reason for this seems evident.

We must, therefore, suspect that the manifest disagreement between the parties conceals, and yet expresses, an underlying agreement. Both have agreed to act as if only a universalistic society must exist. What they differ on is only the sort of universal that shall prevail. The groups seem disposed to a moralistic-hedonistic universal, the leaders to a moralistic-intellectual universal.

The parties, then, for all that they seem split, also agree: they agree to split. We have encountered this contrivance before. In order to unmuddy the waters, members try to separate mud from water, assigning half one place, the other half another. In the present situation, the leaders seem inclined to assign hedonism to the group, viewing themselves as conscientiously intellectual persons; the group assigns the wish to know to the leaders. Each party, having reassigned ownership in this way (you take the red checkers, I'll take the black), has a uniform, clear, unconflicted universal to work with. But having made their assignments and having agreed to disagree, the leader and group are still uncomfortable. Neither can now tolerate the mutually acknowledged separateness, even though they agree upon it. Why not? This question is in fact two questions.

To the first question, the answer, it seems, must be that they do not get rid of the orientation which they reassign because it is valuable. It is a valuable encumbrance. As such, they wish to conserve it, but not to be burdened by it. It is as though they want to be rid of it temporarily because it interferes but not to abolish it permanently, since it was once and may be again a factor of worth.

If this is the case, the answer to the second question—why they do not consider the exchange of orientations a good trade—quite reasonably follows. If they wish to get rid of their intellectual or their hedonistic qualities, respectively, because they are not now valued, they nevertheless know that they may want them again. The trade, therefore, cannot be final. The leaders want to keep their intellectual stance and to be rid of their hedonistic wishes lest they succumb and, abandoning their separateness from the groups, join in on the fun. The groups do not want knowledge lest it cramp their style by putting them into conflict. Both use one another as a dumping ground.

But if this is so, it signals that something further has also taken place. The members of the groups are less concerned with the criticism offerable by their inner "others." Previously, the cavalier disposition of the unwanted quality, now taking place, would have threatened retaliatory behavior from fearsome inner aspects of themselves. At the moment, however, the leader and these inner aspects are neither congruent nor in need of protection from one another (much as one parent will stand up for the other). The division of labor seems rather more commensal; the members seem to regard the leader as equal to themselves. The spirit is competitive; the issue is whose view shall prevail. This spirited pursuit of assertion is not encumbered with malice. It seems more a declaration of independent co-equality: the groups seem to assert that their members claim as much right to their hedonism as the leaders do to their intellectual orientation.

Yet this stance appears to be vulnerable, easily toppled. It is as though the members also mourn the omnipotent possibilities which the leader previously was given. Agreeing to disagree and going on to pursue different courses induces a degree of sadness and loss. The undertone in the discussion is wistful. One thinks of a child asking Mommy to hold his Teddy so he can race and romp. But once Teddy and Mommy are left behind, the child abruptly feels a bit forlorn. Couldn't Teddy come too? But the child does not ask. He knows what Mother will say, and doesn't want to know it. Though he departs without Teddy, he maintains to himself that it would have been possible to have both the animal and the romp. Yet the very assertion he so staunchly maintains makes him the more lonely, for it stands between himself and Mother.

For the groups, too, one senses, knowledge means choice and choice the renunciation of certain hopes in favor of other ones.

CHAPTER EIGHTEEN

THE HOME STRETCH

As hedonism rises among group members, so does moral fervor. A theoretical model for this evolution.

There remains another matter to turn our attention to in the home-stretch sessions: the earnest preoccupation with morality—"who is right," "what is the right thing to do"—is there as much as it was in the beginning (Kohlberg 1971). Yet the groups are in a hedonistic mood. The hedonism, however, does not leave the loaf of morality. It exists in contrast, sometimes in conflict, with it.

This fact sets us a new puzzle. The old puzzle is: why this concern with morality in the first place? The new one is: why has hedonism emerged without being mitigated by or mitigating the morality? Indeed, why has moral fervor increased?

Our previous answer to the old puzzle was that the absence of supposed-to's necessitated the activation of inner morality and constraint. While this seems to us still to be true, it does not fully explain why there had to be such a shifting of inner compunction to restore the equilibrium which was disturbed when the leaders failed to be moral leaders. Why couldn't people relax and enjoy the climate of freedom? One answer is that they came to the groups feeling somehow that they were bad and wished to be improved. Though here, too, we have no reason to doubt the answer, it does not explain why the members of the group spend so much time reassuring one another that they are perfectly good (or normal) people. Why not morally castigate or uplift one another? We have to assume that those giving reassurance suppose that the recipients want it and do not want to be castigated or uplifted. The reassurers are saying it's O.K. to be as you are.

If this is true, we will have to reformulate our explanations as follows. People come to the groups because they feel a need to be improved, but they hate that need. The need, they prefer to think, is spurred by a hypercritical inner other. The leader, they expect, is an outside other who shares views with their inner others. If he took over the job from the inner others, the latter could go to sleep. The selves of the members would simply have to contend with the leader. But when the leader fails to objectify the inner others, these quickly waken and set up a clamor of conscience. The members then attempt to strengthen one another against this insistent disapproval. The feeling seems to be that if they can do this, hedonism will be able to flourish untrammeled by inhibition, remorse, or shame.

This theory of the members, however, does not seem to be fulfilled by the ensuing facts. Despite the reassurances, people still feel bad: "There is still prejudice within me which I hate." It seems, indeed, that no amount of reassurance will help. Can it be, then, that the members *insist* on feeling bad? At first blush, this hardly seems a credible hypothesis. No one really likes feeling bad. But do people like *being* bad? To this question we find a different answer. There is something attractive about being bad, the more so if one can be bad without feeling bad, or, at least, without feeling *too* bad.

Let us, accordingly, try out this thesis on the material we have. If people are finding being bad attractive and report some questionable bit of behavior, what does reassurance that they have been good do for them? "Yes, even while I am here in this group, I have been prejudiced (*but* I am here to correct this badness)." Well, clearly, it helps them feel less bad—this we have already agreed upon. But does not this minimization of the sense of having been bad detract from the stir and attractive sensations that being bad is designed to convey? Whereas if their reply to a confession was "Oh, how perfectly dreadful!" would it not tickle the senations even while stirring up guilt or shame?

Given this line of reasoning, we come to the further view that the preoccupation with morality remains because it expresses the members' abashed intentions to be bad. For were such intentions abandoned, the morality which rides herd on them would be *de trop*. We can, therefore, regard the group's preoccupations with morality as the smoke which obscures the finest of the intentions.

It follows, then, does it not, that as intentions strengthen, so will moral fervor. Were the two—the pleasures of being bad and the crusading morality—to achieve a synthesis, a genuine mitigation of each other, both would be reduced. But the members, it seems, once again take a stand against such compromise. Their position seems, rather, to be this: "O.K., we have to suffer for our misdeeds, but that only goes to affirm that our deeds are, as we wish, misdeeds. So that is a tradeoff. But it is a better tradeoff than a more trivial misdeed condemned by a fainter sense of compunction, because though a fierce sense of compunction hurts our selves more, think of what fierceness this compunction delivers unto others who misdo!" This position is somewhat reminiscent of the situation in which one child says to another: "My old man can beat up your old man, 'cause look what he did to me." The fierce inner other is not, then, simply a mean, harsh, spoil-sport; at times he (or she) can join with the self so that together they become an avenging angel.

No one needs to be reminded how much evil is done in the name of good. The things that even the most mild of our inner others forbids us to do, not to speak of those actions that are proscribed by all our inner others combined, can be done in the name of goodness, justice, mercy, or charity. But for such evil to be unleashed, we need right on our side. We need to be or feel sinned against. Given this sense of injustice to ourselves, we can feel entitled to do unto others as they have done unto us.

We set out to account for the rising hedonism in the groups. We set out also to account for the rising tide of moral fervor. The puzzle we faced was, why both simultaneously? Perhaps we are now in a position to solve the puzzle. Does not the vigilance of the moral fervor serve as a radar which can pick up and pick out transgressions against the members which, once recorded, in turn buy the rights to hedonism? Isn't it more a self-indulgence not to face the hard task of the group of working to understand what is happening?

With this conclusion, the groups' assignment of intellectual orientations to their leader, which we noted in the preceding discussion, takes on new light. If he is being bad and ruining everything with his preachy-teachy-know-it-all qualities, do we (the members seemed to have asked and answered in the affirmative), do we not have the right to restore the equilibrium by being the more hedonistic? Doesn't his badness offset ours? Isn't he just asking for this?

From our vantage point we can see the value of the solution at which the groups arrive. It frees them to do what otherwise they could not. But the solution is based more on circumvention than on resolution. The members buy off, indeed, enlist their inner others in a campaign of retribution. Why not do the fun things plain and simple?

The answer to this lies, we must suppose, in the members' continuing relationship with their inner others. They have not yet been able to free themselves of the prominence of their presence. Or, more precisely, they cling to their inner others in order to feel less lonely, less lost in their own skins, islands, not touching other human beings in depth, and by tying the inner others to themselves they are tied by the inner others. To preserve the joy of being at one with the inner others or, alternatively, being loved and regarded by them requires of the members the convoluted strategies we have observed.

CHAPTER NINETEEN

THE FINAL SESSIONS

Anger, sorrow, frustration. The inevitable anticlimax and the
persistence of hopes in the face of contrary reality.

Group I, Final Session

[Some group members have brought doughnuts for everyone. The smell of
freshly made coffee comes from a large pot brought by other members. People
eat, talk, fall silent; eat, talk, fall silent.]

A: [As if to explain the silences] Like kids we regress and end on a
        happy note.

O: Maybe our expectations are too high for the last day—we came in,
        like in the beginning, with expectations.

N: We are holding back from talking because we don't know what we're
        supposed to do.

O: But that's the point. We're still holding back because we have a fear
        of being judged on what we "should" have done.

A: [Sighs] There's one little thing we haven't gotten to, and maybe we
        won't because it's too far.

K: Are you talking about something specific? I am absolutely baffled.

E: I think I know what A means . . . it's that you can't help feeling a
        sense of potential when twelve people meet, that something positive
        should come out of it. I don't think the potential has to be described
        in order for us to know you haven't gotten there.

O: My goal was to get all twelve people very close—a great concentration
        of strength would have been an ultimate goal.

F: I wonder if I'm realizing we had so much time. We could have put
        more effort into it. Not that we've been apathetic on purpose, but
        maybe we've underestimated the value of relationships and the
        quality that could have developed if we had opened ourselves.

A: So you feel there's something untapped, too.

B: I'd like to read about it, when you write up this experiment.

Leader: What would you like to find out?

B: How Group A compared to Group B.

Leader: We can figure it out here and you won't have to read it. What's your guess? What would you inquire about your own question?

B: I really thought we were going to learn about METCO.

O: [Turning to B] Don't you think we did indirectly?

Leader: What do you want to find out about METCO?

B: What we did. [Uncertainly, groping] I'm sure we did something constructive.

Leader: It sounds as if you're not sure. You don't want to find out what the question is?

B: We've found out a lot about ourselves. I suppose that's what we were looking for.

Leader: I have the feeling that doesn't answer your question.

B: I think we helped each other out by talking, when we *did* talk.

N: [To leader] When you say, "who knows," it's like an invitation to just be. Here we have an invitation to just be and it's difficult because we all come with our ideas of what we are, of others' expectations. Your gesture is an invitation to just be—like the hardest things for kids is just to give them free time.

[Everyone has listened to N with attentive silence.]

E: That's a very good point. It's funny you should come to the end of something and you think of a thousand ways you *could* have acted, a thousand things you *could* have done. I can think of a thousand things I can ask.

Leader: Why don't you ask one?

E: [Turning to D, who has always attended the meetings but never said anything] How much a part of the group do you feel now?

D: I feel a part of it. I feel I know you all very well.

E: That implies we don't know you.

D: You know me more than others do, but you can't accept that—you want me to talk.

Leader: Do you want to take the opportunity to ask something from the group? You want to be accepted as a member of the group without being involved another way. They haven't demonstrated that you can.

D: They don't have to. I know already.

Leader: What about me?

D: I think you know I'm part of the group.

O: [To D] As I got close to the end, I wanted to know about you.

Leader: [To D] Had it occurred to you that the group members wondered if you accepted them?

[Silence]

E: [To D, sighing] I just wish I could have gotten to know you better.

Group II, Final Session

Y: [Jauntily] It's graduation day for the group. Going into the world more sensitive, more aware. Give to them what we got. Be more sensitive to people.

Leader: It sounds like those are all of the things you hoped to get.

F: If people could actually change people, it would be scary to think of what teachers could do to kids.

Y: [Less jauntily] So we're charged with the jobs of changing people . . . kids.

Leader: Isn't that the "scary" idea part of what was going on here with us? You felt there was a gap between us. I wonder if that doesn't represent what happens to people on one side. What they feel is a division—teachers and students, parents and children, whatever . . .

F: Well, like here . . . when someone is not entering in and also not quite—I wasn't confident with *your* role.

Leader: I wonder if there's something that happens when someone wants something from another.

S: In so many jobs, there are bosses. When there's a leader, you wonder what they are like.

Leader: Or what they'll do for you.

Y: [Even less jauntily than before] This idea of sensitivity—it comes with experience and maturity. It takes years and years. By the time you can relate to people, you're too old.

Leader: The question is, then, whether the group has been efficient?

R: I wonder if learning *can* be efficient. I think it's like all other growth—it takes an infant nine months; you can't make a plant grow too fast. I wonder if any kind of learning can be made more efficient than it naturally is.

S: [Protesting] But a teacher does make a difference with children with learning problems.

R: Well, if you fertilize the garden, it grows better.

S: Most of us felt there'd be more discussion here about dealing with people of another kind . . .

Leader: Why was the discussion not about that?

F: Because it would have been a theoretical discussion—on how to deal with black children. But I think it does relate—just dealing with people.

Leader: I'm gathering that your expectations of coming here were that something related to yourselves would change.

Y: *I* find it easier to meet people nowadays. It's brought back the accommodating manner. We're all fighting the same problem, right? [Looks around group]

A: *I've* found it helpful when kids are not getting along, trying to get behind why they don't.

F: *I* find I stop and wonder what's really making me angry. Kids have a wealth of feelings and reasons! It helps you see them in yourself.

R: [As though adding to the list] . . . Or even how could I have said what I said in another way so it could have been listened to by the people I was speaking to.

[Everyone sits back and looks at the leader expectantly.]

Leader: As I've been listening to these different statements, I find myself wondering if people feel they realized everything they hoped for.

A: I'd like to join the group again in the fall; I don't see this as the end.

W: Me too. I look forward to the same thing again in the fall.

I: I do too, *if* we could start with this group. When I think of the *first* twelve weeks . . .

B: I couldn't start with eleven new people like this . . .

W: [Hastily] I can see your point about *us* continuing.

Leader: You'd like to keep this group going and get on to something else.

F: We could get into some people deeper. But on the other hand, it would be interesting to start with a new group and see if there is a transfer.

I: [To F, wonderingly] After what we all went through to get *this* off the ground?

Group III, Final Session

N: I brought some ginger ale. So are we going out?

T: Let's go to Brigham's.

I: Would you go to Brigham's with us? The other section went.

Leader: What if someone didn't want to go?

I: [Laughing] Let's not analyze the group's going to get ice cream.

T: This class gets me into trouble because wherever I go I wind up analyzing people. They get upset and I have to apologize.

H: Why should that make any difference—whether you do it here or "outside"?

T: Because *they're* not ready for it. I always thought things about people and now I say them.

N: Can you take this course twice?

Leader: Some do.

N: We'll know all the angles. They introduced this course all wrong.

Leader: What should they say?

N: It's a gab session.

H: A rap session.

Leader: How can you say that when we have trouble rapping?

T: Before, we didn't talk because we were afraid. Now, we don't talk because we have nothing to say.

Leader: [To T] I remember when you told us of an afternoon that you spent having tea, fighting with the cat and doing nothing.

H: Yeah, that's different from thinking. I guess when I listen to music, it's the same thing . . . *doing* nothing.

N: Everyone, I have to leave early to return these cups.

[N leaves.]

I: [Facetiously] Now the question is how do we feel now that N is gone?

T: She's the most open person here. It's so quiet when she goes. Her presence makes a real difference.

[The others agree.]

Leader: [To I] Are you surprised it was a good question?

[Silence]

T: Anyone doing anything over the summer? Going to Toronto?
I: Yes.
H: What's that?
T: Another Woodstock.
I: [Sadly] No, there will never be another Woodstock.

Group IV, Final Session

Several: Why can't we go outside?
Leader: We're going to have a regular meeting right here. This is our last meeting.
R: Why can't we have one next week?
Leader: Because it's all finished.
P: Who's missing? Looks like lots of kids . . . [looking around]
R: They're taking a test.
Leader: How do you feel about all this ending?
F: We have only thirteen more days of school. I'm going to miss it.
B: I'm not. I can't wait to get out of here.
T: I can't wait till school's over . . . but I think I'll miss the place.
D: Did anyone see [movie]? The part with the kid with the scar, and blood comes gushing out—ooh.
P: Some movies get bad ratings. My father didn't want me to see "Bonnie and Clyde."
R: Why, because of the bedroom scene?
P: No, because of the ending. It was so bloody—those bloody bodies full of holes and bouncing onto the ground from the car.
D: That was fake.
R: Where do you go to see the movies?
P: Where do *you* go?
[Silence. Everyone looks melancholy.]
E: Y'know how teachers fill out reports for us? Well, we should fill them out for teachers as well.
Leader: What would you say?
E: I would say from how much they know and how they present it.
Leader: If you thought that they themselves would read them, would you say the same?
[Silence]

One cannot consider these final sessions without sensing how greatly the group members fear that something like T. S. Eliot's epitaph (1925)— "This is the way the world ends / Not with a bang but a whimper"—may be their own. Even some of the words they sometimes use seem more august and sonorous than usual, as if they intend for the very language itself to weigh in upon the scales of accomplishment. As the groups come to a close, it is clear that the members long, above all, for a feeling of consequentiality.

It is tempting to regard this vigorous quest as something so natural as to warrant little investigation; the groups have been meeting for some time, and if, in the end, they wish to take their own measures in the hope that they have gotten some place and have come away with something to show for it, how can we wonder at that? Would it not be better if we used this moment of reckoning to make some personal estimates of the worth of the experience?

Against this temptation stands one small fact, so easy to lose sight of amidst the more appealing possibilities. The members have come together to discuss, over time, matters of general interest or social concern. Indeed, many topics have been discussed; a range of views has been shared; opportunities for review have been present. People have made their thoughts explicit and listened to these as they spoke them. They have heard similar and contrasting views. Some were based on information they themselves lacked, some on different assemblies of the same general information. Thus there was a basis for revising or maintaining positions on the matters discussed. As the time for this experience comes to a close, we cannot doubt that the groups had the opportunities for which they came. If that were the measure of a venture, then the venture could be regarded as successful.

We are bound to realize, however, the discrepancy between that conception and the conception the members have of the experience. Each of the groups, for example, proposes something in the way of a party for itself, just as W in Group II explained earlier: "We'll have cokes at the end"; Groups I and II avail themselves of food and drink, while Groups III and IV plead for an outing. The fact that each group comes independently to its own conception of how groups should *be* in their closing sessions could give rise to grave doubts about our own, more intellectual, conceptions of the nature of the experience. We appear to be the only ones who do not know what the group experience was to consist of. Our rendition, dealing as it does with matters of talk, topics, and discussion, seems woefully awry compared with a group experience in which feasts or celebrations or at least the expectation of such conviviality have a leading part.

Something needs to be reconciled. Perhaps the talk was not good enough, but we do not hear that the discussions were so poor as to engender different versions of what the experience should be like. In fact, the idea of discussions is noteworthy by its absence—an event all the more striking thanks to the utter lack of self-consciousness with which it is entertained. Here, at the end, the idea that the members came to discuss issues seems to have been abandoned.

In its place have emerged ideas of consequentiality and consummation. The position of the groups seems to be: we have, as patiently as we could, awaited the end of the groups, for with the end we have expected that something would materialize which is at once different from, and an outgrowth of, all that preceded it.

If that rendering of their position is approximately correct, several additional factors must be considered. First, there is the time frame. The end is set off from the other segments of time not as something containing a continuity of experience, but as a distinctive opportunity for culmination. Something in the way of a climax is expected. Second, the time phases preceding the ending seem to have been regarded all along as something to be gone through in order to achieve the ending. The worth of the prelude lies not in itself but in its obligatory relationship to the ending. Somewhere in the time span a transformation was to have taken place, for which all that preceded it was mere prologue. That transformation had at once to happen *in the time* (fifteen to thirty sessions) and *in time* (during the "experience"). We can now see what those extraordinary measures (negativism, seduction, manipulation) of looking in, rather than upon, the leaders (to which we referred in our previous discussion) were all about. The groups had to *create* leaders capable of achieving the transformation for which, it now seems, they had all along come. They had to remove the leaders they encountered (this being their criterion for consequentiality) in order to gain the transfiguration they sought (this being the culmination).

The groups' attitude toward the leaders, which is reflected in this sequence, suggests a very high regard. The leaders are assumed to be capable of performing transformations. But the groups must also contend with what they take to be the leaders' reluctance to effect those fine transformations. They admire the leaders' abilities (both the real ones and the ones assigned to them by the groups) but that admiration turns quickly into envious hatred when those abilities seem not to be confirmed. They cannot accept the leader's inability to perform this transformation. They assume again that he has the ability and has refused to use it on their behalf. Under circumstances of envy, the groups experience the secret consequentiality of the leaders as against their own hopes and, if they cannot enjoy and profit from *their* own consequentiality, strive to divest the leaders of theirs. Thus, we noted, R in Group II, Session 12, speaks of the group as a circle, a container, as it were, which has goodness in it. She regrets that the leader does not avail herself of the good contents of the group, saying: "I would like to gather *her* [waving hand toward leader] in."

But for the most part, it is the contents of the leader to which the groups want access: the groups are to end with a ceremonial feast. Because endings are conventionally celebrated with ceremonial feasting, the meaning of the wish for a feast seems more conventional than it may in fact be. We risk depriving ourselves of an understanding of the groups' hopes if we do not look beyond tradition and regard the tradition as something which makes it possible for the groups, unabashedly, to ask for or avail themselves of the feasting.

R of Group II has provided a clue. She speaks of the group as if it were a container within which are good things . . . things which the leader, by not being "in," is missing. Let us imagine that the groups first think that there are good things, and that these are contained either within the group or within the leader. If they are contained within the group, then certain consequences follow, one of which being that the leader is deprived. Another is that the group has something like a hive full of honey, off which it can feed in time to come; hence the talk of resuming the groups next season. These fantasies must strike us as more wishful than realized when we consider the pervasiveness of the groups' wishes to feed and fortify themselves.

Accordingly, we must recognize that the reverse is true. The groups approach the ending with a feeling of insufficiency. Their cups are not running over, as they might wish to believe. In fact, the contrary is true. The unconscious hope is that within the leader is the stuff for which they yearn, the stuff of which culminations might be made. The fantasy seems to be that the leaders have resources of such sufficiency and creativity as to enable them to remain independent of what the groups have to offer. As the ending approaches, and the leaders will no longer be there to provide these good resources to the groups, the groups' wish is to find a way to get into the leaders, to avail themselves of and consume the stuff the leaders contain.

Still, while this may be the essence of the consummation the groups have in mind, we notice that they are not prepared to consume the leaders. In return for this diffidence, they wish to extract certain ransoms. They want an abrogation of the usual terms of the group so that they may have a more decorous sort of feast; they want, in the end, to have the leader reduce their envy of his great inner resources. The leader can do this by joining the group at the feast, thus confessing he is in need of sustenance too—sustenance other than understanding how, what, and why. In doing so, he becomes more like any other group member than is suggested by his previous behavior.

The groups, then, are prepared to make a certain peace with what they failed to get, which is the Eucharistic hope. They move to this sacrifice of hope, however, only with the proviso that they can now believe the leader to be less desirable than they had formerly believed him to be. They actively diminish the desirability of the leader in order to save the hoped for, desirable leader from themselves. If they subsequently wish to exact compensations (beyond the appeasements of their envy) one can also see that the renunciation of the Eucharistic culmination (in favor of the yielding to the leader of his rights to a continued existence) cannot have been easily made.

The feasting and the discussions of feasting in these last sessions are a weaning, in the same sense that the groups move from a primary preoccupation with the leader's person and that person's qualities to doughnuts or ice cream or cokes. But they seek to establish another consolation as well. This is the counting of their own good qualities and achievements. These too are souvenirs of the encounter. With feasting and achievements, the members seem to feel, they will not come away emptyhanded.

It is clear that this represents a significant, even a radical, change in the use of alternatives. In our survey of the groups at midpoint, they were bent on preserving their hopes, even at the cost of hopelessness and despair and of frustration and deprivation. Now, not so many sessions later, they are prepared to make a kind of peace, based on the renunciation of their primary hopes, in favor of an ordinary party and the consolation of achievement. When previously they feared the half-a-loaf lest it blunt their appetites for the full loaf, now they are prepared to accept it and make do. We hear (most explicitly from Group I) that the groups at last discover what fulfillments they have been wanting, only to recognize simultaneously that these are not to be—"to get all twelve people very close . . . a great concentration of strength." Mournfully, they turn from these potentials to what they can, in fact, manage to garner.

They do not, though, turn from the consolations of achievement—of change. It is not enough merely to have had their discussions, or to have managed the sacrifices which enable them to save the leaders from the members' designs on their "contents." They continue to want from the encounter some sort of transformation, some sort of tangible achievement, some almost quantifiable measure of change. If some feel they can discern some change, they are in that measure gratified. Where tangible achievement seems insufficient, people feel uncompensated and unconsoled. Few can feel it sensible to have gone through the meetings without having been altered.

These reactions seem curious, in that it is not clear why people should be altered. If they are discontent, dissatisfied with themselves, it would seem that they could re-attune themselves with no more fuss than it takes to add a sweater when one is cool. It is clear that it is precisely the fuss that matters, not the significance of the change itself.

Given that desirability of alteration is somehow impressive, it is worth exploring how changes can be measured or otherwise appraised. We could not fail to notice the difference between the groups at the end and the groups a few sessions earlier. At approximately midpoint it seemed almost impossible that the people involved could have even contemplated renouncing the great potentials they believed to be inherent in the experience. At the end, they managed to make a very difficult sort of peace. Put succinctly, the groups had managed to become depressed— more sad than bitter, more mournful than angry, more solicitous than rapacious, more protective than greedy. Since the first words of these pairings have better moral overtones than do the second, the members might have felt a grateful sense of accomplishment if the leaders had described them to the groups. But had the leaders thereupon noticed the gratification, the members might well have felt affronted. They might have wanted the sense of accomplishment (measured by the "distance" between the word pairings) more than they wanted the information the leader would have given them, though the information might conceivably have fomented the opportunity for just such further movement as the members prized.

Assuming our description to be correct, the information concerning the movements from anger to sorrow, etc., was there for everyone to see, to feel—experience—as was the pleasure the members took in whatever other changes they effected. One cannot help feeling, however, that they did not notice movements such as those from bitterness to sadness because they did not value them. Achievement is achievement primarily in moral terms. Accordingly, we are forced to the conclusion that change is, and remains, a moral attribute, and that what the groups experience (insofar as they do not feel fulfilled and transformed) is a moral crisis.

And so we return to where we began—to the supposed-to's. Even in the end, the group members act as if they feel called upon to weigh and measure the degree to which they have achieved what they were *supposed* to achieve. The transformation, rather than the process, is what matters.

Part III

CHAPTER TWENTY

PEOPLE'S FANTASIES IN GROUP SITUATIONS: PSYCHOANALYTIC THEORY OF GROUPS

In 1921 Freud presented his major essay on group psychology (Freud 1921). Since he had not studied groups from the vantage point of the group psychotherapist, it was inevitable that his theory would lack that analysis of unconscious fantasy which is at the heart of psychoanalytic formulation. But, by the same token, it is all the more remarkable that Freud was unable to replace the then-current thinking concerning the group mind or mentality with dynamic and even genetic concepts and to lay the groundwork for a systematic psychoanalytic model. Freud, moreover, never confined his treatment of any subject to a single study. If taken together with the formulations available, notably in his works, *On Narcissism* (1914), *Mourning and Melancholia* (1917), and *Totem and Taboo* (1913b), his original work on groups gains the intrapsychic aspect that was relatively undeveloped in it.

Nevertheless, for approximately forty years, from 1921 until 1961, there was a relative dearth of psychoanalytic contributions to group theory. Jacobson (1945) and Redl (1945) each ventured studies of aspects of group behavior, and there were others, but it remained for Bion (1961) to attempt a thoroughgoing formulation of group psychology, one to which he still adds, as, for instance, in his 1970 book.

Bion had the advantage of conducting groups; and though the earlier papers which constitute his 1961 study deal with the behavior of groups, the later papers offer a close study of the meaning and motivation of that behavior, particularly in terms of Kleinian theories of early object relations and their vicissitudes.

Yet in 1968 Balint observed that in the second half of the forties the psychoanalytic movement faced the question: "Should we psycho-

---

Some of the material in this chapter appeared in different form in H. N. Boris, M. Boris, and N. E. Zinberg, "Fantasies in group situations," *Contemporary Psychoanalysis* 2 (1975):15–45.

analysts accept responsibility for techniques to be used in group psychotherapy?" "The answer," he notes, "was a hesitating 'no' with the
result that group therapy and psychoanalysis developed largely independently of each other, to the great detriment of both."

This situation seems to us still true, not only in the matter of technique but in that of study and theory as well. There is, no doubt, more
than a single reason for this mutual neglect. But one reason may be the
matter of focus. Psychoanalysis is a study of the individual; theories of
groups take something called "the group" as their object. However, what
if one takes as one's focus the study of individuals in group contexts—
does this open the way to a mutual understanding of both individuals
and group phenomena?

This, at any rate, is what we have attempted to do here. And this
attempt accounts also for the approach we have taken in setting down
our formulations here. Rather than offering modifications of or addi-
tions to previous theoretical discussions of groups—which approach
would depend on a close familiarity with the body of group theory to
which we have referred—we make a presentation that seeks to be all of
a piece. Readers familiar with Freud's and Bion's ideas on groups will
readily note our debts to and departures from each of them. Those less
familiar with the work of these men may find it more useful to consider
our presentation as simply a body of inference from the data from which
it is drawn.

For much the same reason we have not attempted to transpose terms
from the psychoanalytic theories of the individual to our own inferences.
Rather, we attempt to describe what we see. If the reader then says,
"That is 'identification' of which they are speaking," we prefer this to
speaking ourselves about "identification," only to have the reader
wonder whether the meaning of the term needs to be altered by the
context.

People in the groups we have studied speak of "making a group." By
that they seem to mean finding or making manifest a good deal in common, each with the others. *Their* theory seems to be that there is such a
thing as a group, and that a group may be constructed if people make it
evident that they have much in common. The energy and persistence
they show in making a group suggests, moreover, that a group is a very
valuable thing to have.

At first blush there seems nothing very remarkable in that theory,
held by the people we have studied. But if we venture to examine it more
closely, it begins to appear rather more remarkable. The first matter one
notices is the extent to which the beliefs are shared. No one seems to
challenge either the belief that there is such a thing as a group or the
belief that the manifestation of things in common can possibly over-

whelm the differences of every sort and variety that, in actuality, exist among the people present. Furthermore, not only is there no challenge to these beliefs; there is a strenuous positive effort to assert them.

It seems, therefore, that a group could be defined as a potential state, which can be realized when the people who compose it find and assert more things in common than things that separate them. This seems a commonplace until we reckon more closely with the differences among the group members. These are of age, sex, marital status, occupation, background, temperament, physique, and cast of mind. It is plain that actual similarities cannot outweigh differences unless a blind eye is turned upon them. Only insofar as all present elect to regard the fact that they are fellow entities—e.g., human beings—as more important than their limitless differences can a group be said to exist.

The belief cannot be faulted: all present *are* human beings. Yet one senses that such a common denominator is not sufficient. "Human being" is too broad a category; it fails to distinguish group members from all those human beings who are not part of the group. Not only must group members have more in common than not in common but there must be more differences from than similarities to others not to be "included" in the "group." The simple fact of being "human beings" does not serve. Just as artifice is required to emphasize similarities and to overlook differences, so those who wish to regard themselves as composing a group must contrive to be a "group" by emphasizing their differences from those outside the group. Thus they are able to ignore the host of similarities which they share with those excluded. From what we have said thus far, we could define the "group" as a number of people who are prepared to accept or contrive similarities and disregard differences—and to accept the resulting perception as the truth. The resulting "group," we could say, is a double invention.

This, however, leaves us with precious little to theorize about! As a theologian depends upon the actuality of God as a basis for theology, the group theorist is equally dependent upon his group. All we have left as a group is an aggregate of people attempting to give substance to a shared fantasy.

Suppose we take that phenomenon as our starting point and attempt to understand the fantasy that so appeals to those who hold to it. What happens in groups is that people labor to actualize a fantasy in order to claim benefits from realizing it. Why and how they labor, and what benefit they derive, may be worth knowing, especially considering the ubiquity of people's beliefs in groups.

We must first define "fantasy." Fantasy, it is fairly plain, enthrones a version of something in preference to the absence of that something or to its factual version. The very function of the imagination is inviting, in that the active and personal mind of the imaginer is necessary, whereas only his senses are required to know of things as they are or are not. And the product of the fantasy delights insofar as it replaces drear fact with versions more palatable.

That this very exercise of fantasy can be delightful is easy to see. Order comes from chaos with but a flick of the mind's eye. A hundred different girls can be made a single "unit" by common costumes and lock-step dances. Life is simplified when numbers of discrete individuals, all different, can be subsumed into categories—black, white; middle class, lower class; normal, psychotic. But the first example differs from the second insofar as the girls must dress and dance alike, while to classify individuals into categories requires only the inventive art of the categorizer.

Apart from mere pleasurable fantasy, something more may define groups. Might it not be that groups are invented as an antidote to the fact[1] of differences? This inference seems logical but at the same time, unreasonable. Differences can sometimes be quite the nicest things in the world: the frightened, hungry child::the comforting, providing mother; the ardent man::the attractive, eager woman. But when we notice that pairings are reciprocal and complementary, we also see that we are dealing only with "good" differences. There are others: the clinging child::the harassed and busy mother; the ardent man::the otherwise committed woman. These differences are anything but complementary and reciprocal. Until and unless they are resolved, they will lead to a fight, a separation, or an otherwise painful relationship. The child may get spanked, sent to his room, or scolded; the man may become intolerably rapacious and the woman he covets may leave the scene. Each member of the pair would no doubt wish first for a reciprocal relationship with the other; failing this, each may be heading for a painful relationship. It is here that "making a group" provides the alternative.

To illustrate: one can see that Dick, the ardent lover, will consent to be just friends, i.e., form a "group," with Jane, as a substitute for loving Jane. Jane is more willing to form a group because she has Tom, from whom her differences are complementary and, therefore, cherished. For Dick, "grouping" with Jane helps avoid complete separation, a painful struggle, or great jealousy. Jane, for her part, rather likes Dick, enjoys the interests and viewpoints they have in common, and even enjoys the

---

[1]Though we say "fact" here, we mean to regard differences much as we do similarities; differences are as much a function of comparisons as are similarities. It is the issue of the selective perception or use of both difference and similarity with which we are engaged here.

affection he still maintains for her. In fact, being a good friend, Dick encourages her in her love affair with Tom. Though she is sure that her parents would like Tom, something in her wonders; she is also sometimes frustrated by Tom's diffidence in their lovemaking.

If we schematize these feelings of Jane's, we see the following. Jane talks of "something in her" which she does not regard as identical with her self. This "something in her" is "in" her, but not of her *self*. It is associated in some way with Jane's parents, but it is not identical with her parents. This "something" causes what Jane talks of as "I" and her "self" to feel doubts about Tom. At the same time Jane's I-self feels very enthusiastic about Tom, and Dick's support helps. Let us call that something in Jane her conscience. Then there is her self. Jane's conscience, though not identical with her "parents," is sometimes identified with them; likewise, though not identical with Jane's self, her conscience can invade Jane's self with doubts and discouragement. Dick, however, can influence these psychic "events."

In like manner, Jane's sexuality wants more satisfaction than Tom will afford "it." Jane is undecided, at times, whether to identify her self with her sexuality against Tom or to take Tom's side, as it were, against her sexuality. Here too Dick is of some help, encouraging Jane's I-self to push sexuality away from her and to accept Tom's attitudes as hers.

So schematized, in deference to Jane's fantasy of being somehow in three parts—conscience, sexuality, and self—we see that Jane feels that she has to contend with things "within herself." Dick helps her contend with these "things" by getting them "out" of her "self," though they remain in her somewhere. Dick seems to come into her self and help her repel the impingement of sexuality and conscience. Clearly that is impossible in the realm of fact, but fantasy, as we have noted, reigns supreme.

If Jane already has fantasies concerning a tripartite going on of things in her self, she also has fantasies that she can take Dick inside her self. What becomes clear, then, is the great value of an external relationship of grouping for the I's-self's internal relationships, much as a good alliance between one country and another could help not only with their struggles with other countries but with problematic factions within each.

Jane could also be rather afraid of Dick as well. Suppose that rather than grouping with her I-self, Dick takes a position in common with either Jane's conscience or her sexuality. The odds, which were so helpful to Jane's self, will certainly have changed. If Jane felt bad to begin with, Dick could, in allegiance with Jane's conscience, make Jane feel *very* bad indeed. Likewise, in allegiance with Jane's sexuality, he could make her feel at one with it, in opposition to Tom's diffident lovemaking.

Dick cannot, of course, effect these changes without the active collaboration of Jane's fantasies. But Jane treats psychic "events" as if they were somehow like physical events. We can guess that when Jane, with help from an inner Dick, repudiates the voice of conscience, she herself will feel less bad. She will also feel more lonely; that is, she will respond to conscience as if it were a person, her mother, and her "estrangement" from this figure will make her feel lonely—quite as if she had lost an actual person. Dick's affection is required to keep her from feeling too lonely for her conscience at those times when she has lost touch with it.

But in following Jane's experience, we have lost sight of Dick and his experiences with and of Jane. Dick did not altogether want to "group" with Jane: he preferred to celebrate their differences in a love relationship rather than establishing so much in common through friendship. On the other hand, he did not want to quarrel with her or lose her. But her repudiation of him both frustrated him sexually and aroused doubts about himself. Dick was thus in much the same boat as Jane, so that Jane's offer of friendship is helpful to Dick in the same way his is to her: Dick employs Jane to augment his self against fault-finding from his conscience and from unmannerly uprisings of his sexuality. His "grouping" with Jane is used by Dick to offset pressures from both directions. In the same way, Dick will, like Jane, be afraid of Jane's becoming identified with either his sexuality or his conscience. Indeed, were Jane to be a little too seductive, Dick's self would feel quite angry at her, nor would he take criticism from Jane at all gladly unless he him*self* agreed with it. Jane and he are to have much in common; differences between them will be anything but welcome.

Jane and Dick make a good group at the moment and will make a better one when Dick finds himself a woman who can enjoy with him their reciprocal differences. But Dick has been through an unrequited love affair once before, with Gloria, and he made the same arrangement with Gloria that he did with Jane. Once he became at one with Jane, he found Gloria intolerable. The anger at Gloria's rejection of him sexually was now active whether she was seductive with him or not. Once he had been pleased to be with and to be seen with Gloria; now he could only be with Gloria provided that he wasn't seen—especially in places he frequented with Jane. He seemed to hate her or himself, hate himself for hating her or hate her for making him hate her or hate himself for hating himself—he couldn't tell which. And yet once they had much the same friendship he and Jane now have.

To account for this reaction of Dick's schematically, we could assume the following. Dick is no longer "himself"—as Gloria might put it. His self now reflects Jane's point of view, or what he takes to be Jane's point of view, concerning Gloria. Thus modified, with Gloria out and Jane in, Dick's self may have several experiences, depending on where Gloria has "gone." If she has gone "outside" and become a differentiated person, Dick may well hate her for the deprivation of him that she represents. But it was to avoid so painful a relationship that Dick moved Gloria inside; thus it is more likely, upon being evicted from self (to make more room for Jane), that Gloria has been moved into his conscience. There she is different, but not as different, separate, but not as separate, as she would be "outside." Though not *of* Dick, she is *in* Dick. Moreover, there are others in his conscience, and, in being merely one of their numbers, though Gloria's presence will be felt, it will be one of several presences, and as such, it will not carry its full weight. Whether Gloria-conscience will despise Dick because he can neither gain fulfillment for his needs nor satisfy women or whether Gloria-conscience will love Dick because he doesn't mess about with romance and sex will depend on what persons preceded Gloria in conscience, how they felt about Dick, and, no less important, how Dick regarded *their* romantic activities.

With this modification, Dick's self is at the mercy of his conscience's view of his failure to win Gloria's consent to a relationship based on differences. Then, too, augmented by Jane's grouping, his self is prepared to tolerate differences between himself and Gloria. Or if these differences between his Dick-Jane self and Gloria are acknowledged, and Dick feels as one with Gloria, Jane and Dick's conscience despise Dick. The *former* position, tolerating differences with Gloria, exemplifies bad differences, while the *latter* position, feeling one with Gloria, illustrates bad similarities. Dick's and Jane's relationship, on the other hand, represents good similarities, while Jane's and Tom's relationship evinces, for the most part, good differences.

If, however, "grouping" is an alternative invented to counteract problems of "internal" and "external" differences, it seems in one respect at least to be a solution to a non-problem. The internal situation, as we have noted in passing, can only be regarded as a fantasy. Thus, it is all very well to infer that the imaginary merger of self and other in a "group" augments the self's struggle with conscience, but this does not account for the fact that conscience is imagined in the first place.

We can account for conscience by positing a reversal of the procedure by which conscience and self become fused as self—that is, an internal grouping. Under those circumstances, the fantasy seems to be that conscience and self are one and the same. But though that fantasy seems to evoke a feeling of great well-being, indeed, sometimes euphoria and elation, it will not work unless the self's relationship with conscience, which previously was based on differences, is replaced with a relationship based on differences with some other figure. Otherwise, a feeling of loneliness ensues. Conscience and self when differentiated give the illusion of an actual relationship.

That actual relationship between conscience and self was modeled on a relationship the person once had with some real external figure. But when it was real and external, it was also problematic in one of the ways we have been discussing. The choices were the usual (schematized) choices: endure, separate, fight, succumb—or group. Of these, grouping was the method of choice, and the individual then imagined himself to be at one with that other person. This, however, though it solved the problem posed by the distasteful nature of the other alternatives, proved not to be a good antidote for loneliness. As a result, another choice is forced: resume the external relationship and conduct it in one of the other modalities—endurance, fighting, etc.—or disgorge the other person from the self and conduct the relationship, *as if it were real*, in imagination. Since, at a given time, the first of the two choices means exchanging one painful situation for another, the second has more appeal. The relationship is conducted as a differentiated one, but in fantasy. If a differentiated relationship can be termed an I-Thou relationship, an I-Thou relationship in reality is replaced by an I-Thou relationship in fantasy.

At this point it should be said that not all of the real I-Thou relationships need be represented internally, nor need all of the I-plus-Thou-equals-Me relationships, which was the mid-stage of the devolution, be allocated to conscience.

The person who is to be imaginatively reconstructed and represented in a fantasied interior need not be assimilated *in toto*. We know that Dick and Jane, and Dick and Gloria, and Tom and Jane continue to conduct actual relationships in spaces which all regard as external, and yet at the same time each maintains figurative, inner relationships with the other inside (see the later discussion of the devolution of "inner" and "outer" spaces and boundaries). Likewise, only some aspects of the Thou person and only some elements of the relationship need to be taken in and moved about there.

The same appears to be the case for movements through internal boundaries. Jane may retain some of Dick for her self and assign some of him elsewhere. Similarly, she may take in Tom's point of view regarding sex and experience it as her own self's view or her conscience's. But it may well strike us that conscience is a word inadequate to describe these creations of fantasy. It suggests something far too forbidding, also too limited and unitary. In fact, people act as if they have a variety of Thou's represented internally and conduct many and varied relationships with them. Our own imaginations cannot be limited if we are to envision the fantasies other people have of the nature of their internal relationships. We are likely to be more accurate if we envision a state of affairs akin to a populous dream—indeed, a series of dreams. The cast may not be quite "a cast of thousands," but it is not a single voice of conscience either.

The separation of I from these internal Thou's is neither absolute nor resolute. Internal "groupings" take place much as external relationships ebb and flow—and, indeed, in fashions complementary each (internal and external) to one another. In creating an internal representation of a Thou, a person creates something akin to the Sorcerer's Apprentice, who, enlisted to solve one problem, lives on to create others. Thus, if the creation of a fantasy relationship makes up for the loss of an actual one, that fantasied relationship may go on to become a problematic one, necessitating external "grouping" to cope with it. This we may imagine was the case for Jane, who created "something (someone) in her" who she imagined could love her under certain circumstances, but who also, it turned out, could make her feel quite bad under others. Dick helped with this by augmenting her self in support of her relationship with Tom. But what if Dick should leave? Jane might continue to "retain" Dick in memory and self as an antidote to that someone in her. But what if, in the end, Jane should change her mind (self) about Tom? Now she will have inner-Dick to contend with as a new source of doubt. Will she be able to part with Dick altogether, sacrificing the good Dick whose approval of Tom makes him now a bad Dick, or, in hoping to hold on to the good Dick, will she have to offset the bad Dick with a new grouping with someone else?

Parsed this way, it can be seen that Jane's original inability to tolerate and endure one of her actual relationships led first to her replacement of that relationship, or aspects of it, with a fantasied grouping in and with her self, and then to a fantasied relationship based on greater differentiation placed within her conscience. These steps, in turn, lead to others—each taken out of the same motivation: to dilute suffering. With each maneuver, Jane hopes to preserve the hope that her dreams for the original relationship can come true, so that with each maneuver Jane replaces a bit of the facts of the original relationship with an additional bit of fiction as well as with the elements that emerge from each new relationship in fact and in fancy.

Much as one "group" may, while opposing another, challenge everything that other group stands for or contains, but may never doubt that the other is a group, so Dick, for his own purpose, may come to oppose Jane in every way but that of challenging the processes of fantasy she uses. His own use of these processes requires that Jane remain un-self-conscious of using them herself; together, therefore, they collude to remain unaware of their substitution of a process of fantasy for processes by which facts are maintained.

Such a collusive endeavor is evident in the very phenomenon with which we began this study of group theory: all those present in the groups we studied believed in grouping; none challenged that belief. These people used the classical hiding place for their belief; they put the belief in that most casual of places: the belief went without saying. Thereafter, the only matters that preoccupied the participants were tactical in nature. The problem was how to assure that others become one with the self and not with any of the internal others to which each participant plays host. The hope attached to this we have already analyzed: it is to augment the self vis-à-vis internal representations of differentiated others. This means that others deemed similar are to be assimilated into the self.

Let us now turn to the groups we have studied. There is a "leader" present, and with this we come upon a new dimension. Not only does each participant's self want augmentation vis-à-vis internal figures, but also each wants augmentation in respect to the external figure of the differentiated leader. Since the leader is external, assimilating others into the self is not the useful thing; each person's self must be attributed to some external locus.

The participants, accordingly, re-invent and then invoke the concept of "the group." And they operate in reverse of Dick's and Jane's mode of "taking in" others: they project their selves out and into the group. The colloquial word they use for this is being "open"—open so that what is within can issue *forth*. The fantasy is that the psychic domain, like the actual physical self, possesses conduits through which substances capable of "making" a group can pass out. The driving fantasy is that the self, or parts of it, can pass from within the boundaries of an individual and fill up the finite space of the group.

Once out there, commingled with the issuances of other "members," the self (or parts) creates an entity called the group. This entity is in one sense an objective correlative of the self; but it is, in another respect, taken to be the whole that is greater than the sum of its parts, as an army is more than the soldiers, a country more than its people, or a team more than its players. Once this entity is formed, *it* rather than its elements can (people seem to believe) be reassimilated into the self, where, far more than Dick could to Jane or Jane to Dick, it can augment the self.

But the now-created group is also believed to have great force in respect to the external object of the group's interests—the "leader," or some other Thou. Jane was not only able to deal better with that "something in her" thanks to her grouping with Dick, but, we should not be surprised to hear, she might have hoped to deal better with Tom. This comes about partly out of the increased confidence she gained within but partly too because Tom might have been more impressed by Dick and Jane together—two against one—than by Jane alone.

The "group" then hopes and trusts that its wish for a differentiated and reciprocal relationship with the Thou they have selected will be the more realizable thanks to their having become a group. The fantasy is that they are now collectively worthy, or at least substantial enough to avoid having to endure, succumb, or separate. If it comes to a struggle, they are strong enough to compel the Thou into a reciprocal relationship.

So cherished and believed is this fantasy, and all the subsidiary fancies that go into its making, that should it prove to be fallacious the whole edifice of fantasy threatens to collapse, leaving behind, like so much rubble, only absolute hopelessness. The leader, of course, does not participate in this reciprocal relationship. The only remaining fantasy is that the external other, the leader, has so much more substance than the "group" that he is awesome indeed. Universal panic results, and separation or flight or a frozen succumbing seems finally the only alternative remaining.

Complete collapse, of course, is not the only alternative. Failing an adequate response from the object of the group's hopes—the Thou— the group can find other objects. It can, for example, divide into two "subgroups," each of which can work out a We-Thou relationship with one another. Such subgrouping is believed to preserve the grouping from "disintegrating" into a series of I-Thou relationships, with the affiliate loss of self-augmentation as a source of effect on inner or external others. And it provides a temporary measure against losing the relationship the participants hope still to find with the original Thou. Because all participants share in the belief in and contriving of this strategy, the grouping remains intact, despite appearances of sub-grouping.

There are other tactics besides subgrouping. All, in any case, are important mainly for the fantasy they are trying to realize. That fantasy, as we have seen, is in two parts, the first of which relates to the object or objective of the "group's" interests, the other of which to the hopes of the individuals who make up the grouping. The first fantasy seeks satisfactions based on reciprocal differences. It is aided by reference to persons deemed to be different and hence outside the perimeter of the group. The second fantasy seeks self- or group-augmentation from within the group.

The two sources of gratification are designed to work complementarily, but it turns out that there is a conflict between them. The conflict is rather similar to that which Jane faced with Tom. If she were to feel at one with Tom, she would have to side with him against her sexuality, striking a compromise between satisfactions requiring difference and those requiring commonality. The hope of people in respect to the group is that this will not be necessary. The belief is that by splitting the two kinds of satisfactions in two and assigning the fulfillment of one sort to the group and the other to the person who is deemed different, both sorts of satisfaction can be received without the need to diminish either one by compromising. Were this hope to work out, there would be no need for choice and hence no conflict.

But hopes can remain hopes only insofar as they remain unfulfilled, whereas satisfactions cannot be realized unless desires are fulfilled. Much as the "group" might wish it to be otherwise, there is an irreconcilable conflict between hopes and satisfactions. Satisfactions suborn and weaken hope by virtue of the immediate pleasures they afford, tempting people to be satisfied with feeling satisfied. Hopes require that the potential be better than the actual.

In the face of satisfactions, the "group" elevates its expectations, while in the face of frustrations it can preserve its hopes. When the self is so augmented, as by grouping it is imagined to be, hopes once abandoned appear to be reassumed, and hope becomes boundless. The hatred of succumbing is experienced with great force, unimpeded by the effective "presence" of inner or external others. When "grouped," people feel themselves able to begin as if for the first time—to begin again with all the private mourning and reconciliations they have gone through, all the enduring and suffering, set aside. They hope that they can now triumph over all those who challenged their dreams in the past.

The concept of satisfaction based on differences is familiar to us, partly because psychoanalytic thinking has focused more on it. But some consideration might, nevertheless, prove useful. We have seen that from time to time people feel it is both necessary and possible to rid themselves of certain sorts of experiences. One of these experiences is that of desire. When experienced, desire can become transformed into satisfaction and fulfillment, but it can also shade into tension, frustration, and deprivation, all of which may prove exceedingly frightening and painful. Since the painful consequences of desire are thought to hinge upon desire itself, people may be tempted to rid themselves of desire.

Desire, however, is extraordinarily difficult to get rid of, rooted as it is in the appetitive and sensual nature of the organism. But the experiencing of desire is something else again: people feel that they can get rid of the experiencing of desire or, failing that, their knowledge of the experiencing of desire, provided only that a place be found for it.

A desire to bite the breast, for example, may be dealt with in the following ways. A baby, let us say a boy, may divide himself into two: a self which does not experience a desire to bite and a not-self which does. The self will be organized to remain in ignorance of this not-self. The not-self may be located in a part of his body, for example, his penis. Since location of desire can change in time, the penis may, at a later time, no longer serve as a useful vessel for urges to bite. The urge to bite may then be reassigned elsewhere—to the breast itself, to someone else's mouth, or to someone else's penis, or to the vagina. Once a place has been found, the urge to bite may be tamed by its new host in ways in which its original owner could not tame it. The new host may, for example, be assumed to have the desire in reverse, now desiring one, as if one had now become the breast. Or the new host, we may assume, wants to free himself of the desire attributed to him or her by insinuating it back into one. Under these circumstances, one may well feel that prudence dictates either the conversion of the desire into its opposite or avoidance of the host currently containing the desire. Thus when the new repository of the desire is someone (or part of someone) other than a part of one's person, that someone is transformed by the addition of the desire. The Thou one dealt with previously, for example, now has a breast that wants to bite one. The previous relationship that obtained will be dramatically changed, and this will prove fateful for the conversion of an actual I-Thou relationship into an "interior" one. The Thou with which one conducts either the actual relationship or the relationship in fancy will no longer be the actual Thou but a Thou transformed by the addition or subtraction of the characteristics of desire.

These fantasies concerning where and how desire can be reallocated are often made before the culture has been able to make its recommendation—as, for example, when the baby is quite young. Nevertheless, the mother who believes the worst concerning the dangers inherent in the breast (or bottle) may be capable of stimulating or reinforcing an infant's disposition to use the breast as a vessel for wishes whose authorship he wishes to disclaim. One mother nurses her baby, offering the breast. The baby roots for the nipple in a series of head-ducking movements. Upon connecting, he sucks vigorously. The mother sees that the baby's nose is pressed close against her breast. She retracts the breast which, as it happens, withdraws the nipple. The baby, rooting, seeks the nipple. The same series of events ensues. Finally, upon the latest loss of the nipple, the baby refuses to suckle. As the mother, leaning toward the baby, brings the nipple to him, he turns away crying. The desire has passed, as it were, from baby to breast.

But the nature of these fantasies may prove to be idiosyncratic in respect to the prevailing culture. The reprocessing of experience which any one individual makes may not be consonant with the processing or revisions others prefer. Insofar as the success of the operations on experience require secrecy, the existence of several versions of experience threatens the security of each one's version. Pluralism or relativism are in these circumstances endangering. People are offered alternative beliefs instead, in order that all may reach consensus, absolutism, and universality. Individuals may find it convenient to replace an idiosyncratic allocation of desire—from one's own mouth to mother's breast—with a culturally "validated" assignment—from our mouths to the enemies' mouths. Even if an individual does not redesign experience to obtain greater consonance with the culture (though if the culture is a breast that bites, he may feel it wiser to do so), he will at least feel tempted to borrow from the culture the fictions with which he replaces those experiential facts that he has found too painful.

That is, under simple sorts of exchanges, as between breast and mouth, the only change is in who desires. But this way of coping with desire may not work very well. Desire may not be so easily got rid of; indeed, desire is quite difficult to get rid of. Easier to get rid of is the knowledge about one's desire. Therefore, knowledge rather than desire is the first casualty in the struggle to revise experience. Knowledge can be denied, forgotten, banished. But in that case it leaves a space where it once was. That negative ("not this") space, from which experience or fact has been subtracted, functions better if filled with a fiction ("not this but that"). Since the fact may be remembered, triggered to recollection by some associational shard, or relearned from subsequent experience, the substitution of fiction for fact helps more than the simple absence of knowledge can. It further helps if the fact that a fact has been got rid of is also forgotten, and it helps even more if, to fill the space left by that now-forgotten item, the fiction that what instead is "so"— the case—was always "so." That "so-ness" is even more invulnerable to the testimony of fact if other people can be induced to attest to it—at least in words, but preferably in actions. Thus if many agree that breasts desire mouths and mothers devour babies, the "fact" that the mouth contains no desire seems truer as a result. If, further, the mother/breast can be induced to devour/desire the mouth/child, the desire may be located without question. Mothers do desire their children as breasts do "desire" being suckled: these facts, however, are employed to sustain a fiction. Mothers with extraordinary desires for their children may thereby assist their children in their efforts to deny their own desires for their mothers; the *quid pro quo* in which the mothers' desires are linked to the children's rather than to the desires of others (the mothers' own mothers, for example) suggests the complicity possible between one person's need not to know and another's. The management of desire and the acknowledgment of desire is a vital activity both in the formation of "groups" and the use of group "membership."

Having discussed desire and satisfaction, let us now come to a discussion of hope. As we contemplate people's fantasies concerning grouping, we gain the impression that people are Platonists: they act and react as though there were an ideal to which all that is real only approximates. It is difficult to account for this conviction. Some people experience the ideal as though it were something to return to—a paradise lost—and some theories have it that such a conviction implies a wish to return to such early times of fulfillment as infancy or the womb. This might be a tenable explanation were there certain evidence that the womb is remembered or that infancy was ideal, but there is no certainty about the first and some certainty that infancy is something less than ideal. Other people experience the hope as one toward which to strive— a paradise gained. Were there certainty about a heavenly afterlife, this belief too might be explicable, but once again the ideal is located in the future by people who do not believe in an afterlife of any sort.

Some theories have it that since the real is so disappointing, people comfort themselves with an ideal, as if to say: "There must be something better than this!" But this leaves the question of what the disappointing reality is compared to. One answer could be that one's own experience is compared to what *others* enjoy. Yet those "others" may neither enjoy nor feel they enjoy more than do those who are comparing themselves to them. If one supposes that a misperception, uncorrected, nevertheless supplies the comparative standard, such a reply does not account for why the overestimation takes place.

Once arguments based on experience fail, it becomes tempting to replace any kind of "nurture" with some sort of nature thesis: perhaps there is something inborn or inherited, something in a racial unconscious. Ethologists have added to our understanding of in-built readinesses or reflexes, showing that much as a newborn duckling will freeze at an overhead shadow, so does the newborn infant turn his mouth to a pressure on his cheek—and it is conceivable that there is an inborn expectation of good things and bad.

This thesis, which requires a mental representation to be conjured up or congenitally "remembered," competes for credibility with theories that rest on creativity. Such a theory might argue that people invent an ideal much as they invent anything else, by making an inductive leap from the experienced to the possible. A theory such as this is akin to structural theories in anthropology and linguistics, and parallels gestalt theories in psychology, in imputing, as it does, an inborn readiness to depart from experience and construct something new or different.

Whatever the explanation, it does appear that people imagine ideal versions of experience and that these versions hold claim on their activities by virtue of the hopes invested in these ideals. Whatever the origins of this idealizing process, it also seems that experiences are ransacked in order both to provide evidence for the ideals and to buttress or insulate the hopes invested in the ideals against erosion by the continuing presence of perceptual-sensory reality. Thus people may choose one instance here and another there, overlooking contrary or modifying examples, in order to fuel their hopes and reinforce their ideals.

Is the belief in groups a reincarnation of such an ideal? Our own inference is that it is. People appear to contrast the group with the differentiated object of their desires, assigning to the object the function of providing them what they want and lack, while to the group they assign their hopes of having (rather than needing) and being (rather than becoming). The group, we have remarked, is an empty potential which people imagine they can fill. Once imagined—hence, presumably, filled—the group is experienced as if it were an entity, present, palpable, sufficient, as if so many fractions have made an integer. The group then appears to be a manifestation of completeness. People feel capable of being both contained by the group, as within something like a circling embrace, and yet having—containing—within the group a sense of fullness and plenty. It is as if, in the group, people at once contain bounty and are contained by it: they have, they are. Or, at least, this is the ideal and the hope.

But the presence of the group's object, the Thou, appears to stimulate longings and, in stimulating longings, questions the fantasy of being complete and replete, jeopardizing hope. Thus, no matter how fulfilling the object, indeed the more fulfilling the more so, the object becomes a source of envy: he or she, containing what the group hopes to contain and be contained by, appears better to approximate the group's hope of being replete and complete than does the group itself. We must conclude, therefore, that the group's attitude toward the object is twofold. It wishes to fuse with that object—to contain it and to be contained by it—but at the same time to *refuse* benefits the object might afford.

If, in the psychology of individuals, investments of hope and pleasure in the self take over when receipts from others fall short, then in the psychology of people's theories about grouping, transactions with "others" only take over when investments in the self prove insufficiently fulfilling. Grouping represents an attempt to supersede needing others and to make those others superfluous.

If our inferences concerning people's fantasies about groups are approximately correct, we should expect to find that their behavior in situations which they take to be group situations follows identifiable patterns expressive of these fantasies. Chief among these patterns should be those expressive of the fundamental duality of hope versus desire. That is, we should expect to see behavior primarily motivated by hope and behavior primarily motivated by desire, with oscillations between these two.

In behavior governed by hope, there will be fantasies that the group is replete and complete, expressed through self-fulfilling activity and an indifference to or scorn of what the group's object has to offer. If we term that object the Thou and for convenience's sake place that Thou vis-à-vis the group as its Eucharistic leader (Slater 1966), we will expect to find the group going on about its business as if that Thou, the leader, had nothing of value to offer. Instead, the group will find sufficiency and value in simply *being*, or, failing that, in engendering experiences for itself.

If the fantasy of people who take themselves to be members of groups is that collectively they embody the be-all and the end-all of things, they will act as though their ability to enjoy and sustain that fantasy is subject to two sources of jeopardy. One consists in the emergence of desire in the members; desire, since it forces an acknowledgment of the desirability of someone or something outside the group, routs the hope that the group contains all that is necessary. The second blow to that hopeful fantasy comes about insofar as the "group" is not desired by others; for if the group embodies all that is desirable, how is it that others do not desire it?

Although the threats are from different sources, they bear a relationship to one another. If, in the first instance, the members wish to "rid" themselves of the stirrings of desire, they can the more easily remain oblivious of their desires by attending to whatever desire may be evinced by others, especially by that other who might otherwise be the object of their desires. Similarly, to be desired can satisfy hope sufficiently so that desire can be the better resisted. The corollary to these is that when the potential object of the "group's" desires fails to desire the "group," the members experience that other as containing more and better of what they hoped to embody, which then stimulates intense desire while shattering hope.

A good deal of activity, accordingly, will be directed to preventing any member from looking to a Thou, especially that Thou who is most easily available and, as such, represents the greatest temptation to abandon a We-Us position for a We-Thou, namely, the leader. If the group cannot prevent this looking-to-a-Thou, it will try to substitute itself for that Thou. One or more members will be stimulated to try and supply the material or services that the straying member or members seek. Subgrouping, as we have seen, is thus one alternative by which to maintain hope within the group.

Failing that, the group will attempt to influence the doubting Thomas to look beyond the leader to some other Thou. God has historically served this purpose; the belief in God made people relatively immune to the demands or delights of Caesar. But whatever the incarnation of the Thou, it will be offered as a palliative, a promise, not a remedy with any actuality or substance. Its offer will be designed to maintain the members' faith in the group by placating them with hopes sufficient to temper their desires.

If this measure also fails to enshrine hope above desire, the object of the errant members' desires will be denigrated and denuded of value, and the implication will be plain that this fate, akin to wearing the scarlet letter, awaits any other member who strays toward that Thou. At the same time the value of what the group contains and is contained by will be escalated. Great value will be found in people's silent thoughts and fantasies, other activities or engagements, relationships with other Thou's. Failing all of this, the group will feel depressed, as if hated and persecuted by the inner Thou's over which they now imagine they have also failed to triumph. This state of affairs will reveal itself in apathetic, dispirited behavior.

At this point, desire is likely to threaten to outweigh hope, for all members of the group are feeling quite hopeless. Where previously it was preoccupied with the leader, now it becomes occupied with him. But what it wants from the leader is a restoration of hope, not gratification of its desires. The group wishes the leader would take in what it is and has been, and then offer to the group, as might an adept portrait artist to his subject or a talented conductor to a composer, a version of itself that restores its flagging hopes. It wants to be made good and nice and sufficient. The leader is thus to be employed as a Mosaic or instrumental leader; the group is not ready to concede to him the possibility of being a Eucharistic leader.

Under the pressure of these wishes and the now rampant criticism from the inner Thou's, the group is prepared to begin weeding out its less than ideal members. This eugenic preoccupation may begin with efforts to convert members to the ideal, but can end with attempts to "purify" the species. Inquisitions, witch hunts, and exactions of good faith will precede, accompany, and follow the effort to have the new Mosaic leader restore the group to its former glory.

The group will, however, feel frightened of the leader: it has tried to repudiate him in the past and still wishes to do so. And it now wishes to have the leader come "into" the group, away from his Thou position into a prime-ministerial position. This is not done with the intention of outright destruction, but it is an attempt to deprive the leader of his actual position by making him into an inner Thou whom the group can use at its pleasure or with whom it can group. None of these efforts are ever wholly renounced but, if they do not succeed, they become latent to, yet modifying of, the pre-eminence of desire. For now desire becomes paramount, and the group becomes frankly occupied with the task of winning gratification from its Thou.

The experience of desire brings with it either envy or jealousy—but in either case, rivalry. The group wants gratification, wants the leader to provide it, but continues to want to have, possess, and control the Thou they now acknowledge to contain or be contained by the gratification they want. As such, they view themselves at odds either with the leader's autonomy over those parts of him (or her) they covet or in competition with whomever they imagine the leader prefers to provide these to. Since these realizations go hand in hand with the acknowledgment of desire, hatred and longing go hand in hand as well. The accompanying hatred arouses guilt, fears of retaliation, fears for the Thou's safety and well-being, and, beyond that, fears for what the group desires from the Thou. Insofar as these fears prove to be unfounded, the group will feel much relieved, but the sense of relief will be set against the group's realization of its impotence and helplessness. This latter realization will further erode the group's hopes for itself, and it may need once more to attempt to buoy up its hopes even at the expense of its desires.

To avoid this contingency, the group goes about attempting to influence its object into requiting its desires in so ample a measure that gratitude will supplant envy and satiety will outmatch jealousy. But the specific desires of each individual will be as different as each individual is from the others. In mobilizing to address the leader-Thou collectively in respect to desire, the members of the group must compose their desires into commonality. This process becomes their first priority.

Next they must compose the means by which their ends are to be fulfilled. This involves, among other things, reconciling each member's preferred and repudiated tactics with the likes and dislikes of the others, and weighing the outcome of these deliberations in terms of each person's theory concerning what will influence the leader-Thou. So formidable is this task that the absolute consensus for which the group strives is not easily, if ever, achieved. If it is not achieved, the united front the group has hoped to present to the leader-Thou and their inner Thou's is weakened. And this, in turn, may require a scaling down of the most ardent desires and boldest means. Scaled down, the original intentions are frustrated, and the frustration gives rise to efforts on the part of the members to convert each other from a status too like the leader of the inner Thou's to one identical with the group "self." These efforts also need to precede, if not the first attempt at gaining satisfactions, then the second, third, and fourth.

But even if the participants can gain consensus on ends and means, and even if they can achieve the satisfaction of their more urgent desires, this satisfaction will be less than they hoped for because their hopes of grouping are so extravagant. So once more the group will feel torn between hope and desire, and once more it may return to a quest for hope in preference to desire.

Assuming such a return to behavior governed by hope—indeed, assuming a series of such oscillations—the group may, in time, return to desire. With that return, the group will have to make a choice between certain of its hopes—for example, its hope for omnipotence vis-à-vis the Thou or the hope for longing unaccompanied by hatred, fear, or guilt. Yet even if it manages these renunciations, it will be confronted with the probability that the very pleasures for which it abandoned its hopes and ideals will prove to be less engaging than it wished and, in its wishes, believed.

That realization can be met either by modifying the belief or by an increase of envy, jeopardy, and hatred. When the group adopts the former stance, it will of necessity weigh once again the issue of whether desire is worth the decrease of hope. Where it adopts the latter stance, it will suffer the very jealousy of hope out of which it came to believe in the group. But perhaps by now the capacity to suffer both the abandonment of hope and the pain of absent pleasures will have increased the group's willingness to take pleasure in those desires that are gratifiable and gratified. If so, there will be fewer, shorter, and less sharp oscillations. When this develops, there will be less of a wish to replace actual Thou's with inner representations, and consequently a diminished need to use grouping as an antidote to problems with inner Thou's.

With the need for grouping vis-à-vis inner Thou's reduced, grouping in respect to actual, external Thou's can proceed in ways more appropriate to the actual requirements of the situation. Greater differentiations can now "take place"—differences can be acknowledged—between members of the same group, and divisions of labor based on those differences can be employed. These divisions, accompanied by greater autonomy for each of the participants relative to others, serve to enhance the ability of the several to pursue their related (probably no longer identical) objectives.

What we see in the final analysis, then, in the fantasies involved in believing in groups is an antidote to the envy and feelings of helplessness aroused when the fantasy that two people are but one and that one, one's own self, gives way to a recognition that people are distinct, separate, and autonomous—and that they are less than fully and mutually reciprocal. The function of a grouping vis-à-vis actual differentiated people is regarded as having an equivalent functional counterpart in "inner people" who behave "within" as also distinct, separate, autonomous, and less than fully and mutually reciprocal to one's desires and who also arouse envy and helplessness instead of gratitude and satiety. What happens in groups is the story of the vicissitudes of these twin antidotes when applied to the actuality of the public situation.[2]

This, then, constitutes our theory of groups, as observed in our experiment. Not all the groups described in Part II had the strong leader necessary to make the foregoing dynamics operate with exact balance and precision, but the ever-present conflict between hope and desire, the conflicts among various inner selves and with the leader, the subgroupings, the I-Thou values—in short, all that we have seen—will be readily recognized by the reader. To illustrate them would prolong this theoretical chapter. There remains but one phenomenon to consider—that of the maintenance of the status quo. This we shall discuss in Chapter 21.

---

[2]For an extended discussion of the theory and therapy of hope, see H. N. Boris, "On hope: Its nature and psychotherapy," *International Journal of Psycho-analysis,* accepted for publication.

CHAPTER TWENTY-ONE

THE STATUS QUO IN GROUP BEHAVIOR

We undertook our study of groups in the late 1960s, a time of social upheaval (Keniston 1965, 1970; Slater 1970). The movements for peace, welfare reform, black unity, women's rights—to take but a few examples—were in full swing. Although we have no objective way of characterizing those teachers who chose to participate in our project, it was clear that a large proportion of them were much concerned with social change. They regarded themselves as activists. Few who thought of themselves as resistant to change would have volunteered.

During the course of the project an interesting relationship developed between those participants who declared their representation of social concern and activism and those who were designated by the "activists" as representing the status quo. In studying this relationship, we acknowledge that an artifically contrived group is clearly different from the larger community (Durkin 1964; Homans 1950) and that we should be cautious in drawing parallels between our group observations and larger social phenomena. However, our observations would seem applicable, at least in some ways, to the social behavior of certain natural groups.

With these reservations, let us take a look at one of *our* groups and then compare it to a natural group in terms of people's feelings regarding the status quo—keeping in mind the group activities we have seen previously, especially the group's complex relationship with the leader and the mechanisms of splitting and projection (see Chapter 2).

Of course, there is something in all of us that needs the status quo. An activist requires viable institutions and opinions to struggle against, just as much as a "conservative" clings to the status quo in the face of pressures for social change. For example, *any* teacher, whether conservative or liberal on the conscious level, will feel anxiety when faced with a newly integrated classroom. If a teacher has been fairly comfortable with the status quo, the black children may be seen as intrusive strangers.

If he has not, they may be seen as potential saviors. In the first instance, the teacher, unable to tolerate the full force of negative "intrusive stranger" feelings, and considering the feelings "unworthy" (a frequent experience in our volunteer sample), might hide them from himself or herself and inexplicably hear anger and impatience from the black children. The teacher who looks to the black children to change the classroom and is disappointed when they do not may deal with this disappointment by exalting the black child and blaming the white child, who (by way of his parents or previous social experience) represents resistance to change. In either case this preoccupation with the status quo joins both types of teachers—at the unconscious level. Consciously, however, the pair see themselves as dissimilar to the point of being in disagreement.

These seemingly opposing teachers tend to have other conscious attitudes in common (Ashton-Warner 1963). They usually share a desire for more direct action, though they would hope for opposite solutions from such action. They long to work toward clearly defined ends and wish to avoid the study and use of the changing, ongoing classroom process. They wish to remain "out there" with definable institutions and opinions to struggle against.

All the teachers we observed were a part of an ongoing process of social change. They were not necessarily aware of each other's feelings, and perhaps did not recognize that each was struggling for a goal antithetical to that of the others. We felt such opposition keenly before we began the project, and we observed that it impeded the achievement of useful social goals. We saw participants trying to heal this rift. Their attempts all too often followed the same pattern. The participants confronted each other, tried to work out a solution acceptable to all, and ended up shouting and gesticulating, urging and exhorting. The confrontations occasionally made the teachers feel better. They seldom produced a solution. Sometimes committees and subcommittees were formed in which theorizing, organizing, investigating, and reporting became ends in themselves.

In general, the group process occurs in the following manner: each group member begins by desiring some sort of betterment. In order to make this clear to the other members and to the leader, an "activist" must distinguish himself as desirous of change. In order to secure this position in the group, other group members must be declared, or induced to represent, the opposition. (Watching this process, an observer might surmise that if the group could not find someone to represent the status quo, it would have to invent such an opponent.) If the status quo representative in the group were to shift position, another representative would have to be found. But it is by no means clear that the allegations supporting the "charge" of supporting the status quo are factual. These distortions often came to the attention of the activists. They were momentarily abashed at the license they had taken with others' positions, but they soon set off on a fresh tack. By requiring more and more proofs of the good faith and good intentions of those they took to represent the status quo, they were able in time to make their demands so excessive that few could meet them. Those who tried would ultimately give up and counterattack, accusing the activists of too much zeal. In this counterattack, the activists were able to "see" the retrograde reactionary trends that they had all along claimed to exist. If this further pressed the status quo group to harden their defensive positions, it was doubtless the fault of the activists. The remarks of both sides seemed calculated to stimulate the opposition. Thus it seemed to us that if the status quo created activists, no less did the activists create the status quo. A symbiosis had been established.

The groups insisted upon divisiveness in order to distinguish and compare themselves. Subsequently, they wanted to repair the intolerable division, for "united we stand; divided we fall." A sense develops that too great an argument, too strong a stand on the conflict will disintegrate the group. Therefore, the members believe that to repair the immediate internal split will bring about a resolution within the group and a chance to decide together how to bring about social change outside of it. Various ways of repairing, getting together, or integrating are offered. But in their desire to find the "right" way to come together, both sides lose sight of the assumptions they originally shared. They are unaware of their intolerance of the struggle, of the fact that allegiances can change, and, above all, of how, in the process of searching for this "right" way, initial goals have become different from and more complex than they were in the beginning.

Let us look briefly again at one teachers' group. A group meeting began with one man reporting on a conference which he had attended on education of minority groups. He reported that the conference came up with a number of do's and don't's for teachers, such as do not judge others; do be open and communicative, etc. The group members listened but responded only minimally. Soon, however, they began to talk of how hard it is to do anything, personally, to change things: all very well to *say* these things, but what to *do*. When the leader wondered why it might be that people feel the need to take action, and at the same time find it difficult to do so, a number of group members said that this was because of the "administration," the attitudes of the less activist-oriented teachers, or other reasons. Most of the group agreed that these outside forces prevented one from accomplishing much.

Mr. W took issue with this position. He stated that while one can't do *everything*, one can at least do *something*. He then told of five consecutive meetings which he had attended. All were meetings of action groups with a particular task to accomplish. The rest seemed somewhat stunned by Mr. W's activities and those of his groups. The group leader wondered how such experiences compare with experiences in *this* group; he wondered whether the group was still pondering the question with which it began: what can and should a group like this—an open group, without any agenda—do? The group began to discuss this; they asked each other whether they should talk about topics or about themselves.

Mr. J said that clearly "selves" took precedence. Others thought "topics" should be the primary subject. Miss Q told of a group she attended which was run very differently: you weren't *allowed* to talk about outside topics. Mr. J described what he had told his wife about several group members. Other group members told what they had first thought of each other.

Mr. J said that he was so pleased that people were talking about selves that he must continue to marvel at the way most people in groups relate to each other. For instance, he said, he went to a meeting on a housing plan where the group was divided into two camps. The very same evening his wife attended a women's liberation meeting where two factions were at each other for the following reasons . . . As the group listened, a number of people began to pick up on the topics Mr. J raised—this or that housing plan, this or that stance for women. They began to discuss these topics. Then the topics waned, the discussion became listless.

The group noticed, with wry amusement, that it had begun discussing topics rather than selves. Everyone resolved that next time they would conduct themselves like the group Miss Q described: they would only talk about the here-and-now of the group experience. All seemed pleased with this resolution.

Even in this capsule session, a number of things are going on. The opening salvo is a characteristic but unconvincing prescription for better relationships among people, which the group passively resists. The members feel a conflict between the need to take action and the need to be sure that it is a *good* action. The group agrees for the moment that outside forces prevent them from taking that "good action." Mr. W does not let this repair last long. He brings in the "do what one can" position that exalts change. The group is disappointed by its lack of unity and by its own failure to take any "good action." The leader responds by asking them to study the process as it occurs within the group, rather than outside of it. Having been identified by Mr. W as the status quo (because of their acceptance of it) the rest of the group looks for a way to "do better," to repair the split in its midst. Mr. J suggests that Mr. W and he, being so much alike, can join paths: alliance and activism. Miss Q offers a "right way" that is a little more acceptable because it is backed by the outside authority of a group designated as active. Since this new solution supports Mr. J as the activist, he proceeds to "do something." But the more Mr. J "takes action," tries to change the group's status quo by talking about "selves," the more the group picks up the issues or topics he mentions in passing. This group, like all groups, tries continuously to repair the damage and to contain possible conflicts. It becomes bland and bored, as though unity will be destroyed if anything is said which allows members to stand for good social change and to do good in the group. When the group decides that it can still try Miss Q's solution, it is charged with new resolve.[1]

Now for the next session: Mr. J, who had discussed himself most directly, and who (the members now say) criticized the rest of the group for "not getting to know each other better," was absent. An argument began about the correctness of his putative criticism. Mr. W maintained that you get to know people better through their talk of topics, issues, events, and opinions from their daily life. Miss Q reacted defensively and reiterated her position of the previous week that you get to know people better through their talk about themselves and how they feel here and now. She got some support, but nothing like the general agreement at the end of the previous session. The old topics-versus-selves argument was extended and became more bitter. The division seemed irreparable. Side A (Mr. W and supporters) had split from Side B (Miss Q's subgroup) by seeming to say: we can't get to know you because your way of getting to know people is not our way of getting anywhere or effecting change. Therefore it must be wrong.

The underlying assumption, shared by both sides, is that something needs to be done—in this case getting to know one another—and that the group must find the "right" way to do it. The members cling to this hope of knowing each other, although neither side is willing to compromise its position and believes itself to be anxious for action and against

---

[1]The "topics" versus "selves" argument is one that teachers must often deal with in their classrooms. The question of whether students learn more through discussing "topics" or through revelation of their own views and feelings on a subject is hotly debated in faculty meetings and classrooms (Bruner 1960; Clark and Erway 1971; Knobloch and Goldstein 1971; Rotter 1954).

Teachers are often confronted with the "good" class—one where the uniformity of the students is only surpassed by their docility. Discussion barely begins before it dies out in bland agreement. This superficial unity and widespread boredom suggests the powerfully divisive feelings that may exist underneath; in the same way our teachers' groups permit discussion to die in order to contain the conflict.

the status quo. Thus the group "decides" to conserve both sides of the question. Each side relentlessly supposes that thoughts and feelings which are intolerable and wrong continue to be espoused by the other side. We might venture that Mr. W, personifying Side A, is anxious to discuss topics and opinions because he is fascinated (revolted) by the possible revelations of feelings that accompany events. Side B, Miss Q, so anxious to explore these very feelings, human relations, might actually be showing a fearful interest in what people really do or do not do. Yet something prevents Mr. W and Miss Q from recognizing that their paths are not so different. With the compelling need for both sides to be maintained, the group comes to a curious, unspoken conclusion: nothing can be changed.

The activist believes himself to be virtuous, and behaves rather badly toward the status quo. He takes it to be the seat of iniquity. But with his eyes firmly on the virtue of *his* cause relative to the evil of the status quo position he can behave badly without being aware of it. The status quo side contains its own sense of virtue—relative to the destructive principles it sees in the activists—and it can also behave badly, and also without feeling ashamed of it. Neither side wants to stop behaving badly to the other. Both want to behave badly without feeling bad and also without recognizing their mutual dependence.

What do we mean by behaving "badly"? Let us assume each side wants to have a school system that is more and better integrated. The topics-versus-selves argument may present itself outside the groups as an argument over whether to teach black history or to put all teachers into a consciousness-raising group. In such an argument, neither side gives any quarter. Neither side can be sure that the other side doesn't want it to be responsible for the current situation—which, of course, is unsatisfactory and which, of course, must be changed, and which is what, in fact, each holds dear. One teacher of the "topics" faction may be willing to change his teaching content but not his method, or vice versa; another teacher, of the "selves" faction, may be willing to trade the intimacy of frank discussion of feelings for the privacy afforded by no specific description of how he acts, or vice versa. Each faction treasures a part of the status quo more than it realizes, and each faction fears that even a desire not to change *certain* things will brand it a traitor. And each person in the group joins first one, then another faction to conceal this secret, often particularly from himself.

We cannot help being impressed by the complementary intricacy of the system the factions devise for themselves. The very system, the very contrivance, is continuous, fixed, permanent. The activists deceive themselves not only by believing that they want to change the status quo but also by not acknowledging their part in the status quo.

Thus we can no longer speak of the status quo faction as those people whom the activists took to be the status quo faction. In fact, they were no more representative of the status quo than were the activists. That the factions imagined there were such differences was a shared illusion. The factual status quo was developed by both factions, equally and jointly. Each depended on it for the preservation of their symbiotic relationship. The group, we could say, *was* the status quo.

All this might be the complete scenario were it not for the fact that the groups had leaders who (as much as possible) wanted nothing for or from the participants. Of course, the group leaders could not *always* be neutral; they were human. They responded to the moods of the group. If someone were to become overtly disturbed, the leader would try to provide direct help. The leaders never doubted that the inequities that so disturbed the teachers existed, and that all would benefit if they were rectified. Their decision *not* to present a program that demanded something specific from the teachers and wanted something for them arose from the group interaction itself. They treated the groups as a shared experience, a voyage of discovery, a joint participation in the study of a process. This involved an agreement about a means to the end—the end being increased self-knowledge, greater tolerance of ambiguity, awareness of group pressures, less reliance on guilt to achieve goodness, and an increased sensitivity to small deceits. These ends, if achieved, are reached surprisingly spontaneously. Insight is a much belabored word but, when achieved, it is always with the surprised start that indicates that it was always nearby had one chosen to look that way. If the groups "worked," it was the leaders' awareness and acceptance of these non-activist goals that became the determining factors.

Because our group leaders wanted less from the factions than the factions wanted from one another or from the leader, they were generally free from the symbiosis. Less objective leaders—those who might have wished followership from members—inevitably would have created a secondary symbiosis which, in turn, depended upon the static continuation of the first symbiosis and the status quo. Objective leaders (like most of ours and, in time, some members) who find and accept symbiotic interests elsewhere (for all human beings are mixtures of longing for change and fear of change, even of moving the spot where one keeps the toothpaste) can remain neutral toward their group, thereby introducing a volatile element in the determinedly static state of the group.

Such volatility stems from the fact that the leader neither needs the members to be as they are nor needs them to be different. Curiously, far from taking this laissez-faire posture as an encouragement to freedom, as might people in a commensal disposition, people in a symbiotic position focus only on the leader's freedom. Since they cannot use freedom for themselves, other people's freedom must be captured and drawn into a symbiosis, as if it set a dangerous precedent and at the same time represented a loss of potential. The relative neutrality of the group leaders in our teachers' groups was no more accepted than was the superintendent's wish, in our next example, to focus on the question of the advantages of open classrooms rather than on his wisdom.

Lures, snares, threats—inducements of every description—ensue. The comparison-competition theme is most particularly played out. In every competition there must be a prize, and this is one great element in the volatility. The group leader is to be won over and revealed as a teacher with a lesson plan. Cast as trophy, the leader provides an incentive for movement away from the status quo ante. But even that momentum, with A and B now competing, is more a foray away from than a renunciation of the status quo. For the leader is to be won and brought back into the status quo position. If he cannot be captured alive, strong tendencies to destroy him awaken. But other consequences also follow. When the leader proves an unwinnable prize, the zest goes out of the competition. The factions begin gradually to undifferentiate themselves, subgroups coalesce. These subgroups emerge because each group member still seeks strength in numbers for his position. The groups shift constantly, though, for the sole object—the only goal of all subgroups—is to draw the elusive and alluring leader into a symbiosis. This is the hope of the group. To fulfill it, the group needs to stimulate the leader's hopes for it and of it. Only—and we cannot overemphasize this point—only the leader's capacity to stand fast can make it possible for the group members to abandon their hopes for symbiosis.

Whether the group will in fact abandon symbiosis is another matter, and one to which the leader of a dynamic group must be indifferent. As observers, however, *we* need not be indifferent to it. Freedom, fraternity, equality, equity—these are noble aims. During the life of the groups few participants professed other goals, just as few wished to allow for envy, greed, rage, sensuality, and fear of closeness and for the conflicts that emerge among such powerful feelings. Even fewer are consciously aware of the proposition that the status quo represents an equilibrium (a solution) that has kept these conflicts in relative abeyance. Tensions between reciprocities of license and jealousy, desire and gratitude, pain and empathy, and claim and restitution prescribe the degree of movement and the acceptance of change possible for anyone. People sense limits. High hopes, when based on unawareness, fear, and self-deceit, descend all too rapidly into hopelessness.

With all these observations in mind, let us now look at a public meeting. The account is taken from real life. Meetings like this one are doubtless familiar to every parent. At a public hearing conducted by the school committee of a suburban community, a group of concerned parents gathers to discuss the superintendent's proposal to inaugurate an "open classroom" program. In his proposal, it is clear the superintendent wants to be fair and at the same time wants to help the program find acceptance.

After he is through, the chairman of the school board calls for discussion. Three people in succession say that since the superintendent is experienced and trained and clearly knows more about these matters than "all of us parents do" they are prepared to support his program. Suddenly a man introduces himself as Mr. F and speaks heatedly. He is utterly against the program. It is too lax; it simply lets children have their own way.

Mr. F's remarks seem to have an incendiary effect. People who merely nodded as the previous three speakers expressed their deference to the superintendent now appear restless. One of those who did speak is heard to mutter, "There's one in every crowd."

Another man then introduces himself as Mr. E. He announces his name in exactly the same way F did, only a little more so. He takes a view opposite to F's. He concludes by saying that our children are the most important things in the world.

If we as classroom observers were able to stop the action at this point and review what had happened, we might find something like this. The superintendent wanted to be fair, but he also wanted to avoid being a target. His presentation was therefore low in profile. He tried to open discussion but avoid controversy. The next three speakers, however, offered support not for the program but for the superintendent, the opposite of what he wished. Suddenly he had become the personification of the issue.

Mr. F, in giving his name, seemed to identify himself as if to counterweigh the superintendent's high status. He was not going to defer as easily as that. The speaker before F made it clear that he was not surprised by F's activity. Did he also guess that his muttered comment would ensure that a man of F's nature would rise to react?

At that point Mr. E spoke. Whatever example the superintendent had tried to set was shunned by Mr. E. He himself was far from conciliatory; instead, he took the matter of children to a rhetorical extreme. We could guess therefore that no man of F's stripe would sit still in the face of this multiple bait. And we could equally guess that, when he next spoke, F would, if possible, further polarize the issue.

Sure enough, after forty-five minutes the meeting had heated up to the point of talking about Commie sympathizers and Birchites. But now most persons looked uncomfortable and restless. Then Mr. L got up. He wanted, he said, to try to get reason back into the room. At this many people nodded. But those who had been speaking nodded most vigorously of all. Mr. L went on to hold up the superintendent as an example of reason, a man who saw both sides of the issue. At this, Mr. E and some of those who had spoken on the superintendent's side of the issue broke into applause. If Mr. L had hoped to replace volatility with reason, it was now plain that he would not succeed. Almost at once Mr. F jumped up to speak.

Let us stop once more to look at the action. Have we been witnessing a failure of communication? To answer yes would seem to yield the comfortable feeling of being charitable. But that answer would also indicate that each of the speakers was ignorant or maladept. And chances are that they were neither. If, for example, Mr. L had wished to inflame matters further, he could scarcely have done a better job. He first called all the previous speakers unreasonable, an accusation which each could tolerate only long enough to cast it over to the other side, as E did pre-emptively with his applause. Second, implying his own superior reason, L went on to defer to the superintendent. F had already shown himself deeply sensitive to such an approach. Once again, the proponents of the open classroom had managed to stimulate opposition to it, and this at a time when, if nothing else, people felt tired of the goings-on and would have liked to resolve the issue.

Mr. F went on to say that he for one did not care what people thought of him. As far as he was concerned, the welfare of children was more important than their opinions of him or of anyone else. And since he felt open classrooms, like open forums, contributed nothing to children, he was against them. Children, he concluded, needed to do what was good for them whether they liked it or not.

After F finished speaking, the chairman of the school committee said that the hour was late, that the discussion had been informative and helpful, and that he and the committee appreciated people's frankness and participation. The meeting was adjourned.

If we further consider what went on at the meeting, we see a curious resemblance in F's last comment to E's first comment. Indeed, we are bound to feel that the two men are at once poles apart and as close as can be. An image comes to mind of F and E backing further and further away from one another until, having gone full circle, E's front is F's back and F's front E's back. The image may not be as surrealistic as it sounds.

Both factions could stand to lose something by compromising. Each tried to conserve his own position in its entirety. This much is obvious. But less obvious and no less true is that each managed to get the other not to give an inch. Nothing from either side was lost to compromise:

all the viewpoints remained intact and present. E felt that the evil attitudes lay in F, and F felt that the evil lay in E. Both were reassured by
this. As observers, we might feel that the open classroom itself somehow
got lost in the shuffle. It had been superseded in importance by the
wish to create the struggle on the part of those who spoke. First each
"dealt" the other the side he did not wish to contain in himself. Then
each, having gotten the other to do his own "dirty" work, made sure the
other did not shirk it.

Our illustration does not show what happens when one faction becomes ready to compromise. But what happens in such a case is simple
and, by now, predictable.

Mr. E: All right. Suppose we try it for a year. Then if you still object, we can get
back to what we have now. Now, can anything be fairer than that?

Mr. F: I can think of a lot that would be fairer. Like improving what we have
now, which we can't do if we're going to put teachers and money into this new
thing. Why don't we improve what we have for a year and then see?

Mr. E: All right. If that's what it'll take for you to see that what we have now is
bankrupt, no matter what is put into it, I'll go along with that!

Mr. F: O.K. Now what we have to do is get some teachers who'll do what it
takes, crack down, if they have to. And they'll have to be given free reign. Then—

By simply moving equidistantly away from wherever one party is
prepared to move, the other can preserve the split between them. We
can be reasonably sure that should the discussion continue and F move
toward E, E could "force" F away, back to equidistance again.

It happened that the controversy over open classrooms continued for
several weeks. One meeting followed another, with feelings running
high and participants dragging their friends along. Not only did one
side not want open classrooms, they wanted to throw out other innova-
tions, such as new methods of teaching social studies, reading, and
mathematics. On the other side, many proponents of the experimental
open classroom program were equally dissatisfied with the school and
hoped the experiment would be only the beginning of far-reaching reform. A stalemate developed. People stopped trading at stores where
they had been customers for years. The superintendent became discouraged; he too raised his voice and gesticulated when people refused to
listen, and soon he was saying, "Nothing ever gets done in this damn
community."

We find in this vignette a familiar symbiosis. Both sides refuse to
move and both in effect cling to the status quo. The leader-superintendent
wanted something for/from the group—open classrooms. He joined the
movement to persuade others of the rightness of his views and at first
tried in every way to conciliate them and to convince them rationally.

But because he wanted something from them, they required something from him: time to present their case. He found himself no longer conciliating, but bargaining. He began to "pay" for even the *appearance* of conciliation. Gradually he found that his wanting something from the other side not only gave them the chance to mount their opposition but strengthened their negativism by giving them a symbol to struggle against. The superintendent became increasingly authoritarian. His posture resulted in a stalemate, and the two opponents began to look more and more alike.

To an uninvolved observer, a great deal seemed to have been accomplished. More people were thinking, talking, and feeling about schools and methods of teaching than in many a year. It is true that this was not the original goal. It is also true that, had the superintendent been aware that he would have to expect disagreements and irrational changes in opinions from even his most enthusiastic constituents, the energy aroused in this controversy might have been constructively channeled.

Perhaps veterans of community battles will read that line and mutter "optimistic nonsense"; perhaps another will mis-hear and think that what was said was "Goals are never important." Not at all. Things must get done. School budgets are passed and some change/innovation occurs. But if this group leader had recognized the symbiosis in his audience, he might have made use of their differences. He might have found another important, controversial topic for discussion besides open classrooms. When many matters are discussed, people usually express different opinions and continually shift sides. When an opponent on one issue finds himself an ally on another, compromises begin to be possible.

Obviously the sorts of things we are thinking about apply to a wide range of groups and may vary in dimension. Some task-oriented groups are artificial, created only to do a specific job, and these easily disintegrate. Community groups have the advantage, or disadvantage, of being natural groups. They may fail in a particular task, but they cannot disintegrate. The leader is an intrinsic part of the group and represents the community task, so that capturing him only means joining a known point of view or changing leaders. His charisma, his enthusiasm for the task, *for a time* heals divisions and convinces some that the consequences of the change are almost all positive. This is a very different procedure from what we described in our teachers' groups. But the example above shows how short-lived that healing can be if the leader is unaware that one cannot shake foundations without paying a price.

It is not surprising that (although unaware that they do so) groups work together to proclaim, "Nothing can be changed; the status quo is acceptable, even though we hate it"; or "The status quo ante was, after all, preferable." If there is failure to achieve or disappointment in what

has been achieved, it will be possible to place the blame on someone
else and then to begin to decide who was justified.

Many of us have experienced a sense of devastation that our vision of
social change has proved so ephemeral. As our understanding of groups
of all sorts increases and we begin to see how these less conscious,
human psychological mechanisms influence the course of social change,
we may shift our interest at least a little. Few of us who have lived
through the recent epoch of hope for quick social change and resultant
disappointment intend to give up our goals. But we may recognize and
accept the fact that the very *process* of working to achieve changes in
institutions and opinions becomes of equal importance and will constitute
the essence of our lives.

CHAPTER TWENTY-TWO

EVALUATION, CONCLUSIONS, AND CAVEATS

This project began as an attempt to produce and study an educational innovation which would have concrete applications for social and educational change (Zinberg and Boris 1968). The Ford Foundation memorandum approving the project made these purposes clear; we have tried to show candidly how we not only did not fulfill these purposes but finally rejected them and adopted others. We knew that our project was funded to stimulate a new approach to teaching, potentially a "good" thing for schools; however, we came to see that mere ad hoc innovation was no solution, either to this situation or to any other. We decided that *implications*—i.e., the understanding of what in a particular place at a particular time made a change interesting or desirable—had more immediate priority than *application*.

Naturally, implications (theory) and application cannot be truly separated. They are interrelated. At some point, implications must lead to application. But we rejected the concept that a study like this one can be expected to end up with a definite, pragmatic judgment about an innovation—whether, for instance, it is "good" or "bad." Any evaluation of our project based on whether it reaches such a final judgment fails to accept the final goal of our project, which is to stimulate rational discussion and debate on (1) the research and (2) the educational "innovation." In our view, perspectives and approaches such as ours ought to be available for such discussion *now*, when educators, social science researchers, and others wondering about the implications of social change are contemplating their status quos. What they then do with our work and their discussion of it will vary with the place and the perspective each hopes to broaden.

THE RESEARCH

Any judgment as to the value of our research—whether it was "good," whether it accomplished its initial purpose, or other criteria—must be a relative one. It must take into consideration the ongoing interaction between research and the social change being studied, and it must take into account how the project worked. Drama critics ponder endlessly a similar question: how to evaluate—and to a certain extent all evaluation or judgment is comparative—a play that attempts a great theme but is flawed. A play that engages some basic human conflict, timeless yet changing, particularly if it takes history into account, cannot be accepted as worthwhile simply on the basis of its efforts. It may be pretentious, technically slovenly, or sophomoric. But given that it is not an obvious disaster, and also not *Hamlet*, how can a critic compare it, for his audience, with the bedroom farce he covered the night before? He can try to establish the play's context, but that may prove to be no easy matter, and willy-nilly he uses quite different standards for his judgment.

Can one make a valid analogy between a play and a social science research project? Are there not, or should there not be, more hard findings in social science—direct, absolute data from which to evaluate a body of research? Yes, there should be, and there are; but what is the standard to use in evaluating them? Can the findings from these groups be compared to questionnaire data, the work of a psychoanalysis, or the results of conditioned learning? If research is evaluated as good, does that mean its findings are valid? Does that mean the research was well done, or the evaluators' bias was confirmed? How do evaluators react when a "good" project, intended to accomplish A, accomplishes B in a different setting, or leads to C, which was unanticipated?

Let us offer a few examples of these complications from our project. James Laue in his evaluative report, quoted so extensively in Part I, found that our project, using group techniques in this area of affectful education, might well be a "good" thing—i.e., applicable—but that our research techniques were not going to "prove" it. With regard to the usefulness of our group techniques in this area, we have the problem of determining what would make it good for whom. Would it be good if the participants learned more facts about sex, drugs, prejudice, and so on? Would it be good if they changed their attitudes about these issues, which then raises the question of what these changes might mean to each individual's general psychic economy? Would it be good if they changed their behavior—if students used more or fewer drugs, if teachers were more or less "polite" to black students? Would it be good if they felt less inhibited about knowing about these issues? And so on and so on. What we found (and "found" is used to mean what our disciplined subjectivity told us) was that the way in which issues were raised and used in groups varied from year to year.

The Arlington groups, for instance, were affected by the changing issues in the larger society. For instance, Zinberg's observation of the

Arlington groups during 1967–1968 (Zinberg and Boris 1968) indicated that student drug use was a "heavy" topic and thus was avoided or brought in fitfully and suspiciously. Likewise, in his report on the 1968–1969 groups, J. M. Starr, a research associate, pointed out that, while students did discuss drugs and pool their information, the discussion often was turned away from the issue (Starr 1970): "If such discussion turned out to be too divisive (the topic tended to become *over*-valued), then all students had the delightful option of joining together in a free-wheeling assault on the stupid and oppressive adults who tempted them with such goodies, and then punished their indulgence in the first place. Each time that the latter kind of discussion emerged, the students were treated to a feeling of mutuality and togetherness (although only by virtue of their common exploitation)."

In his earlier report Zinberg said almost the same thing about sex discussions. He and Starr made the same observations about different issues—how a topic, no matter how important both objectively and in the discussants' own lives, simply lost its import as content and became part of a more enduring group-process issue. How can that be measured? Is it good for adolescents who are insecure and in conflict to have this feeling of mutuality based on their common exploitation? We could raise many such questions, all of which would be answered by saying we don't know.

In Laue's evaluation he says that we should try to determine whether these groups are or are not a good thing, depending on what we "find" in our research. Let us turn back to the Starr Report for a moment:

The most casual observer at Arlington (both high school and junior high schools) couldn't help but notice the martial air which prevails. Surely these schools are little different from any other schools in the U.S.—with their rigidly scheduled activities, hall monitors, lavatory monitors, endless profusion of rules, system of appropriate punishment, carefully articulated standards of proper apparel, youth code, P.A. systems, and segregated facilities for faculty and students—but then those schools look a lot like factories or Army posts too.

The researcher remembers some details with particular vexation. Perhaps worst of all was the whining, carping, badgering tone of many of the P.A. announcements. The official reading the announcement would fly off into an ill-tempered harangue of the students on more than a few occasions. Such an announcement would cut like a knife through whatever rapport the leader had managed to establish in his group. Of course, if all concerned are sensitive to this they can make the appropriate distinctions and adjust accordingly. Nevertheless, such announcements betray something of the total environment with which the students must come to grips, and the behavior often called for is not always consistent with sensitivity and self-respect. Many of these observations, as Zinberg has already indicated, apply to the teachers as well.

Two plaques hang outside the office of the principal of the West Junior High School. One was donated by the Veterans of Foreign Wars and contains instructions for the proper care and display of the flag. It also features slogans and cartoons exalting military virtues and deploring weak-kneed liberal intellectuals. Next to this is a quotation from Kant donated by a local bank: "Unrestrained Freedom is the Most Terrible of All Things." It's hard to tell whose sentiments these displays express. There isn't any evidence that anyone other than the researcher read them during the year of the study. Still, they do seem to fit the ambience of the whole institution. If students find it difficult to let up their guard and take a chance with a teacher and fellow students in a discussion of feelings and issues which are forbidden elsewhere in the school, then we must be ready to see this in perspective. Even a thirsty man will pass up an oasis if he thinks the water is poisoned.

Starr also discusses the many efforts that Roens, the school superintendent, made to change the school's authoritarian rigidity and the resulting conflict, particularly between Roens' approach and that of the older principal. Our groups, then, are part of an ongoing struggle (Kozol 1970; Novak 1970; Silberman 1971). How does that affect the groups, the research, and the struggle between Roens and the principal? All of this was also true of the METCO project, which was a focal point of conflict in most of the participating school systems, as discussed in Part I.

By pointing out the influence of the setting in which our project took place, we do not wish to join the many harsh critics of American schools. *Death at an Early Age* (Kozol 1970), *Crisis in the Classroom* (Silberman 1971), and many other books have put the blame for everything on the schools. They claim the schools themselves—their personnel, mode of instruction, and attitude toward education—are responsible for children's not learning or learning things in a way that interferes with their later integration into our functioning society. Our aim here is only to point out the influence of setting on our project, not to criticize the school system. This was our stance throughout the project, and it annoyed many who wanted to use what we were doing to show what was "wrong" with the existing educational structure.

One method of getting around such complexity in evaluating is to get so deeply into the intrapsychic process of the individual in the group that we lay aside for the moment the question of applicability. Another method is to change the concept of research and evaluation—change, but not eliminate. Although we are not sure which is better, we do think we should avoid pitfalls in communication that make difficult our goal of stimulating *rational* discussion and debate.

We wished to study our groups, but we also wished the participants to find the experience useful. Thus, it was a natural experience and not one contrived for research purposes. There was no effort to control the groups to fit the research protocol. In fact, one of our earliest concerns was the negative effect of the research on the course of the groups (Jones 1940; Zinberg 1964). We were soon aware that we were being too precious and violating our own code: we implied that we knew where the groups *should* be going as soon as we interpreted the research as "interfering." This recognition alleviated our worry to some extent. Nevertheless, the determination to let the groups alone—to notice how they were going but not to manipulate them for research ends as though they were laboratory animals—remained part of our liberal and humanistic operational philosophy.

We concluded that investigators doing quantifiable, statistically oriented research must also *subjectively* select the factors to be studied; that they may try to manipulate and control in order to get useable data; and that the disciplined subjectivity of our social-anthropological techniques was more applicable than theirs to our task of studying a process. Once we had decided that, we felt much easier letting the groups evolve naturally. The immeasurable effects of the conflict about educational innovation in Arlington or the national argument about bussing, both of which we knew must be somehow affecting the groups, ceased to be sources of constant concern. Further, we felt and still feel that, however difficult it is for us to draw larger social implications from this study, those that we do draw derive from a real experience in the real world. These implications, no matter how confusing, can be applied to other real experiences. Thus our disciplined subjectivity may apply more directly to other natural school settings than to laboratory or pseudo-laboratory projects controlled for only a few of the endless variables that must be taken into account. If what is studied in quantifiable research is only that which can be measured with accuracy, it usually faces the "so what" test in the real world because its field has become too small to mean much. Large studies trying to discover, for instance, how many youngsters have tried marijuana in all of Massachusetts can say nothing about how the subject of marijuana use provoked a different qualitative response in Arlington youngsters from one year to the next. And no less than our study, quantifiable research begins with some subjective conviction that something is worth studying, which makes total objectivity as difficult for such researchers as for us. As stated earlier, many projects striving for specific quantifiable results overlook their inherent subjectivity, thus ending up with an objectivity that is more apparent than real.

The effort to think about and describe things as they are, as opposed to finding out what they are supposed to be, is crucial to our concept of research. Originally we had thought about comparing our project to formal sex or drug education courses. However, we found that those courses were not sufficiently standardized to provide a valid standard of comparison. Different teachers, different administrators, different students changed the emphases in each classroom sufficiently to make it impossible to think of these courses as standard. Similarly, among the groups themselves, we had to abandon our initial hopes for some consistency. We began by trying to determine to what extent our groups were leader-proof; that is, we wished to determine what was indigenous to the group process—what would happen in every group no matter what the group leader did or did not do. Part II illustrates how deeply one must go into the human psyche before one gets to human responses that are dependably repetitious. Neither the standard courses nor our groups were executed in a sufficiently standardized form to permit anyone to understand any answers he might get from such questions.

The same problem of lack of a single standard holds true for the setting in which the research took place. It would not be difficult to argue that a course as "loose" or as "innovative" as ours could not flourish in so authoritarian an atmosphere as that of the Arlington schools. We could answer with our suspicion that a group course can only function in an otherwise structured atmosphere, although how structured is a moot point. One can probably only have one class in which the participants talk about what it feels like to be there. Without the surprise value of contrast, such an unstructured discussion would readily get to be a bore. However, if the general tenor of instruction is too punitive and rigid, students may be too frightened or mistrustful of the group-class to open up no matter how often they are reassured. Given the support of Dr. Roens, we surmised that Arlington did not fall into that latter category. But we also recognized that no single word such as traditional, authoritarian, conservative, liberal, creative, and so on, would describe the Arlington schools. The social setting was a mixture of many things which operated differently at different times in different schools. Any researcher who accepted as standard the social setting in which the testing and measuring were taking place would be kidding himself.

Obviously, it is not enough simply to point out that quantitative data in this project depend on subjective judgments and thereby avoid the issue of how a social-anthropological method retains its discipline. One can, though, defend the method and work to ensure its success. A great advantage is to have a research team rather than a single researcher. Then the same data can be looked at as they appear to more than one person. This cross-checking can delineate bias. Observations must be consistent, with a flexible but definite prearranged definition of what to look for. Whenever possible, observations must be cross-checked.

Data gathered from different sources can be used as a check. For instance, we accumulated students' comments about the Arlington groups from teachers we interviewed or from Dr. Roens and compared what was said there with their comments in the groups or in the interviews. Our use of the process that was going on throughout the school system as our field of study made such natural data as much part of the project as anything gathered from the groups.

The team argued. Differing evaluations of data and different perceptions were discussed carefully, so that hypotheses and even perceptions were challenged at every turn. As a matter of course, we developed and worried over a null hypothesis about any positive hypothesis advanced. This effort to pay attention to differences was not undertaken in order to arrive at consensus but to improve the quality and discipline of the observations and obtain clarity and consistency in the acceptance of some data and reasoning and the rejection of others. The research team's need to deal with conflict and disagreement and still remain together as a group echoed mechanisms at work within the project itself.

In effect, once we recognized that one could no more measure the research than one could the project, we made less and less differentiation between the two. As far as we were concerned, we were feeling and finding our way with both. Without worrying about controls, accepting the fact that there was little replication from one group to another or from this project to another, no matter how superficially similar, we established flexibility but changed the entire idea of research. That even this effort at research was, as we have said, an interference with the groups we have no doubt. There was no longer a clear-cut division between cause and effect. The research team's capacity for tact, charm, and human decency, and the conveying of these traits became as important as its methodological skill. The youngsters from Arlington and the METCO teachers were fully aware of how much teachers, parents, principals, administrators, and the like wanted to know how they thought in order to manipulate and coerce them into the "right" channels. The researchers had to be able to differentiate themselves from that multitude and indicate the benignness of their observing and the neutrality of their interest. They could only ask for cooperation from their subjects, particularly when what they asked was private, sometimes embarrassing, and often on issues on which the subjects' opinions, if known publicly, could be sharply criticized and even punished. This was no easy task, and took quite a different sort of view of research, but it is a necessary approach if the goal is to introduce a meaningful innovation.

To complete our defense of disciplined subjectivity, we can quote Charles Gershenson, director of research in the Child Development Section of the Department of Health, Education, and Welfare, certainly one of the most knowledgeable men in the United States about research trends. He pointed out on November 17, 1972, the direction of American research as he saw it: "We are seeing almost total dominance of goal oriented research. The age of learning through doing is past. A-leading-to-B research with an active 'can do' orientation is what will be funded. This is particularly true in education. Compensating education is seen to have failed, so pre-school programs such as Head Start have given way to specific youth development, manpower type programs and studies of whether they accomplish their highly specific goals get funded."

THE EDUCATIONAL INNOVATION

In Part I we discussed the rationale for our decision to use a nonin-formation-giving group method as the way to approach education in affectful areas. We used the metaphor of music *lessons* vs. music *appreciation*—definite goal orientation vs. the exaltation of process—and found that teachers emphasized the music lessons. They became so concerned that the students should know how the ovaries-sperm-contraception mechanisms worked or, in drug courses, just how difficult it was to cure addiction to a bad drug like heroin that they could pay little attention to the students' ability to appreciate the "music." It would be easy to argue that they were simply not very good "music teachers." A good music teacher would automatically sense whether a pupil had a genuine affinity for the world of sound or was merely practicing scales by rote.

But that argument does not take into account the influence of the larger social setting within which these courses took place. The pressure put on those teachers by the public at large and the mass media, while indirect and latent, nevertheless existed. Should their students get pregnant or hooked because of *ignorance*—not having been exposed to the information—they felt culpable. Should the student receive the proper information and still get into trouble, then it was a family or personality problem and the teacher felt exonerated. In such an atmosphere of much heat and very little light, teachers could hardly be faulted for wanting to be sure that students could at least recite the facts—i.e., practice their scales, to continue our musical analogy. Often teachers whom we interviewed admitted they were fascinated by the myths discussed and accepted by whole classes in these courses. We have mentioned the favorite saltpeter story, but other stories of impossible sexual damage, i.e., the girl locked while having intercourse, thus "trapping" the man, had equal currency. But the teachers all reacted the same way.

They let the discussion continue for a while, then felt obligated to tell the class the "truth." One typical teacher said, "I just wouldn't feel right letting young people leave my class believing everything like that without setting them straight. If I didn't say anything, they might think I was agreeing with them."

The problem for the teachers was their confusion between inner states—thoughts, feelings, motives—and behavior. To put our piano lessons/music appreciation metaphor another way, they found it hard to differentiate between ego activity and activity proper (Gill and Brenman 1958; Rapaport 1958). This is one more perspective on the implications/applications duality discussed above. In American education today—at least as it concerns the subjects of sex, drugs, prejudice, and the like, and as long as it operates under conditions of social pressure— the metabolization of information received continues to be treated as though it were a passive process. Our teacher who had to set the student straight would not have thought it adequate merely to raise questions about where and when the student got the information about girls "locking," how he felt about the information, or whether he somehow held onto it without wondering how it worked. And to the extent that the teacher did not see these questions as enough, his model was of the teacher as active giver and the student as passive recipient of precious information. This is an "activity-passivity" behavioral model.

We have suggested a dichotomy between ego activity and activity proper, and we have seen that teachers, in simply handing out information, ignore the students' capacity for ego activity. The dichotomy is real but not total. Action and feeling cannot be considered a total dichotomy any more than can implication/application; while one does not necessarily lead to the other, they are interrelated in complex ways. Many different feelings may lead to the same piece of behavior, just as many different behaviors can stem from the same feeling. This is a psychodynamic model of activity-passivity (Rapaport 1958). An example would be the soldier who vigorously attacks the enemy, never ceasing his efforts. He is active beyond compare, but in his head he has simply followed orders with little of the sense of responsibility that comes from having made a personal decision. By our definition he has shown little ego activity. An opposite example is the hospitalized hyperactive business executive who, when finally convinced that he has had a coronary occlusion (heart attack), accepts bed rest, a passivity which he has always abhorred. By permitting himself pleasure in coping internally with his own inhibitions against inactivity and by accepting responsibility for his own welfare, he shows considerable ego activity. Another example is the group leader who may be silent for the entire session but is busy internally formulating and questioning the behavior and motives of the group. This considerable ego activity may lead to activity proper at some future session, although, if the group begins to cover the same ground, it may never emerge in behavior. These examples illustrate that while ego activity and activity proper can be differentiated as to emphasis, they are not a dichotomy nor are they truly separable within a rational range.

Teachers and students at times resent an emphasis on ego activity. They want to rely on stringent outside controls—the should's, the ought's, do's, and don't's (which are internalized as the conscience)—rather than on ego controls. Particularly when issues became highly controversial and divisive, many of our group members, just like other members of society, sought relief in structures. In our groups this search for external controls brought polarization in the group rather than unity in the group or synthesis in the individual. Calling attention to the futility of what we saw as a search for superego controls may not change such a well-oiled social process in a flash, but it can certainly suggest to people not to resort automatically to a process that indicates their lack of trust in their inner active capacities to wrestle with these knotty choices.

It is our contention, then, that this behavioral model of activity-passivity exemplified by the information-giving teacher mistrusts the role of ego activity, not just in students but in teachers as well. Hence it mistrusts the role of process. The information-giving behavior is piano lesson-oriented. Thus it ends up, of necessity, being goal-oriented, with the goal reflecting specific, so-called normative values and the status quo. In Chapter 7 we show how this goal orientation supports the status quo, whether it purports to be liberal or conservative, by its attempts to coerce "correct" responses. Here our process orientation runs into a conflict with the typical American value system (Ginsberg 1961; Yankelovich 1972). Not only does it accept the role of contemplation and motivation, ego activity, as of the same importance as outcome, but it also unquestionably refuses to spell out for each student what he should do.

Let us turn back to the history of the project for a moment. The Sviridoff memorandum about Arlington and METCO, which caught the spirit of the project's interest in the inner response of students and teachers, quite naturally asked whether this would lead to attitude change and maturation. Let us translate this query into the specific area of drugs. Marijuana use is against the law. Is it more or less mature for someone to use marijuana in this society? In our groups, we found that "conservative" members, i.e., those opposed to marijuana use, were inclined to give ground to more liberal members. We guessed that more people were likely to try marijuana after group discussion than before.

However, the groups were not a one-way street toward "permissiveness." One youngster specifically pointed out that he really had not liked marijuana, had only smoked it because others had, and now wanted to say that he did not like it. To the extent that we define maturity as making up one's own mind and accepting responsibility for such choices, then perhaps group members moved toward maturity. As the encouragement of ego activity means standing against inner impulses as well as outer directives, such encouragement is unlikely to stimulate excessive or outrageous behavior. But because this encouragement means questioning inhibitions and strictures inside one's head, as well as those from the outside world, more members are likely to look for ways of individual expression. That probably means more experimental behavior, and right now, in the United States, that probably means trying more things than accepting strictures as given (Zinberg and Robertson 1972).

As mentioned in Chapter 2, groups can easily become a fad or gimmick. We also pointed out that the effectiveness and stimulation of our process-oriented course rested on its differentiation from the orthodox school curriculum. We must also discuss how our process-oriented educational innovation fits into the current (and at times faddish) interest in contemplation, insight, and general powers of the mind. Most current adherents to "mystical" views hold that critical thinking, when over-emphasized, leads to a belief that one can always get things right. These thinkers see mystical process orientation as an antidote to the excessive American reliance on critical thinking (Reich 1970; Slater 1970). This position reflects one of our concerns about the misuse of our educational efforts because we recognize that this process orientation conflicts with straight, goal-directed, American values. At the moment in the United States there is a new interest in contemplation and mental functions (Weil 1973). Within the youth culture, or at least within the further-out, more hip segment of it, this interest coincides with and, in fact, is fueled by, an interest in consciousness change with or without drugs, mysticism, Eastern religious thought, and the like. This rather resembles our interest in process. But process orientation, if misapplied as it has been by recent devotees of mystical thought, can in an odd fashion lead right back to goal orientation. The mystics and the scientific rationalists both fall into the trap of compartmentalization of mind and behavior. The situation is a bit like that which we describe in our chapter on the status quo, in that the two sides negatively reinforce each other. But the compartmentalization referred to among the young particularly affects ideas about learning and education. On the one hand, the rewards of contemplation of inner functions are recognized. Probably this experience is much closer to what we have called ego activity than they imagine. But it is generally compartmentalized, separated artificially from long-term behavior. In the short term, exercise, diets, readings, and the like are considered helpful for the sought-after mental state. It is as if longer-term behavior is to be postponed until they "get their heads on straight." This postponement is goal-oriented, critical, linear thinking rather than process-oriented thinking. Such hopes minimize one's participation in emotional inner experience. The straight scientists too have their direct goals from their studies of mental processes and find it hard to pay attention to what goes into these more spiritual experiences when seen as part of a "high" created with or without drugs.

An educational innovation such as ours could easily become caught up in that controversy. There were hints in Arlington that the course was seen as an "experience." Probably no one thought of it as a high in the intoxicating sense, but it bordered on being called "unusual," as if considering one's inner process automatically led to "far-out" thinking. Little of this sort of talk, incidentally, came from the participants themselves. They were all too well aware of the discomfort and frustration inherent in trying to face inhibitions in a nondirective setting.

Whatever soundness there is in working with students, teachers, or any group toward the sort of affectful learning intended in our method is not dependent on the outside culture's preoccupation of the moment. At their best, these courses simply consider what the preoccupations are and how people metabolize emotions and ideas around them. As we pointed out, one year drugs were the main subject of interest in Arlington; another year it was sex. The METCO groups in different years clearly reflected the black community's growing interest in separatism rather than integration. The cornerstone of process orientation is the awareness that at different historical periods (which may well, under current mass media pressure, change from one year to the next) different resolutions are offered for what can be seen to be similar conflicts.

When considering how to use our work, it is essential to recognize the social context in which such work takes place. The aim of these courses is to permit students (young or old) to differentiate between music appreciation and piano lessons; it is not to declare process and content to be oil and water. In an atmosphere in which these courses are taken up as a fad and as part of a larger social controversy, they could become directly goal-oriented, one way of attacking straight values and ideas rather than a means of examining how these values work within each individual group member.

Does an educational method centered around awareness of motives and inner response offer something to areas of education other than those dealing with "hot," affect-laden subjects? We have already indicated our conviction that a course taking the form of a relatively nondirective group can only be taught once in a curriculum. But, as we discussed in Chapter 2, a great variety of group activities exists. As we were planning our project and considering how best to work in our course, we found some analogies between other group methods and other educational endeavors. Mathematics, for instance, we reasoned, was taught as though it were a repressive inspirational group. The group searches for an active solution to the problem, pushes aside (represses) any feelings involved as extraneous, and exalts the cleanness and directness of the solution. Under present teaching methods, any effort to develop interest in the feelings involved in the procedure itself would be divisive. But suppose one wished to teach a mathematics appreciation course which was entirely divorced from learning to *do* anything. In this course one might think over infinity, relativity, chance, topological paradoxes, and the like. In this course the students' feelings about what they were doing would be of importance, as they are in English literature courses, yet surely awareness of meter is as important as a study of how a poem affects someone and what he does with the feelings thus aroused.

Naturally, *all* courses in which the discussion centers around emotional responses—whether "heavy" or not—need some process orientation. The teachers and the group leaders who participated in our program became more aware of how group process affected discussion in their other courses. Several of the phenomena discussed in Part II, such as expectations of the leader, splitting, subgroup formation, pairing, and scapegoating, occurred in other courses. Above all, the teachers discovered that inhibitions against learning come not only from students' feelings about the content of their courses but also from conflicts arising from relationships within the classroom. All the teachers agreed that, after their group participation, they were as likely to think about what keeps youngsters from learning as they were about how to get them to learn.

We ended our project feeling that it was important to consider how much teachers should know about group process and how to convey it to them. We have demonstrated two methods, both of which seem to work to some extent. First, the teachers acted as group leaders with supervision and learned by doing. They then applied in their other classes whatever they had learned that was comfortable for them (McKeachie 1958). Second, teachers participated as group members and learned by experiencing (Semrad and Arsenian 1951). Here, too, they could apply their acquired experience at their own rate. In keeping with our entire orientation we preferred methods that let the teachers use group process techniques on their own because this meant choice, ego activity, on their parts. There are many possible complications in this method. For instance, the group member might imitate the group leader reflexly (Kubie 1968) and thus behave actively while remaining ego-passive.

Additional thought by others may further codify the techniques of group teaching. We might offer one warning: we felt after our experience in this project even more strongly than before that good teaching requires, above all, an integrated teacher. Far better an authoritarian teacher comfortable with her method and devoted to her content than one with a superimposed method enhanced by ideology but with insufficient love for the course itself. Neither group process nor any other technique can offer a final answer. Despite our concern about the "music appreciation" of the teacher who came into a METCO group preaching conservatism and left spouting liberalism, we want to know more about the later effect this political shift had upon him. Will he feel more divided internally and more ill at ease with his classes? If the language of his new ideology gets a positive response, will he then be lured to an internal reassessment of his emotional position? Either is possible, and either will happen to different people. *Some* teachers certainly can put a greater knowledge of group process to good use, but surely not all.

In the same way, we hope that some schools will want to try our course, but surely it could not be suited to all. Any that do should remember that, despite our awareness of the heavy burden this course puts on the leader, we elected previously untrained or, whenever possible, indigenous leaders both for Arlington and METCO. Certainly Chapter 20 tells any potential leader about the extent of the group's preoccupation with him, so he should go into a group prepared for total engagement. The teacher should of course remember that self-education—and in essence that is what our courses are—means a growing awareness that each student struggles to a conclusion valid for him as an individual. Dogma from above, even though based on considerable experience and training, might cost more in freshness and a shared struggle than what would be gained by adoption of its smoothness and competence.

There is no fixed backbone in this course. The groups themselves are set up, and their beginning and format are carefully structured, but within that structure there is almost complete freedom. We discussed earlier the problem of METCO sponsorship. The groups were fixed on an area of attention, and this hampered their freedom of operation. In ideal courses the material would evolve from the course itself. There is no laying down of knowledge, but rather a providing of structure within which knowledge can be accumulated.

In this framework the process gets under way. Difficulties become apparent, but, as these are the work of the course, they are equally apparent to all. Each will attack them in his own way. Each member can select, within certain group confines, the depth, intensity, or perspective from which he will tackle the material. As in other courses he ends up with awareness, skills, and tools, but these have been crystallized personally.

As this course does not share the traditional value system of the institution in which it takes place, what is the role of the institution? In our view, this process orientation, which minimizes inculcation of values, makes the institution more valuable to those who need its services—and service is the primary preoccupation of the institution. Conflict arises over who decides the extent to which the service is delivered: the producer, whether school superintendent, principal, teacher, school committee, parent, or legislature, or the consumer, in our case junior and senior high school students and teachers in METCO schools. Once our courses are under way, the consumer, whether he likes it or not, has control over the product, and the representatives of the institutions have little or none. In this case, if our course is not used reasonably, the consumer also has that responsibility, and not the institution. This approach thus works in a healthy way against the placing of blame on bad institutions, bad teachers, or bad pupils.

One of the most useful aspects of this consumer orientation could come from its use within hard-pressed ethnic minority communities. These communities have been asked over and over to let others come in and study their "problems" so that they can be helped to solve them. Our course simply says, let us see if a group of us can agree on what is a difficulty. We can look at it together and see where that takes us. We are not trying to find out whether minority groups' drug use or sex is different from majority group habits, nor are we studying racism in minority group teachers. Rather, we offer a chance to see how some people respond internally to complex situations. To the extent that we have learned to deal with social class, ethnic, and economic differences, personal background will not become a prime consideration for any study except to the degree that participants decide to make it so.

We have pointed out that this sort of process-oriented course in the affectful areas of education may be worth thinking about to some schools and some communities, just as we have hoped that our experience with failing in research will influence some workers who want to do research projects in the areas of potential social change. We have shown that there may be extrapolations from our groups that might help workers think through the ways in which well-meaning efforts to change the status quo in many areas unwittingly become a force to maintain that which is ostensibly under siege. Finally and above all, we have shown that this sort of process orientation cannot act as a panacea, no more than any other goal-directed social change projects.

René Dubos, the biologist, has tried as much as any American teacher to differentiate between shadow and substance in our cultural approach to ambiguous and value-laden issues such as health, normality, and a decent place and way to live. Recently, he said (1972): "The American public has been brainwashed into the belief that progress means introducing into our lives everything we know how to produce." He referred not just to material products but also to the hasty acceptance of values, the pressures on us to choose quickly the better, the faster, the surer. Obviously few people would *prefer* unnecessary fumbling, pain, or discontent, particularly when we touch on the painful social inequities perpetrated by race, ethnicity, or sex. But we want to show that when dealing with the complexity of human psychology, especially in groups, the shortest and most effective approach may not be the apparent straight line. Telling people how wrong it is to be prejudiced, demonstrating it to them rationally, pointing out the enormous personal and social cost of it—in other words, insisting upon the rationality of human equality with difference does not per se dissipate the irrational emotional preoccupations that result in bigotry.

That does not mean that everyone should accept our longer-term assessment that for many people to deal with their specific prejudices against blacks or whites or women or men or long-hairs or short-hairs they need some idea of the roots of their prejudice or, more essentially, the inhibition against alleviation of their prejudice. Otherwise, they simply develop a prejudice against prejudice, and so on. Many people feel deeply the wrongness of prejudice and feel that the prejudice against whites in this society is of quite a different order from the prejudice against blacks. In the same way, because we have attempted an experimental course where teachers function relatively objectively in a value-free atmosphere, this does not mean that we espouse total freedom of values throughout education—not at all. Students, like the rest of us, require many inputs, particularly concerning issues of values and morality. It is hard to imagine the emptiness of a society where no one speaks out about the treatment of a minority group as sinned against as are American blacks.

If our work has social value, it is to point out that teachers and others can know the values and morals they are expressing and can recognize the implications of such expression. Also, we indicate that there is a niche for the study of how such knowledge and the experience of that knowledge are metabolized, just as we studied the process of a relatively value-free situation. Essentially, in a polyglot, multi-input social situation—a fair description of a contemporary school dealing with these "hot" contemporary (and also timeless) issues—we need to do more than assign lessons. It is usually simply too hard to know what they might be. Can we at times just listen to and hear the music, whether soft or sweet, hard and loud, or even atonal, and only then find out how we feel about the performance and how valuable it is? Can we truly learn appreciation?

TRANSCRIPTS OF TWO GROUP MEETINGS

GROUP I, SESSION 4

[Chairs have been placed in a circle, and the group is seated.]

Leader: I wonder whether you find it useful to share the comments you put in your report last time.

O: I forget what I wrote.

Leader: It's a way of asking if it's useful to step back from what we've done and give your impressions about it. Was it good or bad, and where do we want to go?

[No response]

F: Why isn't the tape recorder here?

Leader: I forgot it.

O: I didn't think we were going to start again like this.

Leader: How would you like to start?

O: Like we ended last week.

F: I forget the question we ended off with.

O: I think it was people's experiences.

F: Can you put it into a question to help us out?

O: Experiences in the school as related to ourselves and the children— very vaguely. As far as your question, I keep saying it's the position we put the kids in, trying to put ourselves in a new position and see what a kid has to go through. I wonder what it's like to walk into the environment where there would be other things. Would it be easier if there are materials to show us where to go? With kids it's easy. Here we have to find stuff within ourselves to relate to each other that's good.

Leader: What makes it difficult for you?

O: I don't know. I guess it's that you keep thinking you have to start with very superficial things. We always start out talking about things with no relevance. We have to work ourselves into a good discussion. That's probably just conditioning.

F: As we were coming here, I was thinking how great it would be with food. But if you could smoke and drink coffee, you could be preoccu-

223

	pied for a while. But that would be postponement. By the end we're in full swing. I don't know why the beginning is so difficult.
O:	Because no one wants to say things like, "How's the weather?" So no one says anything.
Leader:	Maybe you can find out here today. You were talking about an application of what women were saying.
O:	You don't want to talk about you; it may be boring to someone else. Certain things we should talk about. So you don't take chances to say it. Since we were kids, we've learned to do this.
Leader:	Does it seem to be that talking with other people will interfere with getting something for themselves or giving it to the kids? Something more satisfying, enjoyable, and easy.
E:	Maybe we're afraid to listen. We may hear some pretty bad things. Sad things maybe. The way some of these children have to live and yet they come to school each day, and we expect them to learn.
Leader:	Do you have an experience?
E:	Yes. Second-grade boys and girls—alcoholic father, etc. They come to school not dressed warm enough and the teacher expects the child to toe the line. The teacher doesn't try to understand the home conditions. It's not really the girl's fault she gets into trouble. She's in the second grade and acts about thirty because she has to take care of the others. The teacher expects her to learn like the others.
F:	Is there any way a teacher can get help for herself in terms of getting insight?
E:	I've tried to talk to the teacher but she wants her class just so—very disciplined.
F:	Can't she be taken out of the classroom?
E:	I suppose she can. I have two grades, but this other teacher is inexperienced and she has her problems too, so I really didn't want to. I can even send her to another school but it's not fair to the children. I wish the teacher would compromise.
L:	Is it your role to talk to the teacher?
E:	I did.
H:	Lots of kids get emotionally deprived. Just adjusting one child in class doesn't answer that. In one community there is less of that, but the parents are never available.
K:	I was talking to a teacher today. He was told he was too much of a disciplinarian and he turned his kids off. I wonder if it isn't part of a larger question of why people go into teaching. The kids meeting the grim needs of the teachers and suffering as a result of it. That's a question we constantly have to be asking ourselves.
H:	Youngsters are doing their share of manipulating too.
L:	That doesn't give us a right to do it.
H:	I agree.
N:	What does it mean when you say kids manipulate teachers?
K:	Youngsters want to smoke so they say they want to go to the john.
H:	Then they come back and act with complete innocence. This is how girls manipulate you all the time. I had a girl who did that last week.

She was gone for fifteen minutes and I asked her why. She said I
was just making it up—absolutely innocently. She said I don't understand girls. I told her she was right.

F: In education there comes a time when people have to assume personal responsibility for their own learning. I was nineteen before I
realized that education was for no one but myself. Only then did I do
it. Before that it was never for myself. I think that with a girl like that—
the huge amounts of discussion that come into play when the teacher
feels it's her responsibility and only her responsibility that the kids get
knowledge. If the situation were reversed, it would make a big difference.

H: But you have to lead them up to it. That's part of their learning.

F: But if you have to discuss being suspicious of someone sneaking
about.

H: You don't ignore it. You open it up and air it out. You're in a framework of an institution.

F: I don't think I ignore it; I think I avoid it.

Leader: How do people feel about this in concrete? I hear the concern about
being kind to children and that responsibilities interfere with the wish
to be nice, but finding yourself involved in manipulations. I would
think this comes up concretely just as it did here. What are the resources here? How do you experience it? The kind of question Mr. E
brought up is a question of kindness. I think people are concerned
about that. It must come up in special concrete situations about your
feelings with kids.

H: I wonder if adolescence isn't a big part of it. Seventh-grade kids are
like elementary school kids. Adolescents begin to use a whole new
bag of tricks.

Leader: How do you feel?

H: I brought up my kids to feel responsibility, that if you don't make a
situation, you don't have one. Sometimes I feel that I have to meet a
situation and not ignore it.

Leader: What do you mean by "make a situation"? How do you feel in it?

H: Just that I'm aware of it. There are lots of feelings. For one thing I'm
a bit amused. I feel responsibility to let her know I'm aware of what
she's doing.

K: I have the feeling that you're trying to put your feelings in acceptable
terms. I feel you're angry when a situation arises.

Leader: Do *you* get angry?

K: Yes, not as much as I used to. I usually let the kids go to the john. I
feel angry when anyone's manipulating me.

Leader: Why?

K: I'm not apologizing for it. Because I think it depersonalizes me. I feel
it's your dilemma with the kids. You want to be good and yet manipulating means you're being taken advantage of.

H: I feel this girl is a cold-blooded creature, with no feelings of responsibility to me or to her environment. I can't deal with her. I feel uncomfortable and puzzled. I feel it's funny. And I'm a little tired of

trying to make contact, but I feel like I'm looking into the eyes of a snake. She's a perfectly nice girl.

Leader: Why?

H: Because she's doing what all the other girls are doing.

Leader: What does she want?

H: Out of it—out of work, out of responsibility. She let one remark slip: "You're just like my mother."

O: In my situation it's related. At our school the principal—last year was my first year. I expected to be manipulated. Our principal leaves us completely autonomous in governing our class. I was floored. I can remember we said, "When is this manipulation going to stop?" We kept feeling it's got to come, but it never did. Our principal gave in. Our class is our personality. It's the most relaxed thing because it's you and what you think is right. It's no manipulation. I think the manipulation comes from somewhere else and we do it to the kids. I had a kid who had a block against reading. I left her alone. The parents came in very displeased. Right away I was on the defensive but they scared me so that I felt myself being very conscious of the kid. I started to think of situations I could get her involved in. Someone was manipulating me to do something to the child. It was terrible. It turned out that there was something physically wrong. For a minute some force comes over you and you take it out on the kids because it's something you don't want to do and it makes you uptight. When it's gone, it's beautiful. If the kids want to smoke, so what? I think education is social for all, especially nowadays. We have to teach to the total individual.

[H says something, and L asks what she said.]

Leader: Were you wishing she had made . . . ?

N: I'm beginning to see what you mean about manipulation—any requirement that is within you, anything that's direction or requirement is manipulation. If you're totally yourself and relaxed, then you're not being manipulated.

L: She's saying you're relaxed if you're not being manipulated. Not necessarily that you're not manipulated if you're relaxed.

N: It's such a different way of being a teacher. You feel that it's important how they feel about you.

O: I want them to feel happy with themselves. They're good kids and can function themselves. That's the way I do it best. For example, one of my kids said he couldn't do it. We tried and he did it. He said the same thing about drawing. This kid needed the confidence to know that I wasn't going to impose anything on him. I don't want them to have hangups—I want them to be happy. I go on the premise that I work best when I'm happy and comfortable, and able to make a mistake. Sometimes it leaves you all bottled up inside. The rest will come, I think.

N: But if you're teaching, there comes a time when you have to point out mistakes. You go about it in terms of feelings.

Leader:	What are you trying to work out? How does it relate to your leaving?
O:	Why did you leave?
N:	I was tired. I felt I was asking the kids to do things they didn't want to do.
Leader:	It sounds like you were asking her to ask kids to do things.
N:	I feel ambivalent about this. I would need more support. I don't think my feelings would be enough to go on.
Leader:	It's an awful conflict. It's tiring.
N:	I just don't know about kids being happy all the time. Being a mother was so different from being a teacher, and now it's so different. That's why I like it better.
L:	She likes to present an atmosphere in the class where the child is learning out of desire rather than out of fear.
O:	There are definite things that you ask them. There are requirements on the child—just by its nature—asking kids what they want to do requires structure. But it's good enough reason for them because they know that's the way it's going to be if they want that situation.
F:	I think something happens when you teach in a grade, like these things called skills—like spelling. You're told you have to memorize. Sometimes I just don't know how important it is to spell properly. This little girl wrote six pages and wrote everything phonetically. I just couldn't tell her she spelled it wrong. I was so conscious of how wrong the words were spelled, but I couldn't tell her.
Leader:	What kept you from it?
F:	She worked so hard on it.
Leader:	What do you think the effect would have been?
F:	Disastrous.
Leader:	How?
N:	She wouldn't tell you what's on her mind next time.
F:	When I see kids stumbling over words that start with "kn" it's so irrelevant.
H:	They're not irrelevant, they're just hard.
K:	Isn't it a part of communication? If someone writes something, it can be misinterpreted. I'm coping with kids who don't know how to spell. That's really annoying.
O:	I think there are times when kids are ready. If the kid can decide when—in the case of this child, she couldn't be told.
Leader:	Is there a way you could have said anything to the child?
F:	Yes, I do it. But I get annoyed that I do it. She wrote a one-page story. It bothered me that I did it. It's what we were talking about in terms of expectations.
K:	It could be projected. Like when a youngster falls down: when the parent jokes, the kid smiles. When the parent feels bad, the kid cries. Could you be projecting your hangup on this child?
F:	That's why I did it.
K:	But you're making a judgment on that child.
L:	She's making far less of a judgment than you are.

Leader: Has anyone experienced what this lady is talking about?

F: You see, I have. If the kid knows his science, why does it bother you if he's spelled wrong?

Leader: What about this experience of the person being hurt? What happens when that happens in this group?

H: It makes you withdraw and become very tight.

B: I've seen it happen here.

O: Did I hurt your feelings [directing her question to H]?

H: No, but I didn't expect to get a revelation here. I just withdrew because you're talking about little elementary-school kids who never had anything before.

R: She gave her reason. She feels the old-fashioned schoolteacher image is shot.

H: But I don't. I teach reading, etc. I teach a very unstructured class, perhaps too much so.

Leader: Let's talk about this. There is a lot of anger associated with it, and a feeling that we won't try again. I think it's quite a common experience. It's part of what people are referring to and there's a kind of taboo about talking about it.

C: It was a very exciting day today.

Leader: What is it that people see in themselves and stress that makes for the vulnerability?

F: What vulnerability?

Leader: I thought I was picking up on your language. What makes one think what one will say will stab someone?

N: Perhaps you're aware of your own fragility yourself, like the children.

C: Sometimes when you were in school and gave wrong answers, someone laughed. Or having an idea shot down and not being able to defend myself because my emotions are wrapped up in it.

F: It can be insecurity of your own. I always get defensive but that's because I always think I'm not sure of what I'm saying like the conversation with the parent.

Leader: I just had a crazy thought. When someone is concerned about not hurting the kids, there must come a point when you want to clobber the kids because you're giving constantly.

C: I just say I'm going for a cigarette. I would hit them otherwise.

N: Don't they manipulate you often because they do want sternness? I can be gushy.

F: Yes, there are all kinds of degrees of love. One kind only likes it if you tell him off. In that case, that's what helps him most. It's still considerate of people's feelings.

Leader: As I hear it, you're supportive rather than loving.

F: I tell them when I'm mad. I guess I just try to relate to them like a human being. They're bright. I have discussions with them like with a friend.

N: It is protective, being afraid to injure someone.

O: I see myself leaving them open and not catering to them.

F: I see it as honesty rather than protection.

O: I think certain things are protecting and not wanting them to grow.

N: I guess it's drawing the line in your own mind. You will not go strong physically but you're afraid mentally.

O: No, with some kids I'm pretty firm. One kid plays games with her whole family, so she needs it. Some kids need me to zip up their coats.

N: You can say, I want you to do it, when you know they can.

O: Yeah, I guess so.

N: So you're making demands on them. We took these things for granted.

F: I think the hardest thing is to make people make demands on themselves.

L: I think this is what this ultimately tries to do. He can't do it without realizing he's an important individual, where he feels he can make decisions himself. Some people feel this is contrived. I find the other way much more contrived, without any results. One thing that is interesting to look at is why education has progressed so far that this is so important now. What about education in the past? Has it produced this?

N: At your level, if you have a child who appears like a big bowl of blubber and always is doing things to get attention, you work and work to show him he can do other things, but it's awfully hard. But how do you bring about changes in his self-image? As teachers there are so many possibilities you can open up for the kid.

L: You can't change him by telling him what he's doing is wrong.

O: But you can't expect them to be all the same. Each kid has his own personality.

N: They find being in a class torture. Am I accepting too much of a role to expect them to change?

Leader: I wonder if people here want to change things about themselves?

K: Theoretically you can talk about it. But it's against human nature to try to resist change.

GROUP III, SESSION 16

[Chairs have been placed in a circle, and the group is seated.]

[Silence]

Leader: Shall I go through my ritual or shall we just begin?

L: B, last week you said you wouldn't go out with a colored girl. Why not?

B: I wouldn't.

L: I asked if you would go out with G, one of the best-looking girls in the school, and you said no. Would you [to N] go out with a colored guy in the school?

N: I would if I liked him, but not to marry him.

H: That's reversal. Usually *she* asks people questions.

L: What about you?

H: I would.

L: What about you, D [addressing the leader by his first name]? If you weren't married?

Leader: In general, yes, though I'm up tight about the black-white issue. I feel excluded. I would wonder whether the black girl would want to go out with me, or something else.

L: Would anyone else but B not like to go out with a colored person?

B: Everyone should do their own thing.

K: But not get married. You have to think of the children.

[N and L discuss whether parents would affect this. N says her parents would influence whom she married. L says he doesn't care about his parents.]

N: This generation is less prejudiced than the last one. I haven't been brought up to be prejudiced against anyone, not blacks or Jews. I have an Italian friend and I make jokes about Italians, and she gets hurt sometimes but I'm not prejudiced. What do *you* [to leader] think? You're in between our generation and the last one. Do you think we're less prone to prejudice?

Leader: I'm glad you didn't put me in the last generation. You want me to say who's more prejudiced. What do you think I'll say?

N: I hope you'll say it's getting better.

L: There are more race riots now. People get more prejudiced by the violence and the news about it. There's just as much white rioting but whites are in the majority, so the news pushes the black ones.

N: Do you think they can get anywhere without riots?

L: No. They're in the same position as a hundred years ago.

N: My mother works in the post office and they have Civil Service exams. She said they lowered the test since she took it for the intelligence of the black people so they can work there. My father got upset and said the country is going down, down, down in intelligence. But even when they lowered the test, the black people couldn't pass it.

L: But they come from an environment which is against them. In the ghetto they get the worst teachers, etc.

N: But if I were a teacher, I wouldn't want to teach in a black area— knives, etc. It's not so sweet.

[I and L say they've been in black areas and nothing happened, that whites beat each other up, too.]

N: I think it's the environment: not blacks or whites. The government tried projects and gave them a nice place to live in but they don't take care of it, they're not used to it.

L: How can they keep it nice with twenty-five dollars a week?

N: You can't give them a decent education until the environment changes.

H: It doesn't help if they go home to ignorant people.

I: That's like saying a kid can't be not prejudiced if his parents are.

[N and L say all they need is to know black people.]

L: How many blacks do you know?

B: Four.

L: I know hundreds.

B: Good.

L: Black people have better personalities than whites; they're friendlier.

N: Why should color make a difference in personality?

Leader: I wonder if it's possible to be prejudiced against ideas as well as against color of skin?

N: My father thinks the country is getting worse.

L: Tell your father there was more draft evasion in World War II than now. It's just television that lets him see the riots in California. Tell your father it's getting better.

N: There are more colleges now. That's where you get most of your radical ideas—from professors or kids.

Leader: It seems to me there's a difference between walking to the ghetto and saying I'd like to understand you and saying to B, I'd like to understand you. We've cut him off.

L: No, he wants to make believe they don't exist.

Leader: But have you been so willing to get to know B as the [names an organized group] in [a nearby town]?

B: People reverse themselves too. I worked in a gas station and this black guy used to come in and say, "Fill it up, boy; give me change, boy."

L: If you got punched in the face, wouldn't you punch back?

H: If we shouldn't do it [call them "boy"], why should they?

L: Black people are striking back.

H: Is that the best way to stop the other guy from punching you?

L: Yes, now he's being recognized.

H: Is violence working?

L: Yes, violence got them more.

H: That or peaceful things like Martin Luther King's way.

L: You can't expect change right away.

I: You have to fight for what you want.

H: It's social Darwinism—to stay on top. Carnegie and Ford scrunched down white people, but that's not prejudice. I disagree that violence is the best way.

L: It is.

H: Doesn't violence alienate people?

I: It scares people.

H: Is that good?

N: They've been fighting a long time.

H: Name one black leader before 1950.

L: Brooker J. [*sic*] Washington, the guy who did the stuff with the peanuts. Read a black history book. The blacks tried peaceful ways but that didn't work.

N: My mother said the blacks in the post office have priority over people who come back from Vietnam. That's a problem with wars.

L: How many presidents weren't war heroes?

N: None, I guess.

L: How many weren't millionaires?

N: Eisenhower? Nixon? O.K., Lincoln.

L: He had money.

N: He made it on his own. You need money to go into office.

L: No, you don't.

H: Now you're arguing not against prejudice but putting the wrong people in office for the wrong reasons.

L: The blacks and poor haven't been able to prosper because they put all their rich friends in office.

N: But most people go into politics because they are lawyers and make money. They're smart. They had an education because they had money.

L: J. Paul Getty is the richest man in the world. How far did he go to school? He dropped out in the third grade. They say, "We'll get rich and the rest can stay poor."

H: So is that prejudice or is that wanting power?

Leader: Also, why has it seemed so important that everyone agree with us? It seemed selective to who would carry on the conversation. A couple were never invited in. Why must everyone agree with us?

L: Because unless they agree there won't be tranquility, but whites against blacks.

Leader: Do we come in thinking our side is right?

L: People do.

Leader: Can we try out ideas?

L: People don't want to admit they're wrong. Do you [to N] admit when you're wrong?

N: Yeah. Yesterday my sister and I made a lot of noise and my father came up and smacked us. I thought he was right.

L: Did you tell him he was right? Do you tell people they're right?

N: It depends. If they'll put me down, I won't, but if they don't, I might.

APPENDIX II

SAMPLES OF RESEARCH FORMS

FORM A

PRE-TEST*

Name_____

Introduction:

On each of the yellow pages inside this booklet there are four words. By *omitting one word*, and rearranging the other three, you will be able to construct a meaningful sentence or phrase. In each case we want you to look at the words briefly, and then quickly turn the page and write down the first meaningful sentence that comes to mind.

Professor ————— will give you further instructions about the time to be taken over each item; when to begin; and when to move on to the next item in the booklet. *Please do not turn over this page until he tells you to.*

see hear the bird	_____
it's announced forgotten been	_____
the swat hear fly	_____
ticket the punch take	_____
bargain a drive find	_____
grapes the pack crush	_____
busy he stupid is	_____
it's plot a joke	_____
a give him seat slap	_____
snobs dislike meet I	_____
paper cut the bring	_____
nails the count hit	_____
you me tell annoy	_____
egg cook the beat	_____

*This form was administered to both groups.

your use fist pencil   _____
always prying frying they're   _____
hear I you hate   _____
out him let knock   _____
liar a woman she's   _____
window the open break   _____
seam rip sew the   _____
fight out point if   _____
lock the smash fix   _____

FORM B

POST-TEST*

Name: _____

Introduction:

On each of the green pages inside this booklet there are four words. By *omitting one word*, and *re-arranging the other three*, you will be able to construct a meaningful sentence or phrase. In each case we want you to look at the words briefly, and then quickly turn over the page and write down the first meaningful sentence that comes to mind.

Professor ———— will give you further instructions about the time to be taken over each item; when to begin; and when to move on to the next item in the booflet. *Please do not turn over this page* until he tells you to.

the see slap mosquito   _____
ticket the punch take   _____
bargain a drive find   _____
grapes the pack crush   _____
foolish he working is   _____
man a cheat he's   _____
a give him seat slap   _____
snobs dislike meet I   _____
the hit bring ball   _____
orange the squash taste   _____
you me tell annoy   _____
egg cook the beat   _____
your use fist pencil   _____
often accused tempted I'm   _____
me you disgust convince   _____
him hell time give   _____

*This form was administered to both groups.

out sort bawl them
price the cut learn
cloth sell tear the
fight out point it
lock the smash fix

_____
_____
_____
_____
_____

Name: _____

Date: _____

Group leader is: _____

What are your impressions at this point, based on your experience in the group?*

———————————————————————————————————

Name: L. L. _____

Date: 2–24–70 _____

Group Leader is: Ms.———— _____

What are your impressions at this point, based on your experience in the group?

I have both enjoyed and become frustrated by my own experience in the group. Talking, thinking, and discussing the black problem with others has forced me in a way to begin sorting out my own feelings about black people, my own stereotypes—and begin to realize how little I really know about black people as people. I have begun to read more about the situation, and to talk more freely with others about how I feel.

I feel that this group experience, as a place where teachers and others can meet to begin to look at themselves and some of their feelings about blacks as well as other issues, can be invaluable—what I do from this point seems as important. I feel somewhat more at ease expressing my own opinions, and I feel that I can admit more of my prejudices—now I can at least begin to recognize these prejudices— I feel more sensitive to blacks, maybe overly so—

Talking with others and realizing that they have feelings similar to my own—that they are unsure of what they feel and think—has helped me in some ways.

———————————————————————————————————

*This form was used for the teacher groups: a form with a typical answer follows.

BIBLIOGRAPHY

Abrams, A. 1973. *Accountability in drug education, a model for evaluation.* Publication HS-1. Washington, D.C.: Drug Abuse Council.

Allport, G. W. 1954. *The nature of prejudice.* Cambridge, Mass.: Addison-Wesley.

Ashton-Warner, S. 1963. *Teacher.* New York: Simon and Schuster.

Assimakos, J. 1965. Experimental seminars in sex education for seventh-grade girls. *Social Casework* 46:352–57.

Bales, R. 1951. *Interaction process analysis.* Cambridge, Mass.: Addison-Wesley.

Balint, M. 1968. *The basic fault: Therapeutic aspects of repression.* London: Tavistock.

Bass, B. M. 1960. *Leadership in psychology and organizational behavior.* New York: Harper.

Beisser, A., and Harris, H. 1966. Psychological aspects of the civil rights movement in the Negro professional man. *American Journal of Psychiatry* 123: 72–87.

Bell, G. B., and French, R. L. 1965. Consistency of individual leadership position in small groups of varying membership. In A. P. Hare, E. F. Borgatta, and R. F. Bales, eds., *Small groups, studies in social interaction.* New York: Knopf.

Bennett, V. D. C., Taylor, P., and Ford, S. 1969. An experimental course in sex education for teachers. *Mental Hygiene* 53:625–31.

Bennis, W. G. 1964. Patterns and vicissitudes in t-group development. In L. P. Bradford, J. R. Gibb, and K. D. Benne, eds., *T-group theory and laboratory method: Innovation in re-education.* New York: Wiley.

Berman, L. 1956. The educator and mental health. *American Journal of Orthopsychiatry* 26:204–7.

Bernard, V. W. 1965. Some principles of dynamic psychiatry in relation to poverty. *American Journal of Psychiatry* 3:260–67.

Berzon, B., and Farson, R. 1963. The therapeutic event in group psychotherapy: A study of subjective reports by group members. *Journal of Individual Psychology* 19:204–12.

Bion, W. R. 1961. *Experiences in groups.* New York: Basic Books.

———. 1962. *Learning from experience.* New York: Basic Books.

———. 1963. *Elements of psychoanalysis.* New York: Basic Books.

———. 1965. *Transformations.* New York: Basic Books.

———. 1970. *Attention and interpretation.* New York: Basic Books.

Blatt, M., and Kohlberg, L. 1973. The effects of classroom discussion on the development of moral judgment. In L. Kohlberg and E. Turiel, eds., *Recent research in moral development.* New York: Holt, Rinehart and Winston.

Boris, H. N. 1966a. Proposal to NIMH for support of a project to research and demonstrate methodologies for community-wide mental health consultation programs. Plainfield, Vt.: Goddard College. Mimeographed.

———. 1966b. Report of progress: Project OM 00662, the college-rural school-community mental health consultation project, March 29, 1965–March 31, 1966. Submitted to National Institute of Mental Health—Research Utilization Branch. Mimeographed.

———. 1970a. On spreading mental health. *Psychiatry and Social Science Review* 4:37–41.

———. 1970b. The medium, the message, and the good group dream. *International Journal of Group Psychotherapy* 20:191–98.

———. 1971. The seelsorger in rural Vermont. *International Journal of Group Psychotherapy* 21:159–73.

———. 1973. Confrontation in the analysis of the transference resistance. In G. Adler and P. G. Myerson, eds., *Confrontation in psychotherapy.* New York: Science House.

Boris, H. N., Boris, M., and Zinberg, N. E. 1975. Fantasies in group situations. *Contemporary Psychoanalysis* 2:15–45.

Boris, H. N., and Zinberg, N. E. 1970a. Are piano lessons different from the appreciation of music? The social education and METCO projects: progress and prospectus. Submitted to The Ford Foundation. Mimeographed.

———. 1970b. The group consultation program for teachers; report of progress, September 1968–July 1969. Submitted to METCO. Mimeographed.

———. 1970c. The social education project; report of progress, September 1968–July 1969. Submitted to The Ford Foundation. Mimeographed.

Boris, H. N., Zinberg, N. E., and Boris, M. 1975. The pull of the status quo. Manuscript.

Boris, M. 1971. A group consultation program for teachers; a review of 1969–70. Submitted to The Ford Foundation. Mimeographed.

Boy, A. V., and Pine, G. J. 1971. *Expanding the self: Personal growth for teachers.* Dubuque, Iowa: Brown.

Bruner, J. S. 1960. *The process of education.* Cambridge, Mass. Harvard University Press.

California Teachers Association. 1968. Educating activist youth: A challenge to research. Proceedings of the Twentieth Annual State Conference on Educational Research. Burlingame: California Teachers Association.

Carkoff, R. and Pierce, R. 1967. Differential effects of the therapists' race and social class upon patient, depth of self-exploration in the initial clinical interview. *Journal of Consulting Psychology* 31:632–35.

Caswell, H. L. 1964. The nature of good teacher. In M. Crow and R. D. Crow, eds., *Vital issues in American education.* New York: Bantam Books.

Chance, E. 1971. Varieties of treatment contracts. *International Journal of Group Psychotherapy* 21:91–94.

Child Study Association of America. 1954. *Facts of life for children.* New York: Bobbs-Merrill.

Clark, M., and Erway, E. 1971. *The learning encounter.* New York: Random House.

Coles, R. 1972. *Children of crisis.* New York: Delta.

Conger, J. J., and Miller, W. C. 1966. *Personality, social chaos and delinquency.* New York: Wiley.

Coombs, R. H. 1968. Acquiring sex attitudes and information in our society. In C. E. Vincent, ed., *Human sexuality in medical education and practice.* Springfield, Ill.: C. C. Thomas.

Corsini, R., and Rosenberg, B. 1955. Mechanisms of group psychotherapy: Processes and dynamics. *Journal of Abnormal and Social Psychology* 51:406–11.

Corwin, H. A. 1973. Therapeutic confrontation from routine to heroic. In G. Adler and P. G. Myerson, eds., *Confrontation in psychotherapy.* New York: Science House.

Dubos, R. 1972. *A god within.* New York: Scribner's.

Durkin, H. E. 1964. *The group in depth.* New York: International Universities Press.

Eliot, T. S. 1925. The hollow men. In *Complete poems and plays.* New York: Harcourt, Brace, 1952.

Erikson, E. H. 1959. *Identity and the life cycle.* Psychological Issues Monograph 1. New York: International Universities Press.

——. 1969. *Gandhi's truth.* New York: Norton.

Fayette County Public Schools. 1968. A senior high school sex education research guide. Lexington, Ky.: Department of Instruction.

Feldstein, H. 1969. Program possibilities relating to youth, alienation, drugs. Submitted to Board of Directors, The Ford Foundation. Mimeographed.

Foulkes, S. A., and Anthony, E. J. 1957. *Group psychotherapy: The psychoanalytic approach.* London: Penguin.

Frank, J. D. 1957. Some determinants, manifestations and effect of cohesion in groups. *International Journal of Group Psychotherapy* 7:53–62.

Freud, S. 1913a. On beginning the treatment (further recommendations on the technique of psycho-analysis I). Standard edition 12:123–44. London: Hogarth, 1958.

——. 1913b. Totem and taboo. Standard edition 13:1–161. London: Hogarth, 1955.

——. 1914. On narcissism: an introduction. Standard edition 14:73–102. London: Hogarth, 1957.

——. 1917. Mourning and melancholia. Standard edition 14:237–58. London: Hogarth, 1957.

——. 1921. Group psychology and the analysis of the ego. Standard edition 18:69–143. London: Hogarth, 1960.

G. A. P. Report. 1968. *The dimensions of community psychiatry.* New York: G. A. P. Publications. No. 69.

Gill, M., and Brenman, M. 1958. *Hypnosis and other related states.* New York: International Universities Press.

Ginsberg, E. 1961. *Values and ideals of American youth.* New York: Columbia University Press.

Hartmann, H. 1950. Notes on the psychoanalytic theory of the ego. *Psycho-analytic Study of the Child* 5:74–95.

Herndon, J. 1970. *How to survive in your native land.* New York: Simon and Shuster.

Hollingshead, A. B., and Redlich, F. C. 1958. *Social class and mental illness: A community study.* New York: Wiley.

Holt, J. 1972. *Freedom and beyond.* New York: Dell.

Homans, G. C. 1950. *The human group.* New York: Harcourt, Brace.

Jackson, M. 1963. *Theory of social change: A research plan and supporting data.* Bethesda, Md.: National Institute of Mental Health.

Jacobson, E. 1945. Transference and group formation in children and adolescents. *Psychoanalytic Study of the Child* 1:359–66.

Jerome, J. 1970. *Culture out of anarchy.* New York: Herder and Herder.

Jersild, A. 1952. *In search of self.* New York: Teachers Village Press.

Jones, H. E. 1940. Observational methods in the study of individual development. *Journal of Consulting Psychology* 4:234–38.

Jones, M. C. 1959. A study of socialization patterns at the high school level. *Journal of General Psychology* 93:87–111.

Keniston, K. 1965. *The uncommitted.* New York: Harcourt, Brace.

———. 1970. The sources of student dissent. In P. H. Musser, J. J. Conger, and J. Kagan, eds., *Readings in child development and personality.* New York: Harper and Row.

Klein, M. 1932. *The psycho-analysis of children.* London: Hogarth.

———. 1948. *Contributions to psycho-analysis, 1921–45.* J. Riviere, ed. London: Hogarth.

———. 1952. *Developments in psycho-analysis.* London: Hogarth.

———. 1957. *Envy and gratitude.* London: Tavistock.

———. 1961. *Narrative of a child analysis.* New York: Basic Books.

———. 1963. *Our adult world and other essays.* New York: Basic Books.

Klein, M., Heimann, P., and Money-Kyrle, R., eds. 1955. *New directions in psycho-analysis.* London: Tavistock.

Knobloch, P., and Goldstein, A. 1971. *The lonely teacher.* Boston: Allyn and Bacon.

Kohlberg, L. 1969. Stage and sequence. The cognitive-developmental approach to socialization. In D. Gaslin, ed., *Handbook of socialization: Theory and research.* Chicago: Rand McNally.

———. 1971. From is to ought: How to commit the naturalistic fallacy and get away with it in the study of moral development. In T. Mischel, ed., *Cognitive development and epistemology.* New York: Academic Press.

Kozol, J. 1970. *Death at an early age.* Boston: Houghton Mifflin.

Kubie, L. 1968. Unsolved problems in the resolution of the transference. *Psychoanalytic Quarterly* 37:331–36.

Laing, R. D. 1967. *The politics of experience.* New York: Pantheon.

———. 1969a. *Self and others.* New York: Pantheon.

———. 1969b. *The divided self.* New York: Random House.

Laue, J. 1970. Analysis of METCO and Arlington social education projects (69–130). Report to The Ford Foundation. Mimeographed.

Lerrigo, M. O. 1962. *Facts aren't enough.* Chicago: American Medical Association.

Lewis, D. C. 1970. The drug experience; data for decision-making. Boston: City Schools Curriculum Service.

Lieberman, M. S., Whitaker, D. S., and Lakin, M. 1967. Groups and dyads: Never the twain shall meet. Chicago: University of Chicago. Mimeographed.

McKeachie, W. J. 1958. Students, groups and teaching methods. *American Psychologist* 13:580–84.

Maryland State Department of Education. 1968. Principles and guidelines for family life and sex education programs in the local systems of Maryland. Baltimore: Maryland State Department of Education. Mimeographed.

Maslow, A. 1963. The need to know and the fear of knowing. *Journal of General Psychology* 68:111–25.

Meade, G. H. 1934. *Mind, self and society.* Chicago: University of Chicago Press.

Myerson, P. G. 1973. The meanings of confrontation. In G. Adler and P. G. Myerson, eds., *Confrontation in Psychotherapy.* New York: Science House.

National Association of Independent Schools. 1967. Planning and program of sex education. Boston: National Association of Independent Schools. Mimeographed.

North Carolina Department of Public Instruction. 1968. Sex education, a policy statement. Raleigh: North Carolina Department of Public Instruction. Mimeographed.

Novak, M. 1970. *The experience of nothingness.* New York: Harper and Row.

Oakeshott, M. 1968. Lecture, London School of Economics.

Ohio Department of Education. 1968. Education symposium on social issues: Narcotics, smoking, sex, alcohol. Columbus: Ohio Department of Education. Mimeographed.

Piaget, J. 1948. *The moral judgment of the child.* Glencoe: Free Press.

——— . 1962. The stages of the intellectual development of the child. In P. H. Musser, J. J. Conger, and J. Kagan, eds., *Readings in child development and personality.* New York: Harper and Row.

Pinderhughes, C. A. 1969. Understanding black power. *American Journal of Psychiatry* 125:77–81.

Postman, N., and Weingartner, C. 1969. *Teaching as a subversive activity.* New York: Delacorte.

Rapaport, D. R. 1958. The theory of ego autonomy: A generalization. In M. M. Gill, ed., *The Collected Papers of David R. Rapaport.* New York: Basic Books, 1967.

Redl, F. 1945. The psychology of gang formation and the treatment of juvenile delinquents. *Psychoanalytic Study of the Child* 1:367–78.

Reese, H. W. 1963. "Perceptual set" in children. *Child Development* 34:157–59.

Reich, C. 1970. *The greening of America.* New York: Random House.

Reiss, I. L. 1968. Sex education in the public schools: Problem or solution? *Phi Delta Kappan* 59:52–56.

Report to the Massachusetts State Legislature. 1967. Boston: Department of Education, Commonwealth of Massachusetts.

Rosenthal, D. 1955. Changes in moral values following psychotherapy. *Journal of Consulting Psychology* 19:431–36.

Rotter, J. 1954. *Social learning and clinical psychology.* New York: Prentice-Hall.

Scheidlinger, S. 1955. The concept of identification in group psychotherapy. *American Journal of Psychotherapy* 9:661–67.

School District of Kansas City. 1968. Kansas school district television: Seventh grade health education. Kansas City: School District. Mimeographed.

School Health Education Study. 1967. *Health education: A conceptual approach to curriculum design.* St. Paul, Minn.: 3M Education Press.

Segal, H. 1964. *Introduction to the work of Melanie Klein.* London: Heinemann.

Semrad, E. V., and Arsenian, J. 1951. The use of group processes in teaching group dynamics. *American Journal of Psychiatry* 108:358–62.

Sherif, M. 1958. Group influences upon the formation of norms and attitudes. In E. E. Maccoby, T. M. Newcomb, and E. L. Hartley, eds., *Readings in social psychology.* New York: Holt, Rinehart and Winston.

Shmuck, R. 1971. *Group processes in the classroom.* Dubuque, Iowa: Brown.

Silberman, C. 1971. *Crisis in the classroom.* New York: Random House.

Slater, P. 1966. *Microcosm.* New York: Wiley.

————. 1970. *The pursuit of loneliness.* Boston: Beacon Press.

Starr, J. M. 1970. Report on The Ford Foundation program of social education in Arlington, Mass., 1968–69. Mimeographed.

Stock, D. 1964. A survey of research on t-groups. In L. P. Bradford, J. R. Gibb, and K. D. Benne., eds., *T-group theory and laboratory method: Innovation in re-education.* New York: Wiley.

Stock, D., and Thelen, H. H. 1958. *Emotional dynamics and group culture.* Washington: National Training Publication.

Stock, D., and Whitman, R. 1957. Patients' and therapists' apperceptions of an episode in group psychotherapy. *Human Relations* 10:367–83.

Students Speak on Drugs. The high school student project. 1974. Publication HS-3. Washington, D.C.: Drug Abuse Council.

Szasz, T. G. 1968. Psychoanalysis and the rule of law. *Psychoanalytic Review* 55:248–58.

Tryon, C. M. 1939. Evaluations of adolescent personality by adolescents. Monographs in Social Research. *Child Development* 4:79–86.

Weil, A. 1973. *The natural mind.* Boston: Houghton Mifflin.

Weinstein, G., and Fantini, M. D., eds. 1970. *Toward a humanistic education: A curriculum of affect.* New York: Praeger.

Whitaker, D. S., and Lieberman, M. 1964. *Psychotherapy through the group process.* New York: Atherton.

White, R. W. 1959. Motivation reconsidered: The concept of competence. *Psychological Review* 66:297–333.

White, R. W., and Lippit, R. 1962. Leader behavior and member reaction in three "social climates." In D. Cartwright and A. Zander, eds., *Group dynamics: Research and theory.* New York: Row, Peterson.

Yalom, I. D. 1970. *The theory and practice of group psychotherapy.* New York: Basic Books.

Yalom, I. D., and Rand, K. 1966. Compatibility and cohesiveness in therapy groups. *Archives of General Psychiatry* 13:267–76.

Yankelovich, D. 1972. *American value systems.* New York: Washington Square Press.

Zinberg, N. E. 1964. The psychiatrist as group observer: Notes on training procedure in individual and group psychotherapy. In N. E. Zinberg, ed., *Psychiatry and medical practice in a general hospital.* New York: International Universities Press.

——— . 1967. A group approach with the schoolteacher in the integration crisis. *Mental Hygiene* 51:2–7.

——— . 1969. A group approach with the schoolteacher in the integration crisis. Expanded version. In M. G. Gottsegen and G. B. Gottsegen, eds., *Professional school psychology III.* New York: Grune and Stratton.

——— . 1973. The technique of confrontation and social class differences. In G. Adler and P. G. Myerson, eds., *Confrontation in psychotherapy.* New York: Science House.

——— . 1975. Addiction and ego function. *Psychoanalytic Study of the Child* 30:567–88.

Zinberg, N. E., and Boris, H. N. 1968. Proposal to The Ford Foundation: A group approach to prejudicial attitudes in teachers of METCO schools for September 1968–August 1969. Boston: Metropolitan Council for Educational Opportunity (METCO). Mimeographed.

Zinberg, N. E., and Glotfeldty, J. 1968. The power of the peer group. *International Journal of Group Psychotherapy* 18:155–64.

Zinberg, N. E., and Robertson, J. A. 1972. *Drugs and the public.* New York: Simon and Schuster.

Zinberg, N. E., and Shapiro, D. 1964. A group approach in the contexts of therapy and education. In N. E. Zinberg, ed., *Psychiatry and medical practice in a general hospital.* New York: International Universities Press.

INDEX

Abrams, A., 4, 5
Activism vs. status quo: confrontation, 194–96, 197–206, 221; symbiosis, 196, 200–201, 204–5
"Activity-passivity" behavioral model, 215–16
Activity proper, vs. ego activity, 215–16
Addict groups, 29, 37, 38–39
Adolescence, problems of, 122–23
Affective education, 8, 208, 214, 218, 221; Ford Foundation project, 11
Alcoholics Anonymous, 29, 30
Allocation, 134, 156–57; reallocation of desire, 184–86
Alter ego, 127
Anger, in groups, 117–19, 124; anatomy of, 120–23; metamorphosed into sorrow, 170; reassignment to leader, 121, 128
Anthony, E. J., xi
Anxiety, in groups, 117–19
Applied research, x, 207; criterion of success, 82; project failure as, 82
"Are Piano Lessons Different from the Appreciation of Music?" (Boris and Zinberg report to Ford Foundation), 17
Arlington, Mass., School District, 7, 8, 19, 209–10, 212
Arlington "Social Education" groups, 8–9, 13–14, 23–24, 53–69, 121–22, 208–9, 212, 213, 218; aim of, 12, 13, 70; announcement of, 8–9, 14; compared to METCO groups, 121–23, 146–47; diagrammatic representation, 20–21; Ford evaluation of (by Laue), 72, 74–75; leader-member relationship in, 54–55, 56–57, 59–64, 78, 146–51; number of groups, 13, 20–21; parent reaction to,

15; post-group interviews, 66–67; research objectives, 70; silences, 58; size of, 9; student participants, 9, 15, 52–54; students' age level, 14, 52, 54, 146; students' expectations, 122; students' motives for joining, 64–65; supervision of group leaders, 9, 14–15, 18, 56, 60, 67–68; teacher/leaders of, 9, 11, 14, 18, 52, 54–64, 67–68, 90, 146–147; teacher/leader assessment, 64; teacher/leader manipulation by children, 146–51; teacher/leaders' nondirective approach, 9, 52, 55, 60; teacher/leaders' pay, 14; topics, 52–53, 58, 209, 218; transcripts of, 86–87, 95–97, 102–4, 109–10, 115–16, 130–31, 140–42, 154–55, 164–65, 223–32
Arsenian, J., 219
Ashton-Warner, S., 195
Assimakos, J., 5
Attitude formation and change: behavioral counterpart of, 18, 72, 73, 77–78; difficulty of quantifying, 51, 70, 71, 72–73, 75–78; as early goal of project, 12, 14, 17–18, 23, 70–71, 72, 73; effect of group approach on, 12, 17. *See also* Social attitudes; Status quo

Baby-to-breast reallocation of desire, 184, 185
Bales, R., 45
Balint, M. 173
Basic research. *See* Pure research
Bass, B. M., 45
Batson, Ruth, 7, 8, 10, 15, 20, 48, 50, 74
Behavior, in groups, 173–74; as mirror of preoccupations of group, 91–92, 132; motivated by desire, 188, 190–92; motivated by hope, 188, 189–90, 192

245

Library of Congress Cataloging in Publication Data

Zinberg, Norman Earl, 1921–
    Teaching Social Change

    Bibliography: pp. 237–43
    Includes index.
    1. Group work in education.   2. Students—
Attitudes. 3. Sex. 4. Drug abuse 5. Prejudices
and antipathies. I. Boris, Harold N., joint author.
II. Boris, Marylynn, joint author. III. Title.
LB1032.Z48   301.18'5   75-26746
ISBN 0-8018-1771-4